SERIES EDITORS
Sumit Ganguly and E. Sridharan

After a long period of relative isolation during the Cold War years, contemporary South Asia has grown immensely in its significance in the global political and economic order. This ascendancy has two key dimensions. First, the emergence of India as a potential economic and political power that follows its acquisition of nuclear weapons and its fitful embrace of economic liberalization. Second, the persistent instability along India's borders continues to undermine any attempts at achieving political harmony in the region: fellow nuclear-armed state Pakistan is beset with chronic domestic political upheavals; Afghanistan is paralysed and trapped with internecine warfare and weak political institutions; Sri Lanka is confronted by an uncertain future with a disenchanted Tamil minority; Nepal is caught in a vortex of political and legal uncertainty as it forges a new constitution; and Bangladesh is overwhelmed by a tumultuous political climate.

India's rising position as an important player in global economic and political affairs warrants extra-regional and international attention. The rapidly evolving strategic role and importance of South Asia in the world demands focused analyses of foreign and security policies within and towards the region. The present series addresses these concerns. It consists of original, theoretically grounded, empirically rich, timely, and topical volumes oriented towards contemporary and future developments in one of the most populous and diverse corners of the world.

Sumit Ganguly is a Distinguished Professor of Political Science and Rabindranath Tagore Chair in Indian Cultures and Civilizations, Indiana University, Bloomington, USA.

E. Sridharan is Academic Director, University of Pennsylvania Institute for the Advanced Study of India, New Delhi.

THE OXFORD INTERNATIONAL RELATIONS IN SOUTH ASIA SERIES

India Rising

A Multilayered Analysis of Ideas,
Interests, and Institutions

Edited by
Johannes Plagemann
Sandra Destradi
Amrita Narlikar

OXFORD
UNIVERSITY PRESS

OXFORD
UNIVERSITY PRESS

Oxford University Press is a department of the University of Oxford.
It furthers the University's objective of excellence in research, scholarship,
and education by publishing worldwide. Oxford is a registered trademark of
Oxford University Press in the UK and in certain other countries.

Published in India by
Oxford University Press
22 Workspace, 2nd Floor, 1/22 Asaf Ali Road, New Delhi 110 002, India

ISBN-13 (print edition): 978-0-19-012116-7
ISBN-10 (print edition): 0-19-012116-5

ISBN-13 (eBook): 978-0-19-099021-3
ISBN-10 (eBook): 0-19-099021-X

Typeset in Adobe Jenson Pro 10.5/13
by Tranistics Data Technologies, Kolkata 700 091
Printed in India by Rakmo Press, New Delhi 110 020

Contents

Tables and Figures

Tables

Figures

Introduction

Ideas, Interests, and Institutions in India's Foreign Policy on the Global Level— A Framework for Analysis

JOHANNES PLAGEMANN, SANDRA DESTRADI, AND AMRITA NARLIKAR*

R ISING POWERS HAVE BECOME KEY ACTORS in all fields of global governance, and India, in particular, has emerged as an increasingly visible player in international affairs. In fact, India has remained, together with China, the only BRICS (the block of Brazil, Russia, India, China, and South Africa) country that is actually still perceived as rising, with growth rates of over 7 per cent and a self-confident posture abroad. In terms of its international engagement, New Delhi has a long tradition of foreign-policy activism on a global scale. It 'has become a hub of diplomatic interaction— network as well as club diplomacy' (Cooper and Thakur 2014, 268)—and has contributed in shaping debates and negotiation outcomes in several areas of global governance, such as drafting the Universal Declaration of Human Rights and the creation of the multilateral trading system. At the same time, and across different issue areas, India has often displayed an inflexible attitude, becoming the 'India that can't say yes' (Cohen 2001, 66). Its negotiation stance in the General Agreement on Tariffs and Trade, and now the World Trade Organization, has historically earned it the

* We are grateful to Cordula Tibi Weber for excellent research assistance.

reputation of being a difficult negotiator (Narlikar 2006). Similarly, when it comes to global climate governance, the Indian government has long refused binding commitments of targets to curb emissions, privileging instead the notion of 'common but differentiated responsibilities' and highlighting the historic burden and responsibility of the 'West'.

The main question we pose is: *What drives rising India's global-level conduct?* We seek to understand India's often ambivalent approach to global governance by considering three potential factors—ideas, interests, and institutions—that have an impact on India's foreign policy making in seven issue areas at the global level. We examine possible explanations for India's varying compliance with global regimes and for its varying contributions to the development and change of those regimes—in the fields of nuclear non-proliferation, counterterrorism, maritime security, cyber-governance, trade policy, climate change, and democracy promotion.

On leaving the realm of international relations (IR) theory and looking into concrete policy fields, it quickly becomes clear that none of the three factors can stand alone in explaining Indian foreign policy. Ideas, interests, and institutions are interrelated and may result in both contradictory and mutually reinforcing pressures. In fact, each individual factor, too, is an abstraction of complex and at times competing forces. Moreover, we presume that it is not only domestic interests, institutions, and ideas that matter, but constraints, pressures, and expectations from the regional and global level of politics that play a role as well.

We are interested in India as a rising power. The focus of our analysis is Indian foreign policy making from the early 2000s to 2016, that is, throughout the United Progressive Alliance I and II governments under Prime Minister (PM) Manmohan Singh (2004–14) and the first half of the current government's mandate under PM Narendra Modi. We think a study of this period is especially useful because the global financial crises during those years in a variety of ways exposed the new role India can—and hopes to—occupy in global politics. Whereas Western nations have been preoccupied with fighting the economic fallout of the financial crisis, growth of the Indian economy has continued unabated. And PM Modi's unexpected activism in foreign policy and economic diplomacy has changed India's traditionally rather inward-looking image further. On the one hand, we have observed a more determined approach towards the South Asian region, with a range of policy initiatives vis-à-vis smaller countries such as the settlement of the contested border with Bangladesh or a further improvement of relations with Afghanistan. On the other hand, on a global scale, the Modi government saw an intensification of bilateral relations with all major international players—from a strengthening of relations with the United States, to a parallel improvement of bilateral ties with all major competing powers in the Middle East: Saudi Arabia, Iran, and Israel. On a rhetorical level, the Modi government explicitly distanced itself from previously predominant Nehruvian discourses, so much so that Modi took the controversial decision to not participate in the Non-Aligned Movement (NAM) summit in September 2016.

Against this backdrop, the notion of change is particularly important to us. Indeed, indications are that some of the underlying forces shaping Indian foreign policy are changing. We seek to uncover how India's new status—from a leader of the developing world, to being a global power in a multipolar world—translates into concrete policy fields, and vice versa.

In the following sections, we will briefly review the existing literature on India's and other rising powers' approaches to global governance, and discuss the main gaps in that literature. We will then proceed to develop our multilayered analytical framework that focuses on three levels of analysis (the domestic, regional, and international) and on three explanatory factors (ideas, interests, and institutions). We conclude by highlighting how this approach—through the inclusion of ideational factors—goes beyond conventional analyses of India's policies and provides a more nuanced understanding of India's approach to global governance. Importantly, the framework will help us in comprehending change—and continuity—in rising India's global-level conduct. Finally, we discuss how our analysis can be useful beyond the case of India to assess other rising powers' approaches to global governance.

State of the Art

While the study of rising powers traditionally focused on power transitions and on the consequences of their rise for the structure of the international system, the past few years have seen the emergence of a body of literature that analyses rising powers' contribution to global governance (for example, Jentleson 2012; Kahler 2013). Despite the growing interest in this topic, however, only a few studies have so far focused specifically on explaining the origins and drivers of rising powers' global policies. Some liberal analyses of rising powers' policies address domestic preference formation. For example, Schirm (2013) finds that societal interests and ideas about economic governance are better able to explain divergent economic-policy positions among G20 countries than are structural conditions. Some studies analyse the influence of specific actors on rising powers' policies. Never (2012), for example, studies the impact of 'communities of practice'—networks composed of officials, scientists, and business representatives—on climate governance in rising powers. The ideational dimension of rising powers' policies has generated greater academic interest in recent years. Several studies have focused on the world views of rising powers (for example, Nau and Ollapally 2012) as well as on their aspiration for recognition and status in global affairs (Nel 2010; Paul, Larson, and Wohlforth 2014). Some comparative studies take into account ideational factors to explain rising powers' approaches to different fields of global governance such as security (Onderco 2015; Thakur 2013a), economic governance (Stephen 2012), or foreign-policy discourses (Nymalm and Plagemann 2018). According to Nölke et al. (2015), Brazil, China, and India represent a distinct type of capitalism dubbed 'state-permeated market economy'. Thus, state-centric development strategies within these countries are conceived as a result of a common institutional model governing their economies and determining their stances in global economic governance. However, attempts to study the interplay of different kinds of influence— of ideas, interests, and institutions—on rising powers' approaches to global governance are missing. Similarly, we lack a more systematic understanding of how different levels of analysis interact in shaping those policies. While several authors have looked at the regional dimension of rising powers' policies (for example, Nel and Nolte 2010), we still know little about the interplay of factors at the regional and global, as well as the domestic levels of analysis.

Given the complexity of such interrelations, it is not very surprising that the conventional canon of IR theories offers only limited guidance in making sense of rising powers' foreign policies across policy levels and fields. Realism, for instance, fails to explain both India's reluctance to substantially reform and expand its military, on the one hand, and its wariness to fully buy into a military alliance–like cooperation with the United States of America (USA) and against China, on the other. Liberalism, with its emphasis on domestic constituencies, may explain why New Delhi's investments in its military capabilities remain somewhat limited. Yet, it fails to explain a variety of other consistent elements in India's foreign policy, from New Delhi's aspirations for regional hegemony, to its insistence on non-interference and close relations with Russia. Constructivism appears to be better equipped for dealing with such foreign-policy specificities related to postcolonial history and particular ideologies adopted by India's main political parties—the Congress and the Bharatiya Janata Party (Nehruvian internationalism and Hindu nationalism respectively). And institutionalist approaches may explain India's consistent support for the UN, as well as, more recently, the BRICS process. Yet, they also face challenges resulting from the inconsistencies in India's foreign relations. For instance, India's outspoken support for multilateralism globally conflicts with its preference of bilateralism over multilateralism regionally, as well as with India's intransigent position on national sovereignty in a variety of international fora and important bilateral relations (with China and Pakistan, in particular). Finally, whereas constructivists may refer to India's self-understanding as one of the world's major civilizations, rather than nation states, in order to explain New Delhi's aspirations for a global status, one wonders why despite such ambitions New Delhi's diplomatic apparatus remains so small in size and, correspondingly, capacity.

With few exceptions,[1] the more specific literature on India's foreign policies across issue areas is characterized by similar gaps. New Delhi's positions and policies on global governance have frequently been justified with India's domestic priorities and its goals as a developing country, for example in the fields of food security and intellectual property or in the promotion of the idea of 'common but differentiated responsibilities' for climate change. While several excellent studies exist on India's domestic politics (for example, Mitra 2011; Rudolph and Rudolph 1987), on the historical evolution of India's foreign policy (for example, Cohen 2001; Mohan 2003), or on India's troubled relations with its neighbours (for example, Ganguly 2001), we lack more systematic knowledge about the determinants of India's policies at the global level. The criticism articulated by Ganguly and Pardesi (2010) some years ago—that the literature on South Asia is mostly descriptive–analytical and that only rarely are theoretical insights gained from the empirical analysis of cases from this region—is still largely valid.

[1] For an explicit treatment of the role of ideas and interests in institutional change in Indian economic history, see Mukherji (2014).

One of the few attempts to explain India's foreign policy by systematically taking into account factors from different levels of analysis is the edited volume by Ganguly (2010), which includes some chapters on selected global-governance issue areas. But generally, still very few studies address in detail the actual processes of foreign policy decision-making in India (for example, Mattoo and Jacob 2009). One major exception is a recent study by Schaffer and Schaffer (2016, 82–106), who discuss the role and competencies of the Indian Foreign Service, the national security advisor, and a range of other institutions and actors involved in foreign policy making. Nonetheless, our knowledge about the influence of single actors, lobby groups, think tanks, state governments, or ministries across specific global issues is still limited. By contrast, the ideational foundations of India's policies have been explored somewhat better. Existing studies include analyses of the impact of identity politics on India's approach to South Asia (Singh 2013); the impact of single norms or principles such as non-alignment on India's foreign policy (Pant and Super 2015); role-theoretical assessments of India's maritime security and climate policies (Prys and Plagemann 2018) or its understanding of humanitarian norms (Hansel and Möller 2015); and the analysis of the cultural origins of India's negotiating behaviour in different fields of global governance (Narlikar and Narlikar 2014). However, a comprehensive analysis investigating both domestic material (interests and institutions) and ideational influences that shape India's global ambitions and strategies is missing. And just as important is the gap in our understanding of the interactions between the different layers of analysis, that is, domestic, regional, and international factors, and their impact on India's rise.

This collection of papers aims to address these gaps by offering an analysis of the changes accompanying India's rise, embracing a multilayered approach. The contributions bring unique value addition to the scholarly and public debate on India by systematically factoring in the role of (frequently ignored) ideational variables and their interaction with interest-based and institutional factors.

Analytical Framework

This volume addresses India's global policies by using a common analytical framework. The framework includes three levels (domestic, regional, global) and, for each of them, three basic explanatory factors:

ideas, interests, and institutions. All three of those factors are key terms in IR literature, but their meaning is contested. Moreover, all three are interrelated: ideas (for example, notions of state sovereignty) form the basis of institutions (for example, the United Nations): as Béland and Cox (2011, 9) put it, 'Institutions do more than establish routines that rational individuals must negotiate; they also nurture peoples' identities, helping them to construct their fundamental values, which, in turn, shapes their beliefs and interests.' Ideas shape the interests of those in power—and will be shaped by institutional developments as well as interests.

By *institutions*, we refer to formal regulatory frameworks and forms of political organization relevant for individual policy fields. Informal institutions are included to the extent that they directly refer to the political processes and the praxis of foreign policy making, as for instance in routines such as informally established lines of reporting or practices of multilateral coalition formation. Obviously, relevant institutions differ from the domestic to the regional and global level. Domestic, regional, and global institutions—with differing degrees—predetermine the array of alternatives and actions in international politics, establish communities of practice, and determine which actors New Delhi will communicate with. Institutions, therefore, shape India's global-level foreign policy menu and co-determine eventual policies.

Analogous to the institutional factor, differing sets of *ideas* exist across levels of analysis. Most forcefully, domestic intellectual traditions, historical narratives, and epistemic concepts define the world views of Indian policy makers and the wider public alike. As stated previously, sources of relevant ideas range from religious and philosophical traditions to political ideologies and convictions. As will be illustrated in the following chapters, India's specific intellectual resources—from ancient Hindu texts, to modern nationalists' thought, and the contemporary amalgam of both—continue to shape Indians' negotiation behaviour across policy fields and understandings of the national interest. Of lesser impact but nonetheless politically meaningful in some cases are regionally shared and developed ideas, that is ideas *from* the region. Moreover, in liberalizing and globalizing India, ideas diffusing globally across policy fields, arguably, play an ever more important role in shaping Indian foreign policy.

Finally, by *interests* we refer to the core security and welfare objectives held by national governments. The interests we consider here as factors shaping India's policies within individual areas of global governance are of a conventional material and geopolitical nature, typically circumscribed in realist literature under the terms 'national interest' or *raison d' état*. Both terms are open to interpretation, and domestic intellectual traditions (ideas) co-define the national interest in India as elsewhere. Moreover, foreign policy makers in most areas must reconcile a variety of often competing domestic or 'national' interests (Thakur 2013a). Nonetheless, we found it useful to treat India's interests in fundamental matters of national welfare, security, and autonomy on the domestic, regional, and global levels within individual policy fields as an analytically separate factor independent from the ideas factor.

In this volume we seek to enhance our understanding of the components contributing to India's global policies. Therefore, we do not treat regional and global interests of, say, regional powers (for example, Pakistan) and global powers (for example, the USA) as exogenous factors analogous to domestic, regional, and global institutions or ideas. Instead, we examine *Indian* interests at these three levels. In other words, whereas in this framework regional and global ideas are somewhat exogenous factors, Indian interests at the regional and global levels are as endogenous as India's domestic-level interests. India's regional security interests, for instance, influence New Delhi's global policies in areas such as nuclear non-proliferation or fighting terrorism. Likewise, both India's domestic interests in social welfare and its interest in global status influence New Delhi's position in global negotiations on issues ranging from trade to climate.

By considering all three factors—interests, ideas, and institutions—the reader may be reminded of past IR debates between realists, constructivists, and institutionalists. Surely, in today's complex and multipolar world, all three schools of thought retain some explanatory value. Yet, we believe that neither one is sufficient on its own in providing an understanding of India's (and other major powers') global actions. While the precise relevance of each factor varies from one policy field to the other, each carries at least some relevance in each of the policy fields considered here. Rather than siding with one camp or the other, we developed this framework with an open question in mind: to what extent and in what ways have ideas, interests, and institutions shaped rising India's global policies? Thus, our objective is not to collect evidence for one or the other of the aforementioned schools of thought. Instead, we seek to, first, explore the determinants of India's global policies and, second, develop a research framework that is applicable to cases beyond India. In each of the following contributions, this framework is applied to explain India's policies in specific issue areas. Figure I.1 illustrates the interplay of the three factors on three levels of analysis.

Domestic Level

The interplay of ideas, interests, and institutions in India's global policies is perhaps most obvious at the domestic level of politics. By domestic *institutions* we refer to the distribution of competencies and authority with regard to foreign affairs amongst Indian ministries as well as the Prime Minister's Office (PMO) and the National Security Advisor (NSA). The characteristics of India's foreign-policy bureaucracy and the armed services comprise further important institutional factors co-determining eventual global-level conduct. Literature on bureaucratic politics has established the importance of bureaucratic organization for foreign policy outcomes (Halperin and Clapp 2006). In the case of India, for instance, several studies explain the remarkable persistence of India's foreign-policy principles or ideas with reference to the relatively autonomous foreign-policy elite and other institutional specificities (for example, Chatterjee Miller 2014; Narang and Staniland 2012). However, the foreign-policy bureaucracy is not static per se. There have been changes recently, as, for instance, with regard to the role of the national

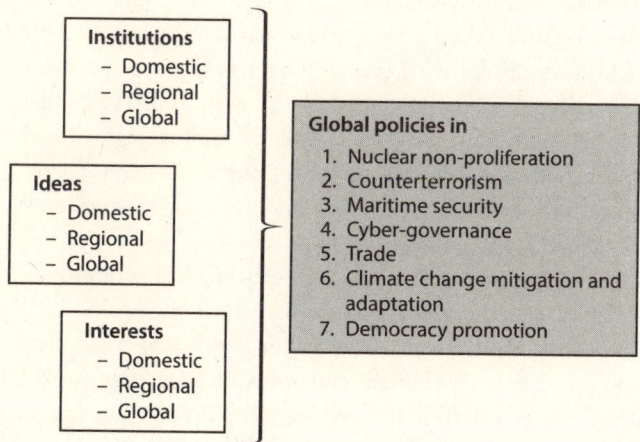

Figure I.1   Authors' framework for analysis

security advisor. Moreover, India's federal set-up—with (some) powerful individual states in pursuit of their own external interests and numerous regional parties with bargaining power on the national level—is increasingly important for understanding Indian foreign policy making (Plagemann and Destradi 2015).

The permeability (or its absence) of foreign policy institutions with regard to non-state actors—from businesses, to civil society organizations—are part of a country's institutional set-up and determine how domestic institutions transform and transmit diverse societal interests. Domestic level *interests* refer to societal preferences as identified by political economy approaches to foreign policy analysis. For instance, the Indian economy's characteristic reliance on oil shipments from Gulf states has ensured close relations with oil exporting countries and a pronounced interest in the cooperative maintenance of safe sea lanes across the Indian Ocean Region. Similarly uncontested is India's interest in a global climate regime flexible enough to not inhibit domestic economic growth. However, societal interests may also diverge. As a result, Indian foreign policy makers at times encounter contradictory demands. Abandoning India's infamous import restrictions, for instance, hurts those powerful companies built around such restrictions. On the other hand, manufacturing companies with interests in export markets and imported capital goods lobby for further liberalization.

Finally, domestic preferences interrelate with ideas and values transmitted by culture. We understand *ideas* as a mix of norms and world views broadly relating to India's external relations including both ancient Hindu tradition with contemporary resonance and more recent lines of thought characterizing India's strategic culture. For instance, a reading of India's classical treatises in political and strategic thought, such as Kautilya's Arthashastra, will underline the 'realist' content of Hindu thought and its sensitivity to power and force in international affairs (cf. Zimmer 1951, 87–139). Narlikar and Narlikar (2014) illustrate how classical Hindu texts such as the Mahabharata continue to impact India's negotiating culture and bargaining behaviour. Again, the diversity of India's history of ideas may account for competing principles equally rooted in contemporary Indian culture. Consider that in 2004 PM Manmohan Singh referred to 'cooperative pluralism' as India's global philosophy enshrined in the Sanskrit phrase 'Vasudhaiva Kutumbakam'—the whole world is one family. Statements such as this suggest, in the words of David Malone (2012, 264), 'a cooperative outlook ideally suited to multilateral institutions, the desire to transform them and a recognition that with greater power and influence comes responsibility in international affairs'. However, in practice, Indian references to the moral high ground do not necessarily lead to effective results in international politics. In Malone's words:

> A noted denizen of India's Ministry of External Affairs (MEA), a keen bilateralist at that, when asked what India does best internationally replied without a moment's hesitation 'multilateral diplomacy'. And yet queries about Indian performance at the UN and elsewhere in the multilateral sphere hardly validate that judgement: 'arrogant', 'moralistic', and 'confrontational' are terms more invoked by developing and industrialized counterparts, despite recognition that Indian negotiators are rarely less than 'impressive' and often 'brilliant'. (Malone 2012, 270)

As will be laid out in more detail in the following chapters, domestic ideas and institutions are at times closely interrelated. For instance, the oft-noted lack of capacity on behalf of India's foreign policy apparatus plays into upholding established frames of reference and ideas and is one explanation for continuity in terms of guiding ideas—from non-alignment, to the 'common but differentiated responsibility' (CBDR) in climate change negotiations. On the other hand, a Chinese-inspired sense of 'mercantilism' has become the underlying idea for much of India's economic diplomacy, a dynamic that has been reinforced considerably with the election of PM Modi.

Regional Level

Ideas, interests, and institutions from the regional level of analysis also play a role in shaping India's global policies. Regional institutions, albeit with little binding power and constantly threatened by bilateral conflict in South Asia, may impact upon India's global policies. India's limited readiness to cooperate in the framework of the South Asian Association for Regional Cooperation (SAARC), for example, might weaken India's credentials as a responsible player in global affairs. India has also consistently paid attention to avoid an internationalization of its dispute with Pakistan, trying to approach this issue in strictly bilateral terms. The desire to avoid external influences in bilateral and regional affairs connects with India's emphasis on the principles of sovereignty and non-intervention in global politics, which need further investigation. At the same time, regional constraints and interests are important elements in India's approach to global policy fields such as non-proliferation or maritime security. Pakistan's nuclear capability and proliferation of terrorism as well as China's maritime expansion, for instance, are key drivers of India's positioning in global politics. In terms of ideas, the regional level potentially carries insights too. Clearly, India's very conception of its region impacts its global policies, including its relations to extra-regional powers such as the USA or Japan. Countries from adjacent regions with an interest in closer ties, such as Vietnam or Singapore, have contributed to a changing understanding of India's regional responsibilities. The current government's new impetus in regional affairs includes a focus on maritime security and the 'blue economy'—factors that expand India's immediate regional environment from a land-based South Asia to a marine-based Indian Ocean Region that stretches from Africa's eastern coast to South East Asia. 'Learning' experiences—or lack thereof—are also visible in the economic sphere. South East Asia's experiences in economic integration and growth have been important factors in India's trade policies (see Chapter 5 by Biswajit Dhar). Nonetheless, we expect the regional level to be relevant in a limited number of issue areas—which might be an interesting finding in itself as India does not aim to represent its region in global forums and its regional concerns are mostly detached from its position on global governance issues.

Global Level

Finally, we ask how ideas, interests, and institutions from the global level of analysis impact India's global policies. Membership in international institutions can be expected to have a substantial influence. India's ascendance has been accompanied with membership and activism in a variety of global institutions—from the UN, to BRICS—with widely divergent purposes and working cultures. Whereas the IBSA (India, Brazil, South Africa) dialogue forum has lost its initial vigour, India has reinforced its ties with African countries, not least in an attempt to bolster its claim for reform in the UN Security Council. And whereas India continued to be a strong supporter of UN multilateralism in principle (thus its lukewarm reception of the G20 process so far), New Delhi has cherished the leader-level summitry of the BRICS, the establishment of a BRICS development bank, and the diplomatic visibility attached to 'minilateralism'. In terms of interests, India's aspiration to global power stands out. Status-seeking and partnership-building are relevant for most global policy fields scrutinized in this volume. However, indications are that India has been adopting globally shared interests more vigorously too. Consider the outcome of climate change negotiations in Paris 2015, which India helped to facilitate. Finally, in terms of ideas on the global level, we ask to what extent India internalizes 'international' ideas and/or shapes global discourses on governance in selected issue areas. In climate change negotiations, again, the current government has referred to ancient tradition proactively in order to develop a more eco-friendly Indian image abroad—and legitimize a more concessionary negotiating position domestically (Narlikar 2017). At the same time, domestic policy initiatives to address climate change have been influenced by foreign ideas from western donors to NGOs. Global ideas impacting upon India's policy behaviour may also become effective via translation through India's successful diaspora, most notably in the USA.

Choice of Policy Fields

This volume collects insights from seven issue areas, four of which pertain to the security realm as broadly understood. In selecting the issue areas and contributors to this volume, we sought to provide a wide, if not conclusive, overview of India's global governance activities in order to both gain an understanding of the determinants of India's global policies that is as complete as possible and assess the applicability of our framework with as much empirical evidence as possible. Besides aiming at the full spectrum of India's global engagements, we also sought to cover a considerable degree of variation in terms of India's compliance with global regimes and of its own contributions to the development of such regimes. Thus, we included both established, well-documented fields—such as India's engagement with the nuclear non-proliferation, trade, or climate change regimes—and less prominent fields such as cyber-governance or India's limited activities in supporting democracies. Moreover, issue areas comprise fields in which there has been considerable dynamism in recent years (maritime security), and others characterized more by continuity than change (terrorism). Finally, contributions to this volume cover highly institutionalized and densely regularized policy fields (trade) as well as fields in which there are very few or only highly contested international rules in place (cyber).

Outline of Individual Chapters

Kate Sullivan de Estrada (in Chapter 1) explores India's exceptional engagement with the nuclear non-proliferation regime, which has frequently led to its framing as an outsider, a challenger, and even a threat to the normative pillars of non-proliferation centred on the Nuclear Non-proliferation Treaty (NPT). Yet, since 1998, successive Indian leaderships have worked to develop a constructive working relationship with the regime, securing status, institutional recognition, and material advantages. This chapter develops an understanding of the drivers behind India's post-1998 transformation from regime challenger to partner (though not insider). It builds upon existing security-centred and interest-based accounts of India's engagement with the regime, but draws on key ideational factors by employing the twin lenses of nuclear status and nuclear responsibility. The chapter's central argument is that the exceptional nature of India's relationship with the non-proliferation regime derives from an interplay of nuclear autonomy and status considerations at the domestic level; security and status concerns at the regional level; and status recognition as a responsible nuclear power and the threat of social exclusion and material sanctions at the global level. Further, India's complex relationship with the non-proliferation regime has actually served to validate and strengthen several of the regime's key norms, although India remains far from attaining the status of a regime manager or norm-setter.

Sumit Ganguly and Brandon Miliate (in Chapter 2) trace the origins of India's global approach to counterterrorism by looking closely at India's domestic terrorism issues. In particular, they focus on the ongoing conflict in Kashmir, the renewed Naxalite insurgency, and the past insurgency in the Punjab. On the domestic and regional levels, institutional constraints and failures are at the heart of many domestic acts of terror, especially in Kashmir. However, in the Punjab, India has displayed remarkable institutional flexibility and learning in addressing the concerns of Sikh nationalists. Indian interests in stability and concerns to other regions over the spread of separatism give additional impetus to develop a strong counterterrorism policy and to prioritize the topic of terrorism in India's foreign policy. On the international level, the authors explore the links of India with the USA, Saudi Arabia, and Israel, which have been expanded to support cooperation in the field of counterterrorism, especially with regards to intelligence sharing.

In Chapter 3, Rahul Roy-Chaudhury explores New Delhi's renewed interest in maritime security affairs. Although the Indian Navy has traditionally claimed a leadership role for itself in the Indian Ocean, this has not been reflected in government policy until recently. With the Modi government's goal of making India a 'leading power' in the international system, India seeks 'maritime dominance' over the Indian Ocean as a foreign and security policy priority. Its sphere of influence has expanded from the Indian Ocean to the Indo-Pacific area and it has widened its role of being a 'net security provider' to island states in the Indian Ocean, while intensifying naval interactions with the USA, Japan, and Vietnam. India's policies are shaped by its interests in the Indian Ocean, which include safe sea lanes of communication (SLOC), security for economy and energy, the prevention of maritime terrorism, as well as countering China's growing influence in the Indian Ocean. At the same time, India emphasizes the importance of the United Nations Convention on the Law of the Sea (UNCLOS) and the 'freedom of navigation'. The navy, the MEA, and the PMO are the main institutional 'drivers' of India's maritime security, alongside complex centre–state dynamics.

Hannes Ebert (in Chapter 4) assesses India's often overlooked engagement in cyber security. Information and communication technologies (ICTs) have been a key driver of India's post-liberalization economic growth as well as of its claims for great power status. Successive Indian governments have sought to place India at the forefront of the global economy's digitization. In its 'Digital India' initiative, PM Modi's government made increasing internet connectivity and promoting India's global ICT trademark a political priority. Yet, risks and vulnerabilities have augmented in sync with growing opportunities and stakes. Adapting to this environment, the Indian state has taken a middle way in its global internet governance policy, emphasizing 'multistakeholderism' in the realm of internet governance affairs and advocating a dominant role of governments and bilateral negotiations with regard to cyber-security policy making. This chapter inspects the drivers of India's global internet governance policy since 2000. It argues that India has transformed from a 'norm taker' to a 'norm shaper' in global internet governance debates and promoted a policy open to multistakeholder processes. At the same time, India has been insistent on the preeminent role of the state in security-related affairs, primarily driven by the perception of growing cyber-enabled security threats, which in turn contributed to the evolution of security-centred institutions and ideas in India's overall cyber policy.

Biswajit Dhar analyses (in Chapter 5) India's experiences with trade liberalization, a critical element of the policy of economic reforms adopted a quarter of a century ago. India's trade liberalization was a tacit acceptance of the Washington Consensus, the ideational foundation of the latest and the most pervasive phase of global economic integration. A stand-out feature of India's approach to liberalization was the unilateral reduction of the high levels of protection that India had provided to its domestic entities till then. Although, in later years, India's policies were conditioned by the commitments that it had made as a member of the World Trade Organization (WTO), the process of trade liberalization that it undertook was calibrated to suit its economic realities and interests. For instance, India was cautious in lowering the tariffs on agricultural products, in keeping with the imperatives of food security and rural livelihoods. While India was able to deftly balance its domestic compulsions with the demands of the WTO, in recent years, it has been facing serious challenges in manoeuvring its position as trade liberalization processes have sidestepped the multilateral forum to embrace regionalism.

In Chapter 6 on climate change, Sandeep Sengupta analyses India's global policies and shows that the country has indeed been a major player in international climate negotiations. While over the past two decades its foreign policy engagement on this issue has been predominantly marked by continuity—centred on preserving an international climate regime structurally differentiated in its favour—its negotiating positions have undergone considerable change in recent years, particularly in the period from 2009 to 2015. These shifts have been driven by a range of interlinked factors, including a changing understanding of India's interests, the emergence of new institutional frameworks and actors on this issue, and the influence of new ideas. The chapter systematically unpacks these different determinants of India's foreign policy on climate change and analyses how they have operated across multiple levels.

Christian Wagner (in Chapter 7) revisits India's record in democracy promotion, noting that India, the world's largest democracy, has shown remarkably little interest in promoting its democratic ideals in its foreign policy. An assessment of India's relations with other South Asian countries reveals that promoting democracy has sometimes been part of India's relations with some of its neighbours, such as Nepal, but has never been a consistent feature in its foreign policy. The recent debate about democracy promotion was triggered in the context of the rapprochement with the USA since the 1990s. In the 2000s, India joined the UN Global Democracy Fund, and the Election Commission set up an international branch for capacity-building. But despite the emphasis on common democratic values in its relations with the USA and other Western powers, promotion of democracy will remain a weak pillar in India's foreign policy. The idea of non-interference, security interests vis-à-vis neighbouring countries, and the lack of proper instruments can be identified as the main reasons for this continuing weakness.

In the concluding chapter, we summarize the contributors' findings with regard to the interplay of ideas, interests, and institutions in Indian foreign policy making. We look for similar patterns and thereby make a statement about the driving forces of Indian foreign policy beyond individual policy fields. For instance, we ask how far certain established or new ideas have been influential across policy fields. The focus will be on the notion of change: What factors contributed to changes in Indian foreign policy on the global level? How did the interplay of ideas, interests, and institutions affect change? Finally, we also discuss the broader implications of our findings for a more general understanding of rising powers' approaches to global governance.

Globalizing Research

This volume is the result of a workshop with the same title that took place at GIGA German Institute of Global and Area Studies in Hamburg, Germany, in September 2016. It was part of the activities of GIGA's Research Platform India, which was funded by the German Federal Foreign Office in order to support the institution's activities in fostering ties with the region.

Neither the selection of participants nor the research framework are coincidental. As a member of the Leibniz Association, GIGA is mandated to provide the policy and public sphere with sound scholarly analysis and, if asked for, advice. The workshop exemplified this approach.

Besides the contributing authors, three representatives from the Federal Foreign Office took part in the workshop. In Hamburg, we therefore facilitated discussions between diplomats working on and with India, professionals in policy advice from the think tank world, and excellent international scholars from the academic world.

At GIGA we are committed to what we call globalizing research (Narlikar 2016). In academic terms, this is a call for mainstreaming the marginalized sections of global knowledge and experiences. Although we recognize the merits of area studies in providing detailed knowledge of individual polities on their own terms, we study developments in Asia, Africa, the Middle East, and Latin America as potentially highly relevant (and often under-utilized) contributions to global knowledge. In fact, mainstream theories in the social sciences are still based primarily on empirical experiences made in the Global North. Generally speaking, both the social sciences and the policy world tend to overestimate the pervasiveness of the predominantly Western theories or world views at their disposal and overlook inspiring, complementary, or otherwise benign developments and theoretical resources with origins in the histories and intellectual traditions of the other three quarters of global society.

Concretely, mainstreaming the marginalized means developing our research—both grand-scale agendas and detailed frameworks such as this one—with greater sensitivity to the particularities of individual intellectual traditions and local opportunities and constraints, while aiming to improve existing or developing new theories that transgress area studies' narrowly confined geographical containers. In short, we seek to recognize cross-cultural diversity without abandoning the social sciences' ambition to universal knowledge (and its aversion to essentialism or ethnocentrism). Our research framework given earlier exemplifies this approach. Despite some changes recently, rising powers' say in the international institutions, crafted and populated by established powers in many cases, is still limited. Their experiences with international institutions thus differ considerably when compared to European and North American experiences. Political histories of rising powers as colonial subjects diverge fundamentally from those of their former masters—resulting in domestic foreign policy institutions that vary greatly from country to country in terms of effectiveness, permeability, and the power of bureaucracy over politics. The greater influence that some countries from the Global South have gained in recent years exposes such differences—and makes an understanding thereof all the more relevant. Intellectual traditions in those countries are distinct. Sometimes, working with political ideologies originating in the West, such as nationalism or socialism, the result is a fundamentally different one when compared to the original. In terms of the national interests, rising powers from the Global South at first glance exhibit more similarities with established powers. Yet, here too, an interest in security, welfare, and status is translated into diverging global policies due to widely diverging domestic, regional, and global challenges. In fact, rising powers' interests are increasingly complex for various reasons. First, the simultaneity of competition and cooperation amongst them (India and China in particular) has led to diverging policies between the regional and global levels. Second, the growing salience of rising powers for a number of policy fields puts an end to Western powers' monopoly of influence on them. Examples abound—from climate change to fighting piracy. For rising powers being veto powers, it seems, is but a step towards multipolarity. A truly multipolar world, however, involves not only supposedly 'global' ideas spreading from the North to the South, but also ideas radiating from the South in all directions. Contributions to this volume expose the extent to which this is already pertinent.

While this volume is focused specifically on India, we hope that it will offer insights of greater generalizability beyond the Indian case. In fact, what rising powers have in common (or what differentiates them from established powers) is their peculiar position in the international system. They are, on the one hand, the most powerful countries within their regions; on the other hand, they are 'rising' in a global power hierarchy and have gained considerable influence and visibility in global affairs. Global problems simply cannot be solved without their cooperation and their active contribution to the provision of global public goods. At the same time, they still face huge domestic challenges—from poverty and inequality, to structural deficiencies of their economies. We believe that this peculiar constellation leads to a range of trade-offs that rising powers have to deal with when operating as global actors, and that we need a better understanding of how ideas, interests, and institutions from the domestic, regional, and international levels interact in shaping rising powers' global policies. This is all the more relevant as rising powers have increasingly contributed their own ideas and philosophies to different fields of global governance and have thereby played a role in shaping global regimes and their underlying norms.

References

Béland, Daniel and Robert H. Cox. 2011. 'Introduction: Ideas and Politics', in Daniel Béland and Robert H. Cox (eds), *Ideas and Politics in Social Science Research*, pp. 3–20. Oxford: Oxford University Press.

Chatterjee Miller, Manjari. 2014. 'The Un-agumentative Indian? Ideas about the Rise of India and Their Interaction with Domestic Structures', *India Review*, 13 (1): 1–14.

Cohen, Stephen P. 2001. *India: Emerging Power*. Washington, DC: Brookings Institution Press.

Cooper, Andrew F. and Ramesh Thakur. 2014. 'The BRICS in the New Global Geography', in Thomas G. Weiss and Rorden Wilkinson (eds), *International Organization and Global Governance*, pp. 265–78. Abingdon and New York: Routledge.

Ganguly, Sumit. 2001. *Conflict Unending: India–Pakistan Tensions since 1947*. New York: Columbia University Press.

——— (ed.). 2010. *India's Foreign Policy: Retrospect and Prospect*. New Delhi: Oxford University Press.

Ganguly, Sumit and Manjeet S. Pardesi. 2010. 'South Asia and Foreign Policy', in Robert A. Denemark (ed.), *The International Studies Encyclopedia*, pp. 6497–514. Malden, MA: Wiley-Blackwell.

Halperin, Morton H. and Priscilla A Clapp. 2006. *Bureaucratic Politics and Foreign Policy*. Washington DC: Brookings Institution.

Hansel, Mischa and Miriam Möller. 2015. 'Indian Foreign Policy and International Humanitarian Norms: A Role-Theoretical Analysis', *Asian Politics & Policy*, 7 (1): 79–104.

Kahler, Miles. 2013. 'Rising Powers and Global Governance: Negotiating Change in a Resilient Status Quo', *International Affairs*, 89 (3): 711–29.

Jentleson, Bruce W. 2012. 'The John Holmes Memorial Lecture: Global Governance in a Copernican World', *Global Governance*, 18 (2): 133–48.

Malone, David. 2012. *Does the Elephant Dance? Contemporary Indian Foreign Policy*. Oxford: Oxford University Press.

Mattoo, Amitabh and Happymon Jacob. 2009. 'Republic of India', in Hans J. Michelmann (ed.), *Foreign Relations in Federal Countries*, pp. 168–87. Montreal: McGill-Queen's University Press.

Mitra, Subrata. 2011. *Politics in India: Structure, Process and Policy*. London: Routledge.

Mohan, C. Raja. 2003. *Crossing the Rubicon: The Shaping of India's New Foreign Policy*. New York: Palgrave Macmillan.

Mukherji, Rahul. 2014. *Globalization and Deregulation—Ideas, Interests, and Institutional Change in India*. Oxford: Oxford University Press.

Narang, Vipin and Paul Staniland. 2012. 'Institutions and Worldviews in Indian Foreign Security Policy', *India Review*, 11 (2): 76–94.

Narlikar, Amrita. 2006. 'Peculiar Chauvinism or Strategic Calculation? Explaining the Negotiating Strategy of a Rising India', *International Affairs*, 82 (1): 59–76.

———. 2016. '"Because They Matter"—Recognise Diversity, Globalise Research', GIGA Focus Global (1), Hamburg.

———. 2017. 'India's Role in Global Governance: A Modification?', *International Affairs*, 93 (1): 93–111.

Narlikar, Amrita and Aruna Narlikar. 2014. *Bargaining with a Rising India: Lessons from the Mahabharata*. Oxford: Oxford University Press.

Nau, Henry R. and Deepa M. Ollapally (eds). 2012. *Worldviews of Aspiring Powers: Domestic Foreign Policy Debates in China, India, Iran, Japan, and Russia*. Oxford: Oxford University Press.

Nel, Philip. 2010. 'Redistribution and Recognition: What Emerging Regional Powers Want', *Review of International Studies*, 36 (4): 951–74.

Nel, Philip and Detlef Nolte (guest eds). 2010. 'Regional Powers in a Changing Global Order', *Review of International Studies*, 36 (4): 877–974.

Never, Babette. 2012. 'Who Drives Change? Comparing the Evolution of Domestic Climate Governance in India and South Africa', *Journal of Environment and Development*, 21 (3): 362–87.

Nölke, Andreas, Tobias ten Brink, Simone Claar, and Christian May. 2015. 'Domestic Structures, Foreign Economic Policies and Global Economic Order: Implications from the Rise of Large Emerging Economies', *European Journal of International Relations*, 21 (3): 538–67.

Nymalm, Nicola and Johannes Plagemann. 2018. 'Comparative Exceptionalism: Universality and Particularity in Foreign Policy Discourses', *International Studies Review*, 21 (1): 12–37.

Onderco, Michal. 2015. *Iran's Nuclear Program and the Global South: The Foreign Policy of India, Brazil, and South Africa*. New York: Palgrave Macmillan.

Pant, Harsh V. and Julie M. Super. 2015. 'India's "Non-alignment" Conundrum: A Twentieth Century Policy in a Changing World', *International Affairs*, 91 (4): 747–64.

Paul, T.V., Deborah Welch Larson, and William C. Wohlforth (eds). 2014. *Status in World Politics*. Cambridge: Cambridge University Press.

Plagemann, Johannes and Miriam Prys. 2018. '"Responsibility", Change, and Rising Powers' Role Conceptions: Comparing Indian Foreign Policy Roles in Global Climate Change Negotiations and Maritime Security', *International Relations of the Asia Pacific*. Available at https://doi.org/10.1093/irap/lcy028, accessed on 1 June 2019.

Plagemann, Johannes and Sandra Destradi. 2015. 'Soft Sovereignty, Rising Powers, and Subnational Foreign Policy-making: The Case of India', *Globalizations*, 12 (5): 728–43.

Rudolph, Lloyd I. and Susanne Hoeber Rudolph. 1987. *In Pursuit of Lakshmi: The Political Economy of the Indian State*. Chicago: University of Chicago Press.

Schaffer, Teresita C. and Howard B. Schaffer. 2016. *India at the Global High Table: The Quest for Regional Primacy and Strategic Autonomy*. Washington, DC: Brookings Institution Press.

Schirm, Stefan A. 2013. 'Global Politics Are Domestic Politics: A Societal Approach to Divergence in the G20', *Review of International Studies*, 39 (3): 685–706.

Singh, Sinderpal. 2013. *India in South-Asia: Domestic Identity Politics and Foreign Policy from Nehru to the BJP*. Abingdon: Routledge.

Stephen, Matthew D. 2012. 'Rising Regional Powers and International Institutions: The Foreign Policy Orientations of India, Brazil and South Africa', *Global Society*, 26 (3): 289–309.

Thakur, Ramesh. 2013a. 'A Balance of Interest', in Andrew F. Cooper, Jorge Heine, and Ramesh Thakur (eds), *The Oxford Handbook of Modern Diplomacy*, pp. 70–87. Oxford: Oxford University Press.

———. 2013b. 'R2P after Libya and Syria: Engaging Emerging Powers', *The Washington Quarterly*, 36 (2): 61–76.

Zimmer, Heinrich. 1951. *Philosophies of India*. Princeton: Princeton University Press.

1 Understanding India's Exceptional Engagement with the Nuclear Non-proliferation Regime

KATE SULLIVAN DE ESTRADA

To observe that india has had an exceptional relationship with the global nuclear non-proliferation regime is not simply to note that it is different. India's non-proliferation exceptionalism has in the past led to it being framed as an outsider, a challenger, and even a threat to the normative pillars of the non-proliferation regime centred around (but not limited to) the Nuclear Non-proliferation Treaty (NPT). For decades, New Delhi's refusal to sign the NPT and persistent efforts to safeguard the legal and sovereign right to develop and test nuclear weapons positioned India as a prime target of both non-proliferation norms and multilateral technology denial regimes (Chellaney 1993; Frankel 1995; Weiss 2010). Then, in May 1998, India tested nuclear weapons. This breach of a foundational global non-proliferation norm led to widespread international opprobrium. India faced sanctions, condemnation from the United Nations (UN) Security Council and other major international organizations, and increasing pressure from the United States of America (USA) to meet institutionalized non-proliferation benchmarks (Sullivan de Estrada and Wheeler 2016).

Since 1998, successive Indian leaderships have laboured to develop a positive working relationship with the non-proliferation regime. In the process, India has been able to secure status, institutional recognition, and material advantages. The USA categorized India as 'a responsible state with advanced nuclear technology' in 2005, and a bilateral agreement signed between the USA and India in 2006, together with a waiver from the Nuclear Suppliers' Group (NSG) in 2008,[1] opened the way for Indian access to civil nuclear trade (Federal Government of the United States and Government of India 2005). These gains signal India's growing international recognition as a nuclear partner rather than a nuclear challenger. Indeed, in 2018, few states within the 48-member NSG presented obstacles to proposals for India's membership of the grouping, a key indicator of India's nuclear normalization, and a great many more voiced their support for India's inclusion (Roy 2016; Hibbs 2017). In short, India has gained widespread, though not universal, acceptance as an exceptional nuclear state in abidance with key global non-proliferation norms.

The purpose of this chapter is to map out the key drivers behind India's transformation between 1998 and 2017 from a so-called non-proliferation challenger to a constructive partner working productively alongside the non-proliferation regime. In keeping with the common analytical framework advanced throughout this book, the chapter sets out the key ideas, interests, and institutions that drive India's engagement with the non-proliferation regime at three levels: the domestic, the regional, and the global. Existing accounts of India's relationship with the global nuclear non-proliferation regime have almost exclusively focused on the drivers of security and interests as they function at the level of the Indian state, with little attention paid to domestic and international norms and institutions. This chapter expands these accounts by drawing on emerging scholarship on *status* in world politics. Introducing a status lens into the analysis of India's relationship with the non-proliferation regime allows for an engagement with both ideas *and* interests, as well as with the institutions within which they are embedded and/or through which they are expressed.

Overall, this chapter argues that the exceptional nature of India's current working relationship with the global nuclear non-proliferation regime derives from an interplay of interests and ideas at all three levels of analysis: nuclear autonomy and status considerations at the *domestic level*, security and status concerns at the *regional level*, and concerns over material sanctions and a quest for status recognition as a nuclear responsible at the *global level*. However, the key to understanding India's

---

[1] The NSG waiver permitted the operationalization of the US–India Civil Nuclear Agreement.

engagement with the non-proliferation regime is an appreciation of salient international norms enshrined within and beyond the NPT, and India's response to these norms. The chapter's main conclusion is that New Delhi's search for international status as a nuclear responsible, in particular, has served to validate and strengthen several key norms of the global nuclear non-proliferation regime, despite India's complicated position vis-à-vis the regime. India remains, however, far from functioning as a manager or norm-setter within the regime.

Rising India: Status and Nuclear Responsibility

Existing accounts of India's engagement with the global nuclear non-proliferation regime have emphasized the ways in which India has sought to maximize either its security or its interests. On such a reading, Indian elites have sought to retain the flexibility and autonomy of the Indian nuclear programme, foreclose the nuclear options of India's rivals, China and Pakistan, and secure access to trade in civil nuclear materials and technologies in order to enhance India's capacity to produce nuclear energy (Rajagopalan 2013, 2015; Weiss 2010).[2] Rajagopalan (2015, 652), for example, argues that 'India saw multilateral nuclear negotiations as one way to deal with nuclear security threats', with both the Partial Test Ban Treaty (PTBT) and the NPT serving as a way to limit China's nuclear advances in the 1980s and 1990s. Subsequently, India's proposal for the Rajiv Gandhi Action Plan for Nuclear Disarmament (RGAP) in 1988 and early support for the Comprehensive Test Ban Treaty (CTBT) were intended to constrain Pakistan's nuclear development.

Indian assessments of national security requirements are undoubtedly one driver of India's approach to the non-proliferation regime and offer a powerful explanation for India's reluctance to formally join the key institutions of the NPT and CTBT. However, they do not explain India's initial enthusiasm for both institutions; nor why Indian leaders and diplomats have invested so much time and effort in seeking to make a success of multilateral negotiations towards non-proliferation ends;

---

[2] Even A. Vinod Kumar's (2014, see especially pp. 3–5) recent work, which, commendably, aims to foreground the normative framework of the non-proliferation regime, still appears to prioritize India's security concerns as central drivers in its response to the regime.

nor why India today acts in key ways in conformity with central non-proliferation instruments such as the NPT, despite being a non-signatory. Rajagopalan's (2015, 660) assessment that for India 'multilateralism became the default option because the Indian leadership was unwilling to accept the short-term risk involved in taking responsibility for unilateral resolution of its security concerns' reveals only part of the story.

Status and Non-proliferation

A status explanation applied in tandem with a security explanation can shed light on what Indian leaders have hoped to achieve through multilateral diplomacy on nuclear and non-proliferation issues. The major limitation of standard security-centric readings of India's engagement with the non-proliferation regime is that they take seriously neither motivations of Indian state behaviour that offer no clear material gains, nor significant and salient international norms in international nuclear politics which can both shape Indian state behaviour and have real material implications for India's relations with key stakeholder states in the non-proliferation regime.

Recent work on status in world politics and India's status-seeking strategies as a rising power opens one way of drawing in a wider set of influences on state behaviour, including ideas and international normative considerations. First, the status literature makes a distinction between a state's social status and its material position within the international system, and argues that both the material and social compulsions of the international system serve as important drivers of state behaviour (Paul, Larson, and Wohlforth 2014; Larson and Shevchenko 2010; Basrur and Sullivan de Estrada 2017). This distinction signals a break from works on nuclear prestige that understand prestige as deriving from material power. For example, Karsten Frey's (2006) reading of the prestige-based motivations for India's nuclearization, while insightful, remains focused on India's material positioning in the international system, and does not conceptualize the global nuclear order in social terms.[3] By contrast, the

---

[3] As Frey (2006, 20) argues, 'India's attempt to increase the reputation of its power through the acquisition of nuclear weapons clearly aimed at seeking a revision of the international system. The powers that use this strategy are typically those that perceive themselves as the losers of the power competition at the time the international order was established.'

key analytical point in the status literature is that status, defined socially, can be an autonomous domain to material power, and benefits can be derived from status in the absence of the direct exercise of power to coerce or induce (Basrur and Sullivan de Estrada 2017).[4] High or positive status may be conceived of as an instrument for achieving other ends: status can function as a resource for influencing the behaviour of other actors, assist a state in obtaining material goods, or enhance a leadership's domestic political support (Keohane 2010, 19). Moreover, high status also functions as a social good, that is, as an end in itself. High status can provide psychologically rewarding confirmation to a state's leaders and the wider populace that the country is held in high regard (Wohlforth 2009, 35).

Second, the status literature suggests that international norms are central to status seeking. Positive status typically results from the approval received by high-status states for *conformity* to dominant social norms within a given status context while negative status results from *deviation* from dominant social norms (Basrur and Sullivan de Estrada 2017; Larson and Shevchenko 2010; Lebow 2008). In the domain of nuclear politics, international norms pose important constraints on the nuclear behaviours of states (Tannenwald 2007). They can also guide nuclear behaviours and choices, such as India's attempts to gain recognition as a responsible nuclear power.

India's deviation from dominant norms of nuclear responsibly resulted in low status following the 1998 tests (Sullivan 2014b, 2). Meanwhile, Indian conformity, especially successful diplomatic efforts to underscore India's positive track record on the non-proliferation of nuclear materials and know-how to other states, has led to an increase in status, that of a 'nuclear responsible'. Since the late 1990s, as a rising power, India has sought to use conformity with dominant non-proliferation norms to gain recognition as a nuclear responsible from 'elite' nuclear powers within the global nuclear order: the USA in particular, with Russia, France, and the UK also playing an important role, and China serving as a veto player (Leveringhaus and Sullivan de Estrada 2018). The pay-off of such conformity for India is that recognition as a nuclear responsible has been a necessary prerequisite to India being granted privileged civil

---

[4] Basrur and Sullivan de Estrada (2017) argue that the early history of India's status-seeking shows how achieving high status can be a priority for a state which de-prioritizes the use of coercive power in its conduct with other states.

nuclear trading rights (a material benefit), as well as escaping what former Foreign Secretary and National Security Advisor Shivshankar Menon (2016, 51) described as India's nuclear 'outlaw status' (a social benefit).

Third, high status may also derive from *innovation* beyond the dominant norms of a given status context; indeed, status-seeking states may wish to retain and emphasize certain attributes or behaviours that distinguish them from other major or rising powers (Basrur and Sullivan de Estrada 2017; Larson and Shevchenko 2010). States may, therefore, seek status on the basis of alternative criteria. However, those criteria must come to be accepted as worthy by dominant states within a given status context. As we will see, India's attempts to innovate on the basis of norms of nuclear restraint from the mid-1950s to the late 1980s failed to deliver any notable status dividends, which in part explains India's shift to status seeking through conformity, explored in the third part of this chapter.

Domestic Determinants of India's Engagement with the Non-proliferation Regime

Domestic-Level Institutions

In broad terms, the formulation of India's foreign policy originates from the executive branch, comprising the external affairs minister (EAM), two ministers of state for external affairs, the national security advisor (NSA) who heads the National Security Council (NSC), the foreign policy advisor to the prime minister, and, of course, the prime minister himself/ herself. These key individuals work together with bureaucrats from the Ministry of External Affairs (MEA), headed by the foreign secretary, and other advisory structures (Rana 2002). Major transformations in India's nuclear policies, however, have been led from the Prime Minister's Office (PMO). The decision to conduct nuclear tests in 1998 was taken at the highest level, with only a very narrow segment of the Indian leadership under Prime Minister Atal Bihari Vajpayee informed of the clandestine plans (Singh 2007, 231). Meanwhile, Prime Minister Manmohan Singh was a central protagonist behind the domestically controversial US–India Civil Nuclear Agreement, to the extent that he was willing to face (and ultimately, won) a parliamentary vote of confidence over the deal in July 2008 (Menon 2016; Mohan 2010, 141). The significant roles of M.K. Narayanan, serving as NSA from 2005 to 2010, in the negotiation of the agreement, as well as that of Foreign Secretary Shyam Saran, point to the importance of personalities as much as institutions such as the NSC and the MEA (Indo-Asian News Service 2017; Menon 2016).

Other domestic institutions play an oblique role in India's relationship with the non-proliferation regime. India's defence development bureaucracies, in particular the Defence Research and Development Organization (DRDO), do not directly participate in formal decision-making processes on nuclear issues, but they do speak notoriously freely about their technological ambitions and achievements, some of which pertain to nuclear modernization (Narang 2013). Their statements may not enjoy official sanction by India's political leadership, but they hold the potential to signal—whether intentionally or not—both latent, long-term strategic intent, and/or to jeopardize India's self-projection as a responsible nuclear power. The Atomic Energy Regulatory Board (AERB) is another institution that factors into India's engagement on non-proliferation, since a state's standards of national safety and nuclear security play a distinctive role in outside assessments of how responsible its stewardship of nuclear materials and facilities is.

Domestic-Level Interests—Autonomy and Security

India's strategic elite, centred on the individuals and institutions noted earlier and comprising 'a relatively small group of political and bureaucratic elites living in close physical, social, and institutional proximity to one another', generally considers India's interests to be tied up with autonomy and security (Narang and Staniland 2012, 80). Any perceived effort to circumscribe India's autonomy is seen as inherently unacceptable and as a threat to Indian security. Indeed, Rajagopalan (2015, 659) claims, 'Indian negotiators cannot afford to make concessions in international negotiations because of a domestic political culture that will pillory any concession as a "sell-out".' By refusing to sign the NPT and CTBT, successive Indian leaderships have sought to retain India's sovereign autonomy and legal right to test nuclear weapons, in view of India's deterrence needs vis-à-vis its nuclear-armed neighbours, Pakistan and China (Ganguly 1999). Even as India's foreign policy elite engaged in vigorous efforts to portray India as a responsible nuclear power in the wake of the 1998 tests, New Delhi did not comply with demands from the United Nations Security Council (UNSC) and the USA to sign the NPT and CTBT. Instead, Indian interlocutors sought to convince their international counterparts of India's legitimate defence requirements and to secure recognition for

India's nuclear sovereignty, in large part for security purposes (Singh 2007, 231). India has also avoided full participation in the US-led Proliferation Security Initiative (PSI), a consortium of over 100 states who seek to prevent the transport and transfer of weapons of mass destruction, in part over concerns relating to its autonomy (Holmes 2007; Kumar 2009).

How do broader societal preferences impact India's positions and policies on non-proliferation? Historically, foreign policy issues have been insulated from wider Indian political culture (Narang and Staniland 2012, 79). Election campaigns have revolved primarily around social, political, and economic issues, with foreign policy debated only in limited terms (Perkovich 2002, 262). Having said this, the 1998 Bharatiya Janata Party (BJP) election manifesto pledged a pro-nuclear weapons stance, and the 2014 BJP election manifesto made a vague commitment to reconsider India's nuclear doctrine (The Acronym Institute 1998; Burke 2014).

Over the past two decades of accelerated economic growth, heightened foreign trade and foreign investment have led Indian businesses—in both the service and manufacturing sectors—to develop a stronger interest in India's foreign policy (Baru 2009a). Indian firms have funded and participated in Track II diplomatic initiatives (unofficial informal interactions between groups of non-state actors from both nations), particularly in an effort to improve US–India relations in the wake of the 1998 nuclear tests. Successive rounds of the Track II US–India Dialogue, a joint initiative of the Confederation of Indian Industry (CII) and the Aspen Strategy Group, commenced in January 2002 (The Aspen Institute 2017). This dialogue served as an important locus of unofficial talks between the USA and Indian governments before, during, and after the negotiations over the US–India Civil Nuclear Agreement (Malik and Medcalf 2011, 4).

Over the same two-decade period, India has witnessed a revolution in the Indian media, including a marked shift from government patronage to near-domination by the private sector—although there are allegations of 'pervasive, systematic and infringed [government] control' over media owners since the Narendra Modi government came to power in 2014 (Baru 2009b; Press Trust of India 2017). The English-language media and its core middle-class readership became significant for public opinion on certain nuclear foreign policy issues from the mid-1990s, conspicuously in relation to the question of whether India should or should not sign the CTBT (Baru 2009a). More recently, India's declaration of intent to join the NSG in early 2016 and the NSG plenary session in June of the same year captured widespread media attention.

A further growing influence on Indian foreign policy has been the Indian diaspora, 'especially those who have been educated and are politically influential in their country of residence, as in the United States' (Malik and Medcalf 2011, 4). In the nuclear domain, an 'increasingly professional and well-funded "India lobby" among Indian-Americans' played a central role in 2006 in garnering the support of the US Congress for the US–India Civil Nuclear Agreement (Kirk 2008, 275).

Domestic-Level Ideas—Autonomy and Status

Two interrelated sets of domestic norms and ideas significantly shape India's approach to global non-proliferation policies: autonomy and status.

Autonomy has been a concept central to Indian identity both prior to and beyond Independence. The commitment to autonomy that had arisen during the Independence movement—and the grounds upon which that autonomy was seen as legitimate and desirable—was projected into the external sphere. In the context of post-independent India, Narang and Staniland (2012, 79) identify among India's foreign policy elite a continued 'strong preference for security via autonomy rather than security via alliance, engagement in international security organizations, or (to the extent possible) dependence on foreign weaponry'.

Ideas of autonomy are powerful domestically and transcend mere interests. This is underscored by the fact that in the domain of nuclear and non-proliferation policy, India has consistently rejected curbs on its autonomy, often at great cost. In reference to India's refusal to sign the NPT, for example, Rajagopalan (2015, 658) notes how 'India's isolation … carried with it meaningful consequences in the form of reluctance by other powers with advanced nuclear technology to share it or cooperate on it with India'. The emphasis on autonomy as a national staple of foreign policy thinking, but also one with a multitude of connotations, was underscored during domestic debates over the terms of the US–India Civil Nuclear Trading Agreement in 2008. Different party–political positions leveraged notions of autonomy quite distinctively in order to support their own positions on the deal (Sullivan 2008).

Beyond ideational commitments to autonomy, the lens of status helps us to understand how the motivations behind Indian activism in multilateral nuclear forums have exceeded mere security considerations. Early disarmament activism, for example, certainly promised a reduction in global tensions and the removal of the dangers of nuclear war; it also promised to relieve developing countries of the need to devote resources to economic development rather than a costly arms race (Jain 1974, 171). However, beyond these materialist drivers for India's proactive participation, both a prominent role for India in the process of nuclear disarmament and the successful propagation of new, India-designed international norms—such as Jawaharlal Nehru's attempts to press for a ban on nuclear testing in the late 1950s—stood to offer status rewards. Indian diplomats made a significant contribution to the negotiation of the PTBT in 1963, and Nehru's sister Vijaya Lakshmi Pandit sought to underscore India's role before the United Nations in October 1963: as a result of the treaty, she claimed, 'the purpose that India had sought to achieve [a ban on nuclear testing] had been three-quarters accomplished' (cited in Jain 1974, 120). India's attempts at securing high status by brokering agreements to secure robust non-proliferation institutions were foreclosed by the end of the discussions at the Eighteen-Nation Disarmament Committee (1962–69) that set the scene for the—from India's perspective—discriminatory NPT. Later, the failure of the 1988 RGAP further reinforced the hopelessness of India's initiatives to bring normative leadership to the field of non-proliferation.

Both the desire and failure of Indian foreign policy elites to project Indian norms out to the world through their foreign (and nuclear) policies resonate with the concept of status-seeking through innovation outlined earlier. In terms of normative innovation, notions of restraint have played a central role in India's nuclear history, factoring most significantly in India's decision not to develop nuclear weapons until the 1980s, or test them until 1998 (Abraham 2009; Perkovich 2002). In the early decades after Independence, much of India's international identity rested on a strong belief that India had much to teach the world, and particularly the West, about morality in inter-state relations (Sullivan 2014a). Nuclear restraint was, therefore, synonymous with the renunciation of 'immoral' nuclear weapons. The meaning of nuclear restraint gradually began to shift, however. In the 1960s, restraint featured in India's rhetorical campaign before the Eighteen-Nation Committee on Disarmament against the formulation of a non-proliferation treaty that simultaneously failed to secure complete and general disarmament and applied restrictions on the peaceful use of atomic energy by non-nuclear–weapons states. Indian representatives claimed that India was restrained because it was a working example of a state in possession of the technical ability to engage in nuclear weapons proliferation, but which was refraining from doing so (Conference of the Eighteen-Nation Committee on Disarmament 1965, 14). India's 1974 'Peaceful Nuclear Explosion' (PNE), too, was couched in terms of restraint: the Indian leadership sought to project India as a peaceful, nuclear-capable power, rather than a nuclear-armed power. Indeed, a survey of Indian political elite at the time revealed that the vast majority saw India's 'peaceful' atomic capabilities as clear evidence of India's commitment to nuclear restraint (Nandy 1974). A commitment to restraint was even reflected in official Indian statements following the 1998 tests: 'Future actions' would 'continue to reflect ... a sense of responsibility and restraint, but a restraint born of the assurance of action, not of doubts or apprehension' (Government of India 1998b). This understanding of restraint had again shifted: it was borne of the possession of material power, rather than its absence; of strength rather than weakness. An emphasis on nuclear restraint has continued in India's nuclear policies even after 1998, for example, in the pledge of no-first-use and the non-use of coercive nuclear threats for compellence, and in the pursuit of, and—so far—satisfaction with, Small Nuclear Arsenals (SNAs) and de-alerted nuclear forces. These more recent policies of nuclear restraint have been complicated, however, by New Delhi's concomitant drive for the modernization of India's nuclear delivery systems (Leveringhaus and Sullivan de Estrada 2018).

Aside from these innovations, from 1998 onwards, Indian foreign policy elites have sought accommodation for India within the nuclear non-proliferation regime on the basis of conformity to dominant non-proliferation norms, as discussed in more detail later. This is partly to reassure other states that, as a rising and nuclear power, India does not intend to subvert the existing global order, or further subvert the nuclear order (Leveringhaus and Sullivan de Estrada 2018). However, high status is also of clear value in domestic political terms: India's media revolution has occurred in tandem with an expansion of the Indian middle class, a group 'with new aspirations and energies, who seek a new status for India in the world' (Khilnani 2005, 1). Perceptions of unfair discrimination (signalling low status), in the case of the CTBT, and the desire for membership of 'international in-groups' (signalling high status), such as the NSG, have animated public opinion within the English-language media and its core middle-class audience.

Regional Determinants of India's Engagement with the Non-proliferation Regime

Regional-Level Institutions

The impact of formal regional institutions on India's global non-proliferation policies is limited, if not zero.[5] In the nuclear domain, India currently has no confidence-building measures (CBMs) with China, although some do exist with Pakistan. The two countries hold an unbroken 26-year record of exchanging lists of their respective nuclear facilities under the 'Annual Notification of Nuclear Facilities' measure (Press Trust of India 2017). Other CBMs between India and Pakistan were set up in the years following the 1998 nuclear tests, including a mutual provision of advance notification of ballistic missile tests in 2002; however, their implementation has been patchy (Banerjee 2010). The prospect for effective nuclear CBMs does not seem hopeful: Banerjee (2010, 354) argues that the 'mutually exclusive security perceptions and postures of [India, China, and Pakistan] limits the prospects for confidence building between them'.

While a Southeast Asian Nuclear Weapon–Free Zone (NWFZ) was established in 1995 between Southeast Asian states, and the Association of Southeast Asian Nations (ASEAN) has developed other forums and initiatives for cooperation on the non-proliferation of weapons of mass destruction (WMD), no non-proliferation arrangements are currently in effect in the South Asian region or between India and China (Kassenova 2012). Apart from regular statements underscoring a shared commitment to nuclear disarmament among member states, the South Asian Association for Regional Cooperation (SAARC) has had nothing to say about nuclear non-proliferation. Indeed, the summit declaration

---

[5] Basrur (2013) notes similarities in the nuclear thought and practice of the regional nuclear powers China, India, and Pakistan, and these similarities may well be, at least in part, mutually constitutive. However, they are not enshrined in any reciprocal or shared formal institutions.

of the 10th SAARC summit, held in Colombo in July 1998, made no mention of India's and Pakistan's recent nuclear tests despite their *de facto* nuclearization of South Asia (Saez 2012, 102).

Regional-Level Interests: Security

India's general security concerns with regard to China and Pakistan stem from India's territorial disputes with each country. Its nuclear security concerns originate from China's decision to test nuclear weapons in 1964, and from Pakistan, acknowledged as a latent nuclear power from the late 1980s and (like India) an overt nuclear-armed state since May 1998. Indian concerns also stem from Pakistan's 'near-alliance relationship' with China, and China's suspected nuclear assistance to Pakistan (Banerjee 2010, 354). Reciprocally, India's improved ties with the USA are a concern to both Pakistan and China: the USA expended a great deal of diplomatic and political energy on securing access for India to global civil nuclear trade, and both Pakistan and China have viewed these efforts as part of a broader US strategy to support India's emergence as an Asian challenger to China (Perkovich 2005).

Regional-Level Ideas: Status

Two further significant regional determinants of India's engagement with the non-proliferation regime have been India's status rivalry with Pakistan and China. While the former has been fortuitous for India, the latter continues to pose major challenges.

India's and Pakistan's 1998 nuclear tests met with similar international condemnation and sanctions, yet nearly two decades later they differ markedly in their international nuclear status. While both states remain outside the NPT, India enjoys access to civil nuclear trade through the NSG waiver granted in 2008, while Pakistan has continued to face an outright exclusion from civil nuclear commerce, despite both Pakistan and China having lobbied in favour of Pakistani access (*Global Security Newswire* 2011). In contrast to India's familiarity as a democracy and recognition of India's positive record on the non-export of nuclear materials, technologies, and know-how, Pakistan has been perceived as a fragmented state with nuclear installations and materials at risk from terrorist groups that was unable or unwilling to rein in the Pakistani nuclear scientist A. Q. Khan's nuclear black market (Sullivan de Estrada and

Wheeler 2016). To many in the international community, Pakistan's nuclear weapons persist as a source of fear and anxiety. As Dalton and Krepon (2015, 36) note: 'India's nuclear weapons are widely perceived to be less threatening than Pakistan's.' The status dividends for India and the losses for Pakistan over time are clear: a senior White House official reportedly declared in October 2015 that the USA was 'not seeking an exception for Pakistan within the Nuclear Suppliers' Group to facilitate civil nuclear exports', despite rumours to the contrary (*Al Jazeera* 2015).

The story with China is quite different. China enjoys both status and power as one of the five permanent members of the UNSC and as a recognized nuclear weapon state under the NPT, and, as a result, 'has an important voice and role in the process of developing a constructive relationship between India and the non-proliferation regime' (Rajagopalan 2012). China has consistently sought to undermine India's nuclear legitimacy, labelling India a 'nuclear outsider' and a 'nuclear spoiler' (Horsburgh 2015b, 35). In 1998, official Chinese media sources expressed outrage at India's claim that its tests were a response to a threat from China, and labelled India 'irresponsible' and a spoiler of international non-proliferation instruments such as the CTBT. China has played an obstructionist role within the NSG, both in relation to the 2008 India waiver and the more recent discussions over India's bid for NSG membership (Horsburgh 2015b; Roy 2016). Beijing's preference is for the continuation of India's 'outsider' NPT status, and for India to remain an outsider to other nuclear institutions, including the NSG, as a means to check India's rising power and status (Sullivan de Estrada and Leveringhaus 2017). Given China's veto power within both the NSG and other organizations that can grant India insider status, the two countries' status competition stands as a major obstacle to India's fuller integration into the non-proliferation regime.

Global Determinants of India's Engagement with the Non-proliferation Regime: Responsibility and Recognition

Nuclear Responsibility

A useful way of conceptualizing the ways in which international institutions, interests, and ideas are interlinked and can shape state behaviour towards the nuclear non-proliferation regime is through the lens of nuclear responsibility (Walker 2011; Horsburgh 2015a; Leveringhaus and Sullivan de Estrada 2018). Nuclear responsibility can be defined as 'a characteristic of states that fulfil norms of legitimate nuclear behaviour, and whose fulfilment of those norms is recognized by others' (Sullivan 2014b, 2).

At the global institutional level, an assessment of the degree of nuclear responsibility of a given state is, in part, an exercise in examining its nuclear behaviours in reference to a given set of institutionalized behavioural benchmarks (Walker 2010). The NPT is the central institutional reference point: it is one of the oldest[6] non-proliferation treaties, enjoys widespread adherence, and was extended indefinitely in 1995. Different types of responsible behaviours are expected of its signatories, depending on whether a state is recognized as a nuclear-weapons state or a non-nuclear–weapons state under the terms of the treaty. Responsible behaviour for the former entails restraint in the export of sensitive nuclear technologies to non-nuclear states and undefined progress towards arms control and disarmament (Leveringhaus and Sullivan de Estrada 2018). For the latter, responsible behaviour entails forgoing the development of a nuclear weapons capacity while retaining the right to develop nuclear technology and energy for peaceful, civilian purposes. Beyond the NPT, institutionalized benchmarks of national nuclear safety and nuclear security measures—such as liability provisions in the event of a nuclear accident, and the vulnerability of nuclear installations, materials, and know-how to non-state actors—are further markers of nuclear responsibility (Leveringhaus and Sullivan de Estrada 2018).

At the level of global interests, an assessment of whether a state can be considered a nuclear responsible must also pay attention to the degree to which other states recognize or accept that a state's nuclear behaviour meets key, institutionalized behavioural benchmarks within the non-proliferation regime. This means that the values and interests of powerful, architect states in the non-proliferation regime matter because these are the states that typically play a key role in conferring responsible status, particularly the USA (Leveringhaus and Sullivan de Estrada 2018).

Ideas, that is, international norms, factor both into the institutionalized benchmarks of responsible nuclear behaviour and the recognition of the meeting of those benchmarks. The ideas of powerful states tend to win out when non-proliferation norms are enshrined in treaties and institutions,

---

[6] The NPT was opened for signature in 1968 and came into force in 1970.

as the NPT demonstrates. Apart from their role as norm-setters, however, powerful states also ultimately determine who qualifies for the conferral of responsible nuclear status, and, at a more general level, the kinds of states that may be labelled responsible (Medeiros 2007).

Global Institutions

In seeking to understand the relevance of institutionalized benchmarks of responsible nuclear behaviour to India's engagement with the non-proliferation regime, it is important to examine not simply India's willingness to legally accede to non-proliferation instruments, but also India's efforts at conforming to their key normative commitments. India's longstanding refusal to sign the NPT and rejection of the treaty's overall 'discriminatory' nature, due to the NPT's bifurcation of the global nuclear order, should not be mistaken for a rejection of the treaty's provisions. India has long been a supporter of the foundational ideas of non-proliferation as enshrined in the treaty, and since the 1998 tests, its officials have emphasized that India both values and conforms to its central provisions. Indeed, in 2000, External Affairs Minister Jaswant Singh (2000) claimed that 'India's policies have been consistent with the key provisions of NPT that apply to nuclear-weapon states.'

By way of its 1998 nuclear tests, India certainly transgressed perhaps the centremost pillar of the NPT, Article II, according to which non-nuclear weapons states agree 'not to manufacture or otherwise acquire nuclear weapons or other explosive devices'. India also breached the norm of non-testing that emerged from the extension of the treaty in 1995. However, India has upheld a voluntary moratorium on nuclear testing since 1998 (thereby also complying with the CTBT) and has also abided by Article I of the treaty, which commits the nuclear weapon states party to the treaty to desist from the transfer of nuclear weapons or explosive devices to other states or parties and from assisting in any other way in their manufacture or acquisition.

Indeed, it is this aspect of India's non-proliferation behaviour that has drawn the most international attention since its 1998 tests, and Indian officials have repeatedly emphasized India's so-called clean record on the export of nuclear weapon materials, technology, and expertize. Official statements released by the Indian MEA directly after the tests stressed India's 'impeccable' record in exercising 'the most stringent control on the export of sensitive technologies, equipment and commodities especially those related to weapons of mass destruction' (Government of India 1998a, 1998c). India's proliferation credentials have, however, been subject to scrutiny: the Institute for Science and International Security, based in Washington, regularly analyses proliferation behaviours among (primarily) non-Western states and has suggested Indian involvement in 'illicit nuclear trade', although the reports' claims are not echoed elsewhere and are—as the authors themselves note—not comparable to major proliferation episodes such as Pakistan's A.Q. Khan network or China's nuclear cooperation with Pakistan (Albright, Stricker, and Wood 2013). Moreover, India has taken several steps to develop voluntary nuclear export controls. India's 2005 Weapons of Mass Destruction and Their Delivery Systems (Prohibition of Unlawful Activities) Act and update of its national export control list in March 2013 (to fall in line with both the NSG and the Missile Technology Control Regime [MTCR] lists) demonstrate India's keenness to comply with international standards on the export of dual-use items and technologies.

In line with Article III of the NPT, which prohibits the 'diversion of nuclear energy from peaceful uses to nuclear weapons or other nuclear explosive devices' and requires parties to the treaty to transfer nuclear materials and related equipment to other states only under the International Atomic Energy Agency (IAEA) safeguards, India agreed in 2009 to a safeguards agreement with the IAEA to separate its civil and military facilities, as do nuclear weapon states. India has also signed, and in 2015 ratified, an Additional Protocol to the Safeguards Agreement between the Government of India and the IAEA for the Application of Safeguards to Civilian Nuclear Facilities. The purpose of the Additional Protocol for nuclear weapon states (and India) is to inform the IAEA of any nuclear cooperation such that it is better able to detect undeclared nuclear activities in non-nuclear weapon states. Finally, India has played an active role in upholding Article IV of the treaty, which supports non-nuclear–weapons states in their right to the peaceful uses of nuclear energy. India claims also to be committed to Article VI, which commits all signatories to the treaty to the pursuit of negotiations towards global nuclear disarmament. Overall, India's record on NPT compliance—since its 1998 tests, and if it is now held up to the standards of a nuclear-weapons state under the terms of the treaty—appears strong.

Where national safety and nuclear security is concerned, India's nuclear regulatory system has received both domestic and international criticism,[7] and its international ranking, at least according to the methodology of the 2014 Nuclear Threat Initiative Nuclear Materials Security Index—which is questionable to many—is the second lowest (Nuclear Threat Initiative 2014). India has, however, gone to considerable lengths to bolster its nuclear security architecture in line with global norms. First, it has been bringing its domestic legislation in line with UNSC Resolution 1540, which aims to prevent the transfer of nuclear materials to non-state actors. Second, at the international level, it has been signing and ratifying both the 2005 amendment to the Convention on the Physical Protection of Nuclear Material (CPPNM) and the 2005 International Convention for the Suppression of Acts of Nuclear Terrorism (ICSANT). India's participation in all of the Nuclear Security Summits is noteworthy, as is its establishment of a Global Centre for Nuclear Energy Partnership, whose purpose is to deliver training in nuclear safety and security issues. In the domain of nuclear liability, New Delhi has signed the Convention on Supplementary Compensation for Nuclear Damage in 2010 and ratified it in early 2016 (Dixit 2016).

Taken together, these efforts at complying with key international instruments of non-proliferation and nuclear safety and security and demonstrating respect for their constituent norms bolster India's case to be recognized as a nuclear responsible. However, to what extent has that recognition been conferred?

Global Interests

In terms of the outside recognition of India, both the US–India Civil Nuclear Agreement and the 2008 NSG waiver that permitted its operationalization stood as critical milestones in the recognition of India as a responsible nuclear power. The interests of the prime architect and

---

[7] The AERB has received critical reviews following both a 2012 audit by the Comptroller and Auditor General of India (CAG), and an invited audit by the IAEA in 2015 (Mohan and Kini, 2016). Both the CAG and the IAEA audits have questioned the independence of the AERB and recommended the creation of an independent statutory atomic regulator. The Nuclear Safety Regulatory Authority Bill, currently under preparation, plans to legally delink the AERB from the Department of Atomic Energy to address these criticisms.

guarantor of the non-proliferation regime, the USA, were central to the conferral of this status. Support of the USA for the India–US nuclear deal rested on the potential for closer economic and strategic engagement between the two countries given India's impressive economic growth following liberalization and its rising influence in Asia. It was also attractive for domestic political reasons: offering advantages to nuclear energy interests, defence sales, and other suppliers of nuclear and high technology. However, a great deal of the discourse of the US administration in the lead up to the controversial US–India Civil Nuclear Agreement centred on values shared between the two states, such as India's identity as a democracy. Broad US conceptions of India's benevolence, at least in regard to the USA's own interests, also factored (Sullivan 2014b).

To date, India has concluded civil nuclear trading agreements with eight states.[8] With US backing, India became a member of the MTCR in mid-2016, was admitted to the Wassenaar Arrangement in late 2017, and in early 2018 became a member of the Australia Group. Each of these regimes, in some way, serves to bolster non-proliferation and export control regimes, and India's acceptance into them reflects the degree of India's acceptance into the broader non-proliferation regime. At the same time, India remains outside the NSG, despite formally applying for membership in 2016, with deliberations within the NSG over India's membership dating back even earlier, to 2011. Mark Hibbs (2018, 281, 293) has shown how New Delhi has primarily justified its quest for NSG membership in terms of interests—'participation in nuclear non-proliferation and commercial rule making; development of its nuclear-power infrastructure; enhancing its nuclear-exporting capacity; [and] obtaining access to sensitive nuclear technology'—even as status also appears as 'an important driver of New Delhi's quest for NSG membership', as has been noted earlier.[9] India's position outside the NSG shows that there is certainly no international consensus on the politicized question of whether India can be considered a responsible nuclear power. China, in particular, remains resistant to India's membership of the NSG

[8] Argentina, Australia, Canada, France, Japan, Kazakhstan, Mongolia, Namibia, and South Korea.

[9] Hibbs' (2018, 289) useful definition of status recognition through NSG membership overlaps substantially with the definition provided here, although without clear theorization or reference to the status literature.

and India's broader indeterminate relationship with the non-proliferation regime (Sullivan de Estrada and Leveringhaus 2017).

Global Ideas

India has come into clear abidance with many key non-proliferation norms since its 1998 tests. But to what extent has it internalized those norms? The answer depends on whether India's conformity with non-proliferation norms is viewed as an instrumental 'performance' aimed at securing for India status as a nuclear responsible, or whether India's foreign policy elites genuinely attach value to those norms. Given India's longstanding discourses that express a commitment to non-proliferation and disarmament and the psychological rewards of high status as a nuclear responsible, it is likely that many within India's foreign policy elite are invested in the key norms of the nuclear non-proliferation regime. This is not to suggest, however, that it would be impossible, or even particularly difficult to overturn, for example, the norm of non-testing if considerations of security or autonomy should so demand.

A key point to note is that India remains far from occupying a position in the ranks of the managers and architects of the non-proliferation regime. India was not included, for example, in the Six-Party talks on North Korea nor the P5+1 talks on Iran, and remains disadvantaged by its absence of status and power (unlike China) as a nuclear weapon state recognized by the NPT, as a permanent member of the UNSC, and, for the time being at least, as a member of the NSG. India has also not stepped up to the role of a burden-sharer through participation in the PSI, where it could potentially play a prominent interdiction role through its naval reach in the Indian Ocean (Kumar 2009). Moreover, India is far from playing a role as a norm-setter within the non-proliferation regime: while India has sought higher status on the basis of 'responsible' innovations centred around nuclear restraint—such the de-alerting of nuclear weapons—these innovations have not seen institutionalization at the international level (Leveringhaus and Sullivan de Estrada 2018).

***

In the early decades of the twenty-first century, India remains, institutionally speaking, an outlier or 'exception' to key parts of the non-proliferation regime. However, India has succeeded in gaining recognition for its conformity with many of the regime's core norms. This outcome has resulted in dividends for India, although not all would agree that it has been beneficial for the non-proliferation regime. In 2005, when Indian Prime Minister Manmohan Singh and US President George W. Bush issued a joint statement that paved the way for an agreement to permit civil nuclear trade with India, the non-proliferation analyst William Potter (2005, 347) argued that the joint statement was 'likely to promote the further spread of nuclear weapons by eroding the norm of non-proliferation embodied in the NPT.'

Nearly a decade later, while India has not signed the NPT or the CTBT, it has voluntarily committed itself, in principle, to the standards of responsibility expected of their signatories: foregoing the proliferation of nuclear technology to non-nuclear states, and the testing of nuclear weapons since 1998. India has also sought to both align its domestic legislation with international standards on nuclear exports, safety, security, and liability. India's constructive working relationship with the non-proliferation regime shows more prudent non-proliferation behaviour on its part, and in this sense has strengthened it. However, whether other states contemplating an analogous pathway outside the non-proliferation regime are inspired more by India's 'example' than India's 'brand of exceptionalism' is a question yet to be answered (Squassoni 2010, 48). What cannot be denied is that India's exceptional status as a nuclear state but an outsider to the NPT regime signals a vindication of India's decades-long rejection of the terms of the treaty and Indian claims to nuclear exceptionalism.

Important to note is that India is and remains far from being a regime insider. There are no clear means by which India could become a signatory to the NPT in its current form.[10] India's eventual membership of the NSG is probable but by no means assured, given China's strong opposition to India's inclusion. India does not enjoy a managerial role in the non-proliferation regime, nor does it function as a norm-setter. India may have gained an exceptional status outside the non-proliferation regime, but such a status comes with limits on India's power to change what lies within.

---

[10] India has no option to join the treaty as a nuclear-weapons state since the legal status of a nuclear-weapons state under the NPT can only be granted to a state that tested a working nuclear device prior to 1 January 1967.

Overall, India's approach to the non-proliferation regime is clearly shaped by interests and ideas at the domestic, regional, *and* global levels, in keeping with the original assertion that both security and status considerations matter to India. Institutions at the regional level matter barely at all, but are central at the domestic and global levels.

References

Abraham, Itty. 2009. 'Contra-proliferation: Interpreting the Meanings of India's Nuclear Tests', in Scott D. Sagan (ed.), *Inside Nuclear South Asia*, pp. 106–33. Stanford: Stanford University Press.

Acronym Institute, The. 1998. 'BJP Manifesto Pledges Openly Pro-Nuclear-Weapons Stance', *Disarmament Diplomacy*, no. 23, February. Available at: http://www.acronym.org.uk/old/archive/23bjp.htm (accessed 10 September 2016).

Albright, David, Andrea Stricker, and Houston Wood. 2013. *Future World of Illicit Nuclear Trade: Mitigating the Threat*, 29 July. Washington, DC: Institute for Science and International Security.

Al Jazeera. 2015. 'Nuclear Weapons Issue Spoils Sharif's Trip to the US', 24 October. Available at: http://www.aljazeera.com/blogs/asia/2015/10/nuclear-weapons-issue-spoils-sharif-trip-151023220220297.html (accessed 10 September 2016).

Aspen Institute, The. 2017. 'The U.S.–India Strategic Dialogue'. Available at: https://www.aspeninstitute.org/programs/aspen-strategy-group/the-u-s-india-strategic-dialogue/ (accessed 25 July 2017).

Banerjee, Dipankar. 2010. 'Addressing Nuclear Dangers: Confidence Building Between India-China-Pakistan', *India Review*, 9 (3): 345–63.

Baru, Sanjaya. 2009a. 'The Growing Influence of Business and Media on Indian Foreign Policy', *ISAS Insights*, 49 (5). Available at: https://www.files.ethz.ch/isn/96448/50.pdf (accessed 2 September 2016).

———. 2009b. 'The Influence of Business and Media on Indian Foreign Policy', *India Review*, 8 (3): 266–85.

Basrur, Rajesh. 2013. 'China, India and Pakistan: Models for an Intermediate Stage towards Disarmament?' *Australian Journal of International Affairs*, 67 (2): 176–89.

Basrur, Rajesh and Kate Sullivan de Estrada. 2017. *Rising India: Status and Power*. Abingdon: Routledge.

Burke, Jason. 2014. 'Indian Election Alarm as BJP Raises Prospect of Nuclear Weapons Rethink', *The Guardian*, 7 April. Available at: https://www.

theguardian.com/world/2014/apr/07/indian-election-bjp-manifesto-nuclear-weapons (accessed 10 September 2016).

Chellaney, Brahma. 1993. *Nuclear Proliferation: The US–Indian Conflict*. New Delhi: Orient Longman.

Conference of the Eighteen-nation Committee on Disarmament (United Nations). 1965. 'Final Verbatim Record of the Conference of the Eighteen-nation Committee on Disarmament [Meeting 223]', 12 August, ENDC/PV.223.

Dalton, Toby and Michael Krepon. 2015. *A Normal Nuclear Pakistan*. Washington, DC: Stimson Center and Carnegie Endowment for International Peace.

Dixit, Aabha. 2016. 'India Joins the Convention on Supplementary Compensation for Nuclear Damage', 4 February. Vienna: IAEA Office of Public Information and Communication. Available at: https://www.iaea.org/newscenter/news/india-joins-convention-supplementary-compensation-nuclear-damage (accessed 1 September 2016).

Federal Government of the United States and Government of India. 2005. 'Joint Statement by President George W. Bush and Prime Minister Manmohan Singh', 18 July, Washington, DC. Available at: http://2001–2009.state.gov/p/sca/rls/pr/2005/49763.htm (accessed 9 September 2016).

Frankel, Francine (ed.). 1995. *Bridging the Non-proliferation Divide: The United States and India*. Delhi: Konark.

Frey, Karsten. 2006. *India's Nuclear Bomb and National Security*. London/New York: Routledge.

Ganguly, Sumit. 1999. 'India's Pathway to Pokhran II: The Prospects and Sources of New Delhi's Nuclear Weapons Program', *International Security*, 23 (4): 148–77.

Global Security Newswire. 2011. 'China Questions Indian Membership in Nuclear Suppliers Group', 18 July. Available at: http://gsn.nti.org/gsn/nw_20110718_5211.php (accessed 10 September 2016).

Government of India. 1998a. 'Announcement by the Prime Minister', 11 May, New Delhi. Available at: http://pib.nic.in/archieve/lreleng/lyr98/l0598/PIBR110598.html (accessed 29 November 2017).

———. 1998b. 'Evolution of India's Nuclear Policy', *India News*, 16 May–15 June, pp. 3–6.

———. 1998c. 'Planned Series of Nuclear Tests Completed', 13 May, New Delhi. Available at: http://pib.nic.in/archieve/lreleng/lyr98/l0598/PIBR130598.html (accessed 29 November 2017).

Hibbs, Mark. 2017. 'Eyes on the Prize: India's Pursuit of Membership in the Nuclear Suppliers Group', *The Nonproliferation Review*, 24 (3–4), pp. 275–96.

Holmes, James R. 2007. 'India and the Proliferation Security Initiative: A US Perspective', *Strategic Analysis*, 31 (2), pp. 315–37.

Horsburgh, Nicola. 2015a. *China and Global Nuclear Order: From Estrangement to Active Engagement*. Oxford: Oxford University Press.

Horsburgh, Nicola. 2015b. 'Chinese Views of a Nuclear India: From the 1974 Peaceful Nuclear Explosion to the Nuclear Suppliers Group Waiver in 2008', in Kate Sullivan (ed.), *Competing Visions of India in World Politics: India's Rise Beyond the West*, pp. 34–48. Basingstoke: Palgrave Macmillan.

Indo-Asian News Service. 2017. 'Indo–US Civil Nuclear Deal Deadline Will Be Missed: M.K. Narayanan', *The Economic Times* (online edition), 17 April. Available at: http://energy.economictimes.indiatimes.com/news/power/indo-us-civil-nuclear-deal-deadline-will-be-missed-m-k-narayanan/58225592 (accessed 30 April 2017).

Jain, J.P. 1974. *India and Disarmament*, vol. 1, *Nehru Era: An Analytical Study*. New Delhi: Radiant Publishers.

Kassenova, Togzhan. 2012. 'A Regional Approach to WMD Nonproliferation in the Asia-Pacific', *Policy Outlook*, 14 August, Washington, DC: Carnegie Endowment for International Peace. Available at: http://carnegieendowment. org/2012/08/14/regional-approach-to-wmd-nonproliferation-in-asia-pacific-pub-48945 (accessed 7 September 2016).

Keohane, Robert O. 2010. 'The Economy of Esteem and Climate Change', *St. Antony's International Review*, 5 (2): 16–28.

Khilnani, Sunil. 2005. 'India as a Bridging Power', in Prasenjit K. Basu, Brahma Chellaney, Parag Khanna, and Sunil Khilnani (eds), *India as a New Global Leader*, pp. 1–15. London: Foreign Policy Centre.

Kirk, Jason A. 2008. 'Indian-Americans and the US–India Nuclear Agreement: Consolidation of an Ethnic Lobby?' *Foreign Policy Analysis*, 4 (3): 275–300.

Kumar, A. Vinod. 2009. 'India's Participation in the Proliferation Security Initiative: Issues in Perspective', *Strategic Analysis*, 33 (5): 686–700.

———. 2014. *India and the Nuclear Non-proliferation Regime: The Perennial Outlier*. New York: Cambridge University Press.

Larson, Deborah Welch and Alexei Shevchenko. 2010. 'Status Seekers: Chinese and Russian Responses to US Primacy', *International Security*, 34 (4): 63–95.

Lebow, Richard Ned. 2008. *A Cultural Theory of International Relations*. Cambridge: Cambridge University Press.

Leveringhaus, Nicola and Kate Sullivan de Estrada. 2018. 'Between Conformity and Innovation: China's and India's Quest for Status as Responsible Nuclear Powers', *Review of International Studies*, 44 (3): 482–503.

Malik, Ashok and Rory Medcalf. 2011. 'India's New World: Civil Society in the Making of Foreign Policy', *Lowy Institute Analysis*, May. Available at: https://www.lowyinstitute.org/sites/default/files/pubfiles/Malik_and_Medcalf%2C_India%27s_new_world_web_1.pdf (accessed 25 July 2017).

Medeiros, Evan S. 2007. *Reluctant Restraint: The Evolution of China's Nonproliferation Policies and Practices, 1980–2004*. Stanford: Stanford University Press.

Menon, Shivshankar. 2016. *Choices: Inside the Making of India's Foreign Policy*. Gurgaon: Penguin.

Mohan, C. Raja. 2010. 'Rising India: Partner in Shaping the Global Commons?' *The Washington Quarterly*, 33 (3): 133–48.

Mohan, M.P. Ram and Els Reynaers Kini. 2016. 'India's Nuclear Regulators Have Been Audited', *The Hindu Business Line*, 3 January. Available at: http://www.thehindubusinessline.com/opinion/indias-nuclear-regulators-have-been-audited/article8061473.ece (accessed 2 September 2016).

Nandy, Ashis. 1974. 'Between Two Gandhis: Psychopolitical Aspects of the Nuclearization of India', *Asian Survey*, 14 (11): 966–70.

Narang, Vipin. 2013. 'Five Myths about India's Nuclear Posture', *The Washington Quarterly*, 36 (3): 143–57.

Narang, Vipin and Paul Staniland. 2012. 'Institutions and Worldviews in Indian Foreign Security Policy', *India Review*, 11 (2): 76–94.

Nuclear Threat Initiative. 2014. 'Nuclear Materials Security Index, Second Edition', January. Available at: http://ntiindex.org/data-results/2014-findings/ (accessed 10 September 2016).

Paul, T.V., Deborah Welch Larson, and William C. Wohlforth (eds). 2014. *Status in World Politics*. New York: Cambridge University Press.

Perkovich, George. 2002. *India's Nuclear Bomb: The Impact on Global Proliferation*. New Delhi: Oxford University Press.

———. 2005. 'Faulty Promises—The US–India Nuclear Deal', *Policy Outlook*, no. 21, Washington, DC: Carnegie Endowment for International Peace.

Potter, William C. 2005. 'India and the New Look of US Nonproliferation Policy', *The Nonproliferation Review*, 12 (2): 343–54.

Press Trust of India. 2017. 'India, Pakistan Exchange List of Nuclear Facilities', *Hindustan Times*, 1 January. Available at: http://www.hindustantimes.com/india-news/india-pakistan-exchange-lists-of-nuclear-sites/story-WMpXhsXh7Oww6aScmO7iyJ.html (accessed 30 April 2017).

Rajagopalan, Rajesh. 2012. 'Shoring Up the Non-proliferation Regime: The View from India', in Lora Saalman (ed.), *The China–India Nuclear Crossroads*, pp. 121–26. Washington, DC: Carnegie Endowment for International Peace.

————. 2013. 'From Defensive to Pragmatic Multilateralism and Back: India's Approach to Multilateral Arms Control and Disarmament', in W.P.S. Sidhu, P.B. Mehta, and B. Jones (eds), *Shaping the Emerging World: India and the Multilateral Order*, pp. 197–215. Washington, DC: Brookings Institution Press.

————. 2015. 'Multilateralism in India's Nuclear Policy: A Questionable Default Option', in David M. Malone, C. Raja Mohan, and Srinath Raghavan (eds), *The Oxford Handbook of Indian Foreign Policy*, pp. 650–62. Oxford: Oxford University Press.

Rana, Kishan S. 2002. *Inside Diplomacy*. New Delhi: Manas Publications.

Roy, Shubhajit. 2016. 'No Entry in NSG: India Blames One Country (China), Others Said No Too', *The Indian Express*, 25 June. Available at: http://indianexpress.com/article/india/india-news-india/no-entry-in-nsg-india-blames-one-country-china-others-said-no-too-2874377/ (accessed 8 September 2016).

Saez, Lawrence. 2012. *The South Asian Association for Regional Cooperation (SAARC): An Emerging Collaboration Architecture*. London: Routledge.

Singh, Jaswant. 2000. 'Statement to Parliament on the NPT Review Conference by External Affairs Minister Jaswant Singh, May 9, 2000', *Disarmament Diplomacy*, 46. Available at: http://www.acronym.org.uk/ (accessed 20 July 2017).

————. 2007. *In Service of Emergent India: A Call to Honor*. Bloomington: Indiana University Press.

Squassoni, Sharon. 2010. 'Looking Back: The US–Indian Deal and Its Impact', *Arms Control Today*, 40 (6): 48–52.

Sullivan, Kate. 2008. 'Discourses on the Nuclear Deal: Persistence of Independence', *Economic and Political Weekly*, XLIII (3, 19–25 January): 73–6.

————. 2014a. 'Exceptionalism in Indian Diplomacy: The Origins of India's Moral Leadership Aspirations', *South Asia: Journal of South Asian Studies*, 37 (4): 640–55.

————. 2014b. *Is India a Responsible Nuclear Power?* Policy Report, March, Singapore: S. Rajaratnam School of International Studies, NTU.

Sullivan de Estrada, Kate and Nicholas J. Wheeler. 2016. 'Trustworthy Nuclear Sovereigns? India and Pakistan after the 1998 Tests', *Stosunki Międzynarodowe—International Relations*, 52 (2): 289–306.

Sullivan de Estrada, Kate and Nicola Leveringhaus. 2017. 'China's Stance on NSG Membership Shows the Extent of India's Challenge in the Global Nuclear Order', *The Wire*, 30 June. Available at https://thewire.in/152726/india-china-nsg-global-nuclear-order/ (accessed 4 July 2017).

Tannenwald, Nina. 2007. *The Nuclear Taboo: The United States and the Non-use of Nuclear Weapons since 1945*. Cambridge: Cambridge University Press.

Walker, William. 2010. 'The UK, Threshold Status and Responsible Nuclear Sovereignty', *International Affairs*, 86 (2): 447–64.

———. 2011. *Perpetual Menace: Nuclear Weapons and International Order*. London: Routledge.

Weiss, Leonard. 2010. 'India and the NPT', *Strategic Analysis*, 34 (2): 255–71.

Wohlforth, William C. 2009. 'Unipolarity, Status Competition, and Great Power War', *World Politics*, 61 (1): 28–57.

2 Terrorism in India

SUMIT GANGULY AND BRANDON JOSEPH MILIATE

INDIA HAS LONG BEEN A VICTIM of terror and its own experiences with terrorism have substantially shaped its approach to terror in global affairs. For India, terror has emanated from domestic, regional, and, to some degree, even global levels. Before moving to the analysis of India's global-level approach to terrorism, this chapter slightly deviates from the overall analytical framework of this volume by applying the assessment of institutional, interest-based, and ideational factors to the study of domestic counterterrorism in India. The rationale behind this choice lies with the pre-eminence of domestic terror in India's perceptions of terrorism and in its counterterrorism policies on a global scale. Therefore, this chapter will discuss how the following three arenas of terror have haunted the country in the last several decades: the on-going Kashmir insurgency, the insurgency in the Punjab, and the renewed Naxalite insurgency. It will trace the origins of these insurgencies, discuss their trajectories, and conclude with an assessment of their present status. All three insurgencies had their roots in India's domestic politics. They stemmed in considerable measure from real and perceived failures of governance and institutions in the country. Regional forces, to varying degrees, also impinged on all of them. Finally, all three of these uprisings, at various stages, saw the influence of international actors.[1]

The study of terrorism and India's counterterrorism policy making requires some further slight modifications from the framework established

---

[1] For an important statement on how developments at the international level can affect domestic politics, see Gourevitch (1978).

in the introduction to this volume. First, the regional institutions of South Asia remain underdeveloped, particularly when it comes to domestic security concerns. Therefore, we have not addressed regional institutions within the case studies presented here, since there are none to speak of. Second, while the three case studies will allow us to highlight the domestic and regional institutions, interests, and ideas motivating India's counterterrorism behaviour, a separate section on the global dynamics of counterterrorism follows the case studies.

Crises in Kashmir

At the outset, it is important to state that the Kashmir insurgency must be analytically separated from the territorial dispute between India and Pakistan over Kashmir.[2] There is, obviously, no question that the two are integrally related. Pakistan has sought to exploit the discontent within the India-controlled portion of the disputed state, principally because of its territorial claim to the state. However, for the purposes of this chapter, the focus will be primarily on the *domestic* origins of the insurgency and the use of terror on the part of the insurgents.

The roots of the Kashmir insurgency have been discussed at considerable length elsewhere (Ganguly 1997). Suffice it to state that it stemmed from four sources. First, it can be traced to the political machinations of various national governments in New Delhi who had long undermined routine democratic procedures in the state. Second, the outbreak in the late 1980s can be attributed to the emergence of a new, politically sophisticated generation of Kashmiris who were unwilling to countenance the continued denial of their political rights. Third, the movement quickly turned to violence because of the perceived absence on the part of the Kashmiris of the existence of an alternative mode of expressing political disaffection.[3] Fourth, and finally, the strength, scope,

[2] For a discussion of the origins of the territorial dispute, see Ganguly (2001).
[3] In considerable part, an alternative mode of non-violent political mobilization and protest was unavailable in Kashmir principally because of the isolation of the state from the larger stream of the Indian nationalist movement. It was one of the so-called princely states that had recognized the British as the paramount power in India. Its monarch wielded all effective powers barring those of defence, foreign affairs and communications. For a discussion of the end of empire in Kashmir see Copland (1997).

and duration of the insurgency increased dramatically because of Pakistan's swift involvement in the *internal* crisis. Pakistan, which had long maintained an irredentist claim to Kashmir, saw the rebellion as an opportunity to wrest the state from India, initially through support for domestic insurgents (Fair 2014). Shortly thereafter, it inducted a series of Pakistan-based terrorists to foment further discord in the state.

Pakistan's motivations for its involvement in Kashmir were straightforward. It saw the indigenous uprising in the state as a tempting opportunity to inflict significant material costs on India in retaliation for the Indian role in the break-up of Pakistan in the wake of the East Pakistan crisis of 1971. Furthermore, many Pakistani strategists believed that they had successfully formulated a model of a proxy war that had been effectively implemented in Afghanistan with the Taliban. If the might of the Soviet Empire could have been challenged, surely the writ of the Indian state, already under attack in Kashmir, could be further undermined (Blom 2009).

A locally active organization, the Jammu and Kashmir Liberation Front (JKLF), had spearheaded the initial rebellion. It was originally founded by two Kashmiri expatriates, Amanullah Khan and Maqbool Butt, in the United Kingdom in June 1976. The organization had its antecedents in an earlier entity, the Kashmir National Liberation Front, which had been created in the 1960s. It was nominally secular but did not have representation from religious minorities in the state.

The JKLF first attracted significant attention within Kashmir when some of its operatives kidnapped Rubiya Sayeed, the daughter of the then Union Home Minister Mufti Mohammed Sayeed, in December 1989. The kidnappers had demanded that several Kashmiri militants who were in Indian prisons be released to ensure her safe return. After some deliberation, the Indian state acquiesced to their demands and she was set free. This event, in many ways, constituted a critical juncture in the emergence of the Kashmir insurgency. It significantly emboldened both domestic insurgents as well as Pakistan-based terrorists. Shortly thereafter, the valley plunged into a vortex of organized violence and terror.

The JKLF again came to the fore when one of its leaders, Yasin Malik, was implicated in the killings of several Indian Air Force officers in Batmaloo, Srinigar, in January 1990. Its heyday, however, proved to be short-lived. One of the groups that quickly overshadowed them was the Hizb-ul-Mujahideen (HuM). The HuM, though it was primarily composed of Kashmiris, had no secular pretensions. They also made clear that they were, unlike the JKLF, uninterested in an independent Kashmir. Instead they expressed fealty to Pakistan and sought an eventual merger of Indian-controlled Kashmir with Pakistan (Blom 2009, 138).

Over the next several months, the JKLF was quickly sidelined as a host of Pakistan-sponsored terrorists flooded the Kashmir Valley. They included the Zia Tigers, the Ansar-ul Islam, al-Badr, the Allah Tigers, and the Hizb-i-Islam amongst others. These groups proved to be far more vicious in their tactics, enjoyed no blood–soil relationship with the inhabitants of the region, and were well-trained and well-funded. The levels of violence, not surprisingly, escalated dramatically in the early 1990s, especially as Pakistan inducted two other terrorist organizations, the Jaish-e-Mohammed and the Lashkar-e-Taiba, into Kashmir.

Both these organizations enjoyed ample support from Pakistan's Inter-Services Intelligence Directorate (ISI-D) and were prepared to extend their activities beyond Kashmir. Indeed, the Jaish-e-Mohammed was implicated in an attack on the Indian Parliament in December 2001 and the Lashkar-e-Taiba in the swarming terrorist attack across Mumbai in November 2008.

Ironically, Indian security forces, which had had ample prior experience with both counterterrorism and counter-insurgency, nevertheless failed to respond appropriately to the challenge that the terrorists posed in the valley. Instead their initial tactics were crude and ham-handed. Extra-judicial killings, disappearances, and the immunity of the armed forces under Section 7 of the Armed Forces (Jammu and Kashmir) Special Powers Act (1990) (Amnesty International 2015) created a tense atmosphere in the state and did nothing to win over Kashmiri 'hearts and minds'. Not surprisingly, their harsh methods contributed to the further alienation of many of the residents of the valley, expanding the scope and reach of the insurgency.

Despite these initial missteps, the security forces, especially the Indian Army, were able over time to calibrate their tactics. Among other matters, in 1990 the army created the Rashtriya Rifles, a more nimble organization, specifically designed for counter-insurgency operations in Kashmir and elsewhere (PTI 2015). Simultaneously, civil–military coordination improved, the intelligence collection became more sophisticated, and the security forces, especially the army, calibrated the use of force. All these efforts enabled India to bring about a modicum of order across Kashmir toward the end of the decade.

Under the aegis of these changed conditions, the Indian state was able to organize a mostly free and fair election in the state in 1996, thereby restoring more than a semblance of normalcy. Even the Pakistani effort to jump-start the insurgency in 1999 through a series of incursions in the Kargil region of the state failed (Puri 2015). For all practical purposes, in the first decade of the twenty-first century, the insurgency in the state with accompanying terrorist acts came to a close despite persistent Pakistani attempts to continue infiltration across the Line of Control (LoC).

The problem that has continued to dog the valley, however, stems from the failure of the Indian state to address the underlying grievances of a generation of young Kashmiris who had grown up within the cauldron of the insurgency. The successful termination of the insurgency had required extensive surveillance of local youth, had involved their periodic harassment on the basis of suspicions of their ties to the insurgents, and had contributed to the militarization of the state.[4]

This reservoir of discontent has continued to pervade the state and is, in considerable part, responsible for periodic outbursts of anomic violence whenever a catalytic event occurs. In 2016, for example, the valley erupted in a series of protests in the wake of the killing of Burhan Wani, an operative of the mostly indigenous terrorist organization Hizb-ul-Mujahideen (Ashiq 2016). The harsh retaliatory tactics of the Indian state only exacerbated the situation, widening the scope of the protests. The sustained, leaderless protests clearly underscored that despite the presence of a freely elected government in the state, much disaffection lurks beneath a veneer of calm and normalcy.

In this context, it needs to be highlighted that the current disturbances that are wracking the state do not fall into the category of terror. Instead these are violent demonstrations in which local, disaffected youth are involved. Of course, as always, Pakistan remains keen on co-opting this movement for its own ends.

---

[4] For one compelling account see Peer (2010).

Domestic Explanatory Variables

As with the other chapters in this volume, we focus our attention on the institutions, interests, and ideas that form the foundation of Indian policies. In this chapter, however, we put particular emphasis on India's domestic counterterrorism behaviour before moving to its global-level policies. In the case of Kashmir, the institutional dimensions are particularly important. It was the decay of political institutions in Kashmir that led to the first outbursts of violence in the state. Politically mobilized and sophisticated youth who had felt rebuffed and thwarted at the ballot box turned to violence. If the mechanisms of normal politics had not been eroded and corrupted, it is entirely possible that their grievances could have been dealt with in an institutional framework. However, the failures of India's political institutions to guarantee the political rights of Kashmiris ultimately pushed their grievances toward insurgency and terror.

India's interest in ensuring its hold on Jammu Kashmir remains firm has been clear enough. While the state might hold some economic and/or geostrategic value, it is more likely that India's primary interests lie in proving that a Muslim-majority region can remain an integral part of a Hindu majority state. In this sense, violence and instability in Kashmir call into question the situation of Muslims and other religious minorities in India as a whole. The fact that some Kashmiri political organizations have expressed loyalty to Pakistan further challenges India's stability. Finally, Kashmir is not the only state in the republic that has played host to a secessionist movement. Indian policy makers, contrary to available evidence about domino effects, fear that Kashmir might provide a model for other movements for increased autonomy and/or independence.

In addition to formal institutions and state interests, ideas also have a clear role to play in understanding Indian policy making in Kashmir. For India, the initial commitment to hold on to Kashmir stemmed from its constitutional commitment to secularism. However, with the decline of the secular credo in the country, thanks to a range of political exigencies, the central *idea* animating its desire to hold on to Kashmir simply stems from a warrant to ensure its territorial integrity.

Regional Explanatory Variables

The interests of Pakistan play a particularly strong explanatory role in the case of Kashmir. At the *regional* level, Pakistan had successfully used terror to advance its goals in Afghanistan. This model, its policy makers—especially its security establishment—quickly concluded could be applied to the Kashmir context. It had obvious applications in the region as Pakistan, to varying degrees, also sought to use it to good effect in the Punjab crisis. The crisis obviously was worsened as a consequence of key material *interests* on the part of both India and Pakistan. Following the initial outbreak of violence in Kashmir, the Pakistani politico-military establishment saw a unique opportunity to exploit a volatile situation in the Indian-controlled portion of the state. They deemed that this was in their interest because a widening insurgency would deliver a body blow to its principal adversary and exact a price for India's intervention in Pakistan's civil war in 1971.

Finally, there is no denying the significance of *ideas* in animating this conflict. For Pakistan, wresting all of Kashmir from Indian hands is simply the 'unfinished business of partition' (Ahmed 2015). This idea has driven Pakistan's irredentist claim to Kashmir since 1947 and has contributed to three wars (1947–8, 1965, and 1999) and multiple crises. Since the resort to the instrumental use of Islam as both mobilizing and legitimizing devices in the country since the final days of Prime Minister Zulfiquar Ali Bhutto, the idea has also become fraught with religious significance. For some groups which are seeking to wreak havoc in Kashmir, such as the Lashkar-e-Taiba and the Jaish-e-Mohammed, the religious dimensions to the conflict are of no minor significance. Their statements and publications routinely emphasize the role of religious ideology in animating their goals and strategies (Afridi 2009).

On 5 August 2019, the ruling Bharatiya Janata Party, using its parliamentary majority, abrogated both Articles 35A and 370, the two constitutional provisions that had granted the disputed state of Jammu and Kashmir a special status. Simultaneously, they bifurcated the state into two union territories (entities that would be ruled directly from New Delhi).

The decision was met with considerable popular and elite opposition in parts of the state and especially in the Kashmir Valley. In an attempt to contain protests and ostensibly to forestall terrorist activity the government initially blocked the Internet, snapped all landline connections, and switched off cellphone towers. Also, a significant number of Kashmir's politicians remained under house arrest.[5]

---

[5] See https://theconversation.com/whats-behind-the-protests-in-kashmir-121833 for more on this issue.

The Punjab Crisis

The origins of the Punjab crisis were complex. At one level, it had deep historical and sociological roots and can be traced to the uncertain relationship between Sikhism and Hinduism. Sikhism, as a number of scholars have noted (Oberoi 1994), was a reform movement of the sixteenth century. The principal purpose of this undertaking—founded by Guru Nanak—had been to challenge the sacerdotal authority of Hinduism and its caste system. Over time, however, Sikhism became a separate faith. One of its later exponents, Guru Gobind Singh, gave the faith its militant features (Oberoi 1994), and was also responsible for drawing clear boundaries with Hinduism through his insistence on the adoption of a set of distinctive cultural markers for Sikh men. This marked a clear break from the Hindu tradition.

Sikhism and its followers had long had an uneasy, but not hostile, coexistence with Hinduism. Given that the faith had originally emerged as an attempt to reform Hinduism, there had long been a fear amongst some members of the community that it could be re-absorbed into the Hindu fold. Indeed, in the early 1970s, discontent had been steadily gathering within segments of the Sikh community about their political status within India. The first expression of these grievances had come with a statement of demands on the part of the principal Sikh political party, the Akali Dal, in September 1981. These claims, it should be noted, were based, in considerable part, on the Anandpur Sahib Resolution that the party, along with some key members of the Sikh diaspora, had passed in 1973 (Leaf 1995). The resolution and subsequent demands called for shifting the capital of Punjab to Chandigarh, the merger of Punjab with all Punjabi-speaking areas, additional protection for Punjabi speakers in neighbouring states, and stronger guarantees on the rights of religious minorities within a federal India (Leaf 1995).

Faced with these demands, Prime Minister Indira Gandhi had asked the party to spell out specific concerns. In response, the Akalis had submitted a memorandum which included fifteen demands ranging from the granting of a 'holy city' status to the city of Amritsar, the home of the principal Sikh shrine, the enactment of legislation for an all-India gurdwara act that would place all historic gurdwaras outside the Punjab under Sikh control, more remunerative prices for agricultural products, the sharing of river waters, and some redefinition of centre–state relations. The Government of India did start negotiations with the Akalis based on these demands. However, these did not prove to be especially fruitful because the two sides could not arrive at any meaningful compromise. The status of Hindi-speakers and Hindus in the Punjab, the status of the capital city Chandigarh, and the division of river waters were particularly controversial and detrimental to these negotiations (Brass 1994). As these discussions stalled, the Akalis resorted to a strategy of mass political mobilization to press for their demands (Patel 1987).

In considerable part, the talks had made little or no headway because Prime Minister Indira Gandhi had two major and related reservations about them from the very outset. At one level, she was innately hostile toward most regional political parties with substantial grassroots political base. This propensity had contributed to significant centralizing choices on her part even if it meant flouting constitutional procedures. In the process, her actions had contributed to considerable institutional decay in India.[6] Key democratic institutions, including the upper and lower houses of Parliament and the courts were substantially weakened by the centralization of power in the hands of the executive. Furthermore, her proclivity for a strongly personal role in politics degraded confidence in democratic institutions and electoral competition in favour or personal loyalties and political dynasty. At another level, she saw the demands embodied in the Anandpur Sahib resolution as being potentially secessionist, as its acceptance and implementation would have dramatically reduced the role and powers of the central (national) government in the state.

The more immediate and sociological sources of the crisis can be found in the transformation of the socio-economic landscape of the Punjab as a consequence of the Green Revolution of the 1970s (Frankel 2015). Among other matters, the Green Revolution generated substantial prosperity amongst significant segments of the Sikh community. Along with this new-found affluence came a propensity to shed many of the distinctive markers of their faith. Gurharpal Singh, drawing on the work of Robin Jeffrey, neatly summarizes these developments:

> It [the Green Revolution] accelerated the emergence of mass society; face-to-face village communities disintegrated; urbanization, consumerism, and mass literacy inflated expectations; ethnic identities

---

[6] For a critique of her centralizing proclivities and their consequences for India's democracy, see Brass (1994).

became firmer emblems of occupational competition; rootlessness, alienation, and graduate unemployment nurtured messianic tendencies, especially fundamentalism; and, above all, a revolution took place in communication, particularly political communication. (Singh 1987)

These social transformations, in turn, created a deep sense of anxiety amongst elements of the Sikh community and provided the basis for the rise of a revivalistic movement. One of the principal exponents of this movement was an itinerant, charismatic preacher, Sant Jarnail Singh Bhindranwale. He focused on the breakdown of these norms and managed to build up a very substantial following amongst a segment of the Sikh community. As his support grew within the Punjab, he chose to make a series of political demands and challenged the local political party, the Akali Dal.

It is widely believed that Bhindranwale received the support and encouragement of Indira Gandhi and her son Sanjay Gandhi to resort to violence against the Akalis (Nayar 2012; Wallace 1995). As Bhindranwale and his followers started to wreak havoc across the Punjab, the leadership of the Congress Party—after having encouraged his rise—came to the realization that its client was no longer controllable. They had unleashed a force that had its own interests and was now a threat to the state and even to India's national security, given its location athwart the India–Pakistan border. In 1983, President's rule, or rule directly through the central government in Delhi, was implemented in response to these threats to India's security and territorial integrity. This, in turn, prompted Indira Gandhi's government to reign in Bhindrawale, resulting in significant fighting between Indian government forces and Bhindrawale's followers.

Bhindranwale and a coterie of dedicated followers took refuge from Indian security forces inside the Golden Temple in the city of Amritsar. He had also brought in a retired Indian major-general, Shabeg Singh, who had ample battlefield experience. From this preserve, he was directing a reign of terror across the Punjab. Meanwhile, talks with the Akalis had mostly stalled. Determined to demonstrate her willingness to take a tough stance against the climate of terror, Indira Gandhi ordered an assault on the Golden Temple to flush out the terrorists in June 1984.[7] The operation, though eventually successful, was nevertheless extremely costly, both in terms of innocent lives and political capital (Dhillon 2006).

[7] For the political backdrop to these events, see Tully and Jacob (1985).

In the aftermath of the military operation at the Golden Temple, rank and file Sikhs in the Indian Army deserted, large numbers of Sikhs who had not been sympathetic to the secessionist cause were alienated from the Indian state, and, ultimately, Indira Gandhi's Sikh bodyguards assassinated her in October 1984. In the wake of her assassination, an anti-Sikh pogrom swept through New Delhi, resulting in the killing of several thousand Sikhs. Not surprisingly, the tempo of the insurgency dramatically increased. In an attempt to find a political solution to the Punjab crisis, her son and successor, Rajiv Gandhi, started negotiations with prominent Sikh leader Harcharan Singh Longowal and then signed an accord with him in July 1985. Longowal, however, was assassinated shortly thereafter. In the next election, the Akalis swept into power in the Punjab. However, for a range of reasons, the Rajiv Gandhi regime was unable to implement the terms of the Longowal accord. As violence returned to the Punjab, the government increasingly adopted a 'law and order' stance toward the problem, favouring heavy policing and restrictions on movement over a political solution.

In 1987 the recently elected government of Surjit Singh Barnala was dismissed and President's rule was imposed once again on the state. As part of the 'law and order' strategy, the government launched a second assault on the Golden Temple, codenamed 'Operation Black Thunder' (Telford 1992). Unlike its predecessor, 'Operation Bluestar', which had proven to be mostly disastrous, this was a far more calibrated operation and proved to be quite successful (Fair 2008). Despite this successful operation, India's heavy-handed counter-insurgency operations continued for some time. It was not until the reappointment of K.P.S. Gill, an Indian Police Service officer, known for his personal courage and ruthless methods, that the strategy underwent a significant change. Unlike the earlier strategy that had relied mostly on the indiscriminate use of force, Gill brought about significant changes. Among other matters, he placed large bounties on the heads of leading militants, resulting in their killing or capture. He also proffered a policy of tacit amnesty for those who were willing to eschew violence. His tactics proved to be quite successful and in considerable measure can be credited with ending the insurgency (Telford 2001).

Domestic Explanatory Variables

In examining the Punjab crisis, it is possible to trace how the breakdown of *institutional* norms and procedures under Indira Gandhi left the Indian government ill-equipped to take on the challenge posed by the Akali Dal. As noted previously, Indira Gandhi's contempt for regional parties and preference for strong central government control meant that she and her government were not willing to consider the Akalis core proposals, which were clearly designed to strengthen regional governments and the ability of Sikhs to govern themselves. Under Nehru, New Delhi was more able to negotiate with regional parties and the interests of the constituent states of the republic, because of strong democratic and state institutions that supported solving these issues through institutional means. However, during the crisis in the Punjab, the Congress Party under Indira had already stripped these institutions of their effectiveness.

The *interests* of the Government of India and key members of the Sikh community, both within India and in the diaspora, were clearly at odds during the insurgency. The Akali Dal's aim to reorganize the political boundaries of Punjab and carve up other religiously specific spaces in the area was not in the interest of the secular leaders of the country. While the roots of Sikh discontentment can be found in the negotiations leading up to partition and the independence of Pakistan and India, the insurgency and terrorist attacks in the Punjab were also influenced by the sudden shift to a more centralized style of governance in New Delhi. This is not only the result of institutional factors, as noted in the preceding paragraph, but also Indira's perception that the stability of India depended on a strong central rule. For the Akalis and other sections of the Sikh population, this conflicted with their stated interests in maintaining the autonomy of their communities in a Hindu-majority India.

With regards to *ideas*, the idea of an independent Khalistan, or an independent Sikh nation state, and rights of the Sikhs to independent statehood play a major explanatory role in this analysis. Some of these ideas had existed in an incipient form in the final days of the Indian nationalist movement. However, national political choices and socio-economic developments in the Punjab in the 1970s contributed to their resurrection and culminated in the insurgency.

Regional Explanatory Variables

Of course, *regional* factors also played a critical role in sustaining the violence. Pakistani decision-makers, sensing an opportunity to widen the scope of the insurgency, provided sanctuary, training, and weaponry to the terrorists. However, India's ability to mostly seal the border dramatically limited their ability to continue their material support.[8]

Ideas, on the contrary, from within the region played no role whatsoever in either fostering or sustaining the Punjab crisis. Neither the People's Republic of China (PRC) nor Pakistan played any role in providing ideological inspiration to the Khalistani movement.

The Naxalite Insurgency: Origins and Redux

The Kashmir and Punjab insurgencies were both ethno-religious in their origins. By contrast, both the original Naxalite insurgency and its more recent manifestation are ideological. The original insurgency obtains its name from the region of Naxalbari in the northern part of the state of West Bengal in 1967. The inspiration for this insurgency had come from the PRC during the peak of its revolutionary phase under Mao-Tse-Tung. Based upon his precepts of revolutionary guerilla warfare, these Indian neophyte revolutionaries sought to stir the peasantry with the aim of spreading revolutionary fervour to major cities (Singh 1995).

The principal exponents of this strategy were Bengali ideologue Charu Mazumdar and his associate Kanu Sanyal, who had sought to mobilize mostly landless peasantry in the villages of Naxalbari, Phansideva, and Kharibari in northern West Bengal. In these areas, land reforms that had been promised after India's Independence had long failed to materialize. Initially, the Communist government that was in power in West Bengal had sought to negotiate with Sanyal. In fact, they had offered to carry out land reform if Sanyal and his supporters would agree to end their resort to the use of violence against landlords in the area. However, Sanyal and his followers did not agree to these terms. At this point, the West Bengal Police were ordered to retaliate against Sanyal's forces (Mehra 2007).

Soon thereafter, the mantle of revolutionary activity spread to the state capital, Calcutta. Young, college-going, primarily upper-middle-class young men (and a few women) spearheaded this movement and unleashed a virtual reign of terror in the city (Gupta 2004). They attacked university administrators, bureaucrats, businessmen, and even ordinary traffic policemen.

---

[8] For evidence of Pakistan's involvement in the Punjab crisis and India's response, see Ganguly and Fidler (2013).

These targeted killings, while instilling fear amongst the general populace, also had the effect of alienating the vast majority of the citizenry from their putative cause. Furthermore, taking advantage of these troubled conditions, common criminals quickly entered the fray. They indulged in bank robberies, theft, and general mayhem. Against this backdrop of a deteriorating public order, the citizenry became quite sympathetic to a harsh, repressive response. This response included summary executions, the use of torture to extract confessions, and cordon and search operations in urban areas that broke the back of the uprising within a few years. Following the end of the terrorist violence in Bengal, for all practical purposes, the movement virtually collapsed.

It has witnessed a resurgence in the first decade of the twenty-first century. Based on the assessment of India's Union Home Ministry, as of July 2016, the Maoists were active in 10 states and 86 districts. This figure represented a decline in their activities from the last several years. The most recent manifestation of this movement has stemmed from the merger of two groups, the Communist Party of India Marxist-Leninist, which was the original exemplar of the insurrection, and the Maoist Communist Centre of India. In 2010, Prime Minister Manmohan Singh described the recrudescence of Naxalite violence to be the 'single most important internal security threat facing India' (PTI 2010).

The precise reasons for the revival of Naxalite terror are the subject of considerable debate. One of the more popular explanations suggests that it is linked to deepening economic inequalities that have been generated as a consequence of India's fitful embrace of economic liberalization since the early 1990s. This argument, while seemingly plausible, is not entirely tenable. Inequality has dogged India since Independence. Hence, this constant feature of the Indian socio-economic landscape cannot be deemed to be the sole causal agent in triggering a renewed bout of neo-Maoist terror. That said, according to some accounts the levels of inequality have worsened. It is the efforts of those imbued with a revolutionary ideology in a manner that strongly resembles Leninist strategies that have led to the mobilization of extant grievances and thereby led to the insurrections that afflict substantial parts of India (Sundar 2012).

Apart from the growth of inequality, it appears that Naxalite violence and terror is also related to the Indian state's willingness to increasingly open up hitherto untouched Tribal areas to private companies interested in the extraction of mineral resources. These efforts have increasingly brought

Tribal groups into conflict with the interests of large corporate entities. The state, at least in the view of some scholars, has colluded with private enterprise, as a result of which these conflicts have ensued (Sundar 2012).

Domestic Explanatory Variables

India's *institutional* response to the Naxalite insurgent groups displays the spatial variation in these institutions. The Indian state's response to Naxalite terror has been mostly repressive (Mehra 2007); however, the strategies of repression have varied, reflecting the federal structure of the Indian state. Some states, especially in the north, have relied almost exclusively upon the use of extensive force (Kennedy 2014). Others, most notably the southern state of Andhra Pradesh, have used more calibrated force, thereby producing better results (Jain 2013). Yet even this effort has not addressed the underlying grievances that the Naxalites have successfully mobilized. Even though no dramatic incidents have transpired in the recent past, it is more than apparent that the movement remains active in significant parts of the country. The regime of Prime Minister Narendra Modi, who assumed political office in 2014 and again in 2019, has yet to announce any novel approach to dealing with the fundamental sources of the movement. Instead, its business-friendly orientation may even militate against adopting any strategy that seeks to accommodate extant grievances.

The Indian government's *interests* with regards to containing the Naxalite movement fall into two categories: (1) stopping the violence and re-establishing stability, and (2) preventing the spread of revolutionary and anti-state ideology. While the immediate goal of India's counterterrorism policy was to stabilize the affected regions and prevent future attacks from Naxalite insurgents, the state was also clearly interested in preventing the spread of the radical ideologies driving the Naxalite conflict.

Obviously, *ideas* played a critical role in the genesis of the original Naxalite insurgency. The terrorists were imbued with the Maoist *idea* of revolutionary transformation and rejected the *institutional* and, more specifically, parliamentary pathway to social and political change. In this regard, they fundamentally differed from the political strategy of the two major Indian Communist parties—the Communist Party of India or CPI and the Communist Party of India (Marxist) or the CPI(M)— both of which eschewed revolutionary violence, and had adopted the parliamentary path to Communism.

Regional Explanatory Variables

It can be argued on the basis of inference and attribution that both Pakistan and the PRC have every interest in seeing India tied down in suppressing the Naxalite rebellion. However, there is no available evidence to suggest that they have played any role in promoting or sustaining it.

With regard to ideas, revolutionary beliefs stemming from Marxism–Leninism and Maoism animate this generation of the Naxalites. However, there is no evidence whatsoever that would link the provenance of these ideas to either Pakistan or the PRC.

Global Factors and Connections

India's domestic counterterrorism policy is increasingly connected to the global fight against terrorism, reflecting the international and transnational aspects of terrorism around the globe. However, India's cooperation with the United States (US) and even Israel has taken a distinct direction from the ways that Indian policy making has worked with regards to the three case studies outlined previously. In this section, we briefly note the primary global aspects of India's counterterrorism strategy focusing on bilateral cooperation with the USA, Saudi Arabia, and Israel, and then apply this volume's *institutions, interests*, and *ideas* framework to look at the explanatory variables driving India's decision-making.

India and the USA have both pursued deeper cooperation in counterterrorism, especially following the November 2008 attacks in Mumbai (Riedel 2014). The following year, during Prime Minister Singh's visit to Washington, the USA and India signed the India–US Counterterrorism Initiative, which prompted increased intelligence-sharing, mutual consultations, and increased capabilities to stop money laundering (Embassy of India 2016). Since that time, declarations of cooperation in combatting terrorism have become commonplace in India–US relations. In September 2015, Prime Minister Modi and President Obama reaffirmed their commitment to combat terrorism in all its forms (US Department of State 2015). Most recently, in August 2016, Secretary of State John Kerry and Indian Foreign Minister Sushma Swaraj declared their intention to further boost counterterrorism cooperation by expanding intelligence sharing (Lee 2016). In 2017, the Trump administration approved India's request for the sale of several predator drones; the US government also announced its continued intent to cooperate with India in the fields of defence and counterterrorism (*The Times of India* 2017a). India's motivations in pursuing this slowly developing partnership with the USA appears largely motivated to increase US pressure on Pakistan and the myriad terrorist groups operating on its soil.

In the Middle East, India is cooperating with players as disparate as Israel and Saudi Arabia. During Prime Minister Modi's visit to Riyadh in April 2016, the Saudi and Indian governments announced that they would be increasing their counterterrorism cooperation, focusing specifically on cutting off financial support for terrorist groups as well the exchange of intelligence (*The Tribune* 2016). This is a particularly interesting, although perhaps limited, agreement, considering Saudi Arabia's long history of cooperation with Pakistan. Despite these recent developments, India has also been deepening its cooperation with Israel in the sphere of counterterrorism. Citing both countries 'as constantly threatened by forces of terrorism and extremism' (Bhattacherjee 2016), the governments of India and Israel have pushed for increased cooperation and coordination in their counterterrorism strategies.

The international dimensions of India's counterterrorism policy have not been limited to bilateral relations. Indeed, India has been a vocal supporter of negotiating a UN Comprehensive Convention in International Terrorism (Krishnan 2015). India's stated interest in becoming a permanent member of the UN Security Council as well as the need to increase international pressure against Pakistan's support of terrorist groups have given further weight to India's international counterterrorism strategy. India has taken a leading role in putting counterterrorism on the BRICS (Brazil, Russia, India, China, and South Africa) agenda, as well. Despite the failure of similar efforts in 2016, in 2017 India convinced its fellow BRICS members to include the Jaish-e-Mohammed and the Haqqani network in its concerns over violence in South Asia (*The Times of India* 2017b). In previous years, China has been careful to avoid any actions, rhetorical or otherwise, against Pakistan. By getting these organizations on the BRICS' security radar, as it were, India appears to have generated regional and international support towards the terrorist threats it faces—threats that China and other BRICS members cannot afford to ignore, even if it puts Pakistan in an uncomfortable position.

While India is the only South Asian state in BRICS, on 9 June 2017, both India and Pakistan were admitted as full members of the Shanghai

Cooperation Organization (SCO). The SCO is the primary multilateral organization in the region, and has been an active tool in counterterrorism cooperation, especially between China and the Central Asian states that border the restive region of Xinjiang in China's far west. The SCO's Regional Anti-Terrorist Structure (RATS) facilitates intelligence-sharing as well as maintaining a blacklist of individuals and groups responsible for terrorist attacks in the region (Rudolf, Julienne, and Buckow 2015). India's membership puts additional negative pressure on Pakistan regarding its support of terrorist organizations, offering India much-needed international support.

International Explanatory Variables

There are no regional institutions for promoting counterterrorism in South Asia. Whatever cooperation has ensued has been strictly ad hoc, sporadic, and bilateral (Ganguly 2009).

Outside of India's domestic interests in counterterrorism, the country also has an interest in becoming a major leader in global counterterrorism campaigns. The US-sponsored programmes such as the Antiterrorism Assistance Programme (US Department of State, n.d.) have given India access to training for its military and law enforcement personnel, as well as substantial aid to increase the counterterrorism capacity of these institutions (US Department of State 2013). Participation in counterterrorism trainings gives India access to training and materials that it would otherwise not have.

Finally, India's idea of itself as a great power in the international state system has necessitated its engagement in the global fight against terror. While traditional great powers have focused on warfare and systemic influence, India has emerged as a regional power in both South and Southeast Asia with increasing ties to East Asian countries as well. This policy of engagement (Pardesi 2015) is no less pertinent in India's counterterrorism policy, where India seeks to not only present itself as a victim of terror but also a leading state in the fight against terrorism on an international level.

***

The analysis of these three cases suggests that terrorism in India has multiple origins. That said, one common factor has been the existence and mobilization of extant political grievances against a backdrop of institutional debility. In at least two of the cases, those of Kashmir and the Punjab, political and social changes coupled with the corruption of *institutions* contributed to the insurgent and terrorist movements. In both cases, the willingness of political leadership to depart from *institutional* procedures provided individuals and organizations with violent ideological agendas to come to the fore.

In both cases, *regional* and even *global* actors also played important roles in aiding terrorist movements. Unfortunately, despite the efforts of the Indian state to highlight the costs that both these terrorist movements exacted, few external actors evinced much interest in helping India curb such domestic terror even when incontrovertible evidence about external involvement was available. Since much of this terror was closely tied to the ongoing Indo-Pakistani conflict, the international community has often seen these movements as domestic or regional issues. They have not been either rhetorically or practically connected to the fight against global terror networks. Consequently, India has had little option but to address these terrorist assaults independently. This has not, however, meant that India has been free from periodic international scrutiny and criticism for the harsh tactics that it has adopted to deal with these terrorist organizations.

The Naxalite movement, however, has different antecedents. In this case, it cannot be attributed to any particular *institutional* failures of the Indian state. Instead, in both its manifestations, it can be traced to the role of particular *ideas* and the mobilization of extant grievances. Also, unlike in the other two cases, the involvement of external actors was minimal. The movement, no doubt, drew its original inspiration from Maoist ideology. However, the direct involvement of the PRC in the original uprising was limited at best.

India's *institutional* responses to the Naxalite insurgencies have also revealed the limits of its commitments to democratic procedures and norms. The primary response of the Indian state as well as its constituent parts has been repression with the promise of promoting economic development. As demonstrated in this chapter, the repressive strategies and tactics have, in fact, in many instances worsened the original problem that they were designed to address.

It is important to note that none of these terrorist movements have succeeded in their stated goals. The Indian state, for its myriad institutional weaknesses and flaws, has demonstrated a remarkable resilience. It has the domestic capacity to stoically accept casualties to fend off efforts on the part of regional actors to exploit internal cleavages and to ward off international disapprobation of its tough-minded tactics designed to quell terrorist and insurgent violence.

That said, these repressive strategies adopted by the Indian state, while having been successful in quelling terrorist violence, have not come without significant material and moral costs. India has been forced to deploy substantial paramilitary forces for extended periods of time in terrorist stricken areas ranging from the northeast, to the state of Jammu and Kashmir. It has also had to pass various forms of draconian legislation that has significantly curbed civil liberties and personal rights of its citizenry (Telford 2001). These laws have occasioned strong protests from segments of India's civil society, but to little avail.

Given India's robust record of economic growth over the past two decades as well as its current trajectory, it is entirely likely that the state will be able to devote more material resources to its repressive apparatus. Consequently, if internal or external actors resort to terror against the Indian state, it is all but certain that the capacity of the state to cope with and repress such challenges will only increase. While the repressive powers of the Indian state are unlikely to abate or ebb anytime soon, it is far from clear that any of its leadership will make concerted efforts to improve its *institutional* capacity. As long as institutional channels for dealing with dissent, inequality, and social discontent remain weak, it appears reasonable to conclude that India is likely to face future terrorist challenges. As seen through its involvement in the insurgencies in both the Punjab and Kashmir, Pakistan remains unreconciled to the territorial status quo in South Asia and will almost invariably step in to exploit these domestic cleavages within India (Ganguly 2016). More to the point, Pakistan can be expected to again deploy its asymmetric war strategy of using various terrorist organizations to strike at targets within India (Kapur and Ganguly 2012).

Whether or not these continuing challenges to political order and the concomitant responses of the Indian state hobble the likely rise of India and its quest for great power status remains an important and open question. The question is far from trivial because ultimately these terrorist movements and their ability to challenge the writ of the Indian state in entire swaths of the country raise a fundamental question about the state's monopoly over the legitimate use of force. In any case, India's own experiences with terrorism have contributed to shape domestic interests as well as domestic norms on terrorism and counterterrorism, which have had major repercussions on the clear prioritization of the issue of terrorism in India's politics on the global stage.

References

Afridi, Jamal. 2009. 'Kashmir Militant Extremists', 9 July. Council on Foreign Relations. Available at: https://www.cfr.org/backgrounder/kashmir-militant-extremists (accessed 21 October 2019).

Ahmed, Ishtiaq. 2015. 'The Unfinished Partition', *The Friday Times*, 23 October.

Amnesty International. 2015. 'India: Accountability Still Missing for Human Rights Violations in Jammu and Kashmir', 1 July. Available at: www.amnesty. org/en/latest/news/2015/07/india-accountability-still-missing-for-human-rights-violations-in-jammu-and-kashmir/ (accessed 16 January 2017).

Ashiq, Peerzada. 2016. 'Wani's Death Triggers Fury, 11 Killed, 200 Hurt in Kashmir', *The Hindu*, 10 July.

Bhattacherjee, Kallol. 2016. 'India, Israel to Scale Up Counter-terror Cooperation', *The Hindu*, 16 November. Available at: http://www.thehindu.com/todays-paper/tp-national/India-Israel-to-scale-up-counter-terror-cooperation/article16445940.ece (accessed 15 December 2016).

Blom, Amelie. 2009. 'A Patron–Client Perspective on Militia–State Relations: The Case of the Hizb-ul-Mujahidin of Kashmir', in Laurent Gayer and Christophe Jaffrelot (eds), *Armed Militias of South Asia: Fundamentalists, Maoists, and Separatists*, pp.135–58. New York: Columbia University Press.

Brass, Paul R. 1994. *The Politics of India since Independence*. Cambridge: Cambridge University Press.

Copland, Ian. 1997. *The Princes of India in the Endgame of Empire, 1917–1947*. Cambridge: Cambridge University Press.

Dhillon, Kirpal. 2006. *Identity and Survival: Sikh Militancy in India; 1979–1993*. New Delhi: Penguin Books.

Embassy of India. 2016. 'India–US Sign Counterterrorism Cooperation Initiative'. Washington, D.C., USA: Press Information Bureau, Embassy of India. Available at: https://www.indianembassyusa.gov.in/Archives Details?id=1292 (accessed 21 October 2019).

Fair, C. Christine. 2008. 'The Golden Temple: A Tale of Two Sieges', in C. Christine Fair and Sumit Ganguly (eds), *Treading on Hallowed Ground: Counterinsurgency Operations in Sacred Places*. New York: Oxford University Press, pp. 37–60.

———. 2014. *Fighting to the End: The Pakistan Army's Way of War*. New York: Oxford University Press.

Frankel, Francine R. 2015. *India's Green Revolution: Economic Gains and Social Costs*. Princeton: Princeton.

Ganguly, Sumit. 1997. *The Crisis in Kashmir: Portents of War, Hopes of Peace*. New York: Cambridge University Press.

———. 2001. *Conflict Unending: India–Pakistan Tensions since 1947*. New York: Columbia University Press.

———. 2009. *Counterterrorism Cooperation in South Asia: History and Prospects*. Seattle: National Bureau of Asian Research.

———. 2016. *Deadly Impasse: India–Pakistan Relations at the Dawn of a New Century*. Cambridge: Cambridge University Press.

Ganguly, Sumit and David P. Fidler (eds). 2013. *India and Counterinsurgency: Lessons Learned*. London: Routledge.

Gourevitch, Peter. 1978. 'The Second Image Reversed: The International Sources of Domestic Politics', *International Organization*, 32 (4): 881–912.

Gupta, Ranjit Kumar. 2004. *The Crimson Agenda: Maoist Protest and Terror*. Calcutta: Wordsmiths.

Jain, Bharti. 2013. 'Andhra Greyhound Model for Other Maoist-Hit States on Anvil', *The Times of India*, 17 February.

Kapur, S. Paul and Sumit Ganguly. 2012. 'The Jihad Paradox: Pakistan and Islamist Militancy in South Asia', *International Security*, 37 (1): 111–41.

Kennedy, Jonathan. 2014. 'Gangsters or Gandhians? The Political Sociology of the Maoist Insurgency in India', *The India Review*, 13 (3): 212–34.

Krishnan, Ananth. 2015. 'India Gets Greater Backing from China and Russia over UN Security Council Seat', *Daily Mail*, 2 February. Available at: http://www.dailymail.co.uk/indiahome/indianews/article-2937182/China-Russia-India-seat-security-council.html (accessed 16 January 2017).

Leaf, Murray J. 1995. 'The Punjab Crisis', *Asian Survey*, 25 (5): 475–98.

Lee, Matthew. 2016. 'United States, India Agree to Boost Anti-terror Cooperation', *Military Times*, 30 August. Available at: http://www.militarytimes.com/articles/united-states-india-agree-to-boost-anti-terror-cooperation (accessed 15 December 2016).

Mehra, Ajay K. 2007. 'Naxalism in India: Revolution or Terror', *Terrorism and Political Violence*, 12 (2): 37–66.

Nayar, Kuldip. 2012. 'How Congress Invented a "Saint"', *India Today*, 8 July.

Oberoi, Harjot Singh. 1994. *The Construction of Religious Boundaries: Culture, Identity and Diversity in the Sikh Tradition*. Chicago: The University of Chicago Press.

Pardesi, Manjeet. 2015. 'Is India a Great Power? Understanding Great Power Status in Contemporary International Relations', *Asian Security*, 11 (1): 1–30.

Patel, Pravin J. 1987. 'Violent Protest in India: The Punjab Movement', *Journal of International Affairs*, 40 (2): 271–85.

Peer, Basharat. 2010. *Curfewed Night: One Kashmiri Journalists' Frontline Account of Life; Love and War in His Homeland*. New York: Scribner.

PTI (Press Trust of India). 2010. 'Naxalism Biggest Threat to Internal Security: Manmohan', *The Hindu*, 24 May.

———. 2015. 'Army's Elite Counter-insurgency Unit Rashtriya Rifles Turns 25 Tomorrow', *The Economic Times*, 30 September.

Puri, Lieutenant General Mohinder. 2015. *Kargil: Turning the Tide*. New Delhi: Lancers.

Riedel, Bruce. 2014. 'India–US Counterterrorism Cooperation'. Brookings, 23 September. Available at: https://www.brookings.edu/research/india-u-s-counterterrorism-cooperation/ (accessed 15 December 2016).

Rudolf, Moritz, Marc Julienne, and Johannes Buckow. 2015. 'China's Counterterrorism Campaign Goes Global', *The Diplomat*, 3 June. Available at: https://thediplomat.com/2015/06/chinas-counterterrorism-campaign-goes-global/ (accessed 29 November 2017).

Singh, Gurharpal. 1987. 'Understanding the "Punjab Problem"', *Asian Survey*, 27 (12): 1268–77.

Singh, Prakash. 1995. *The Naxalite Movement in India*. New Delhi: Rupa.

Sundar, Nandini. 2012. 'Insurgency, Counter-insurgency and Democracy in Central India', in Robin Jeffrey, Ronojoy Sen, and Pratima Singh (eds), *More Than Maoism: Politics, Policies and Insurgencies in South Asia*, pp. 149–68. New Delhi: Manohar.

Telford, Hamish. 1992. 'The Political Economy of Punjab: Creating Space for Sikh Militancy', *Asian Survey*, 32 (11): 969–87.

———. 2001. 'Counter-Insurgency in India: Observations from Punjab and Kashmir', *Journal of Conflict Studies*, 21 (1). Available at: https://journals.lib.unb.ca/index.php/JCS/article/view/4293/4889 (accessed 21 October 2019).

Times of India, The. 2017a. 'US Clears Sale of Guardian Drones to India', 27 June. Available at: https://timesofindia.indiatimes.com/india/us-clears-sale-of-guardian-drones-to-india/articleshow/59331440.cms (accessed 29 November 2017).

———. 2017b. 'Why China Agreed to Include Pak-based Terror Groups in BRICS Declaration', 5 September. Available at: https://timesofindia.

indiatimes.com/india/why-china-agreed-to-include-pak-based-terror-groups-in-brics-declaration/articleshow/60364375.cms (accessed 29 November 2017).

Tribune, The. 2016. 'India, S Arabia to Enhance Counter-terror Cooperation' , 3 April. Available at: http://www.tribuneindia.com/news/nation/india-s-arabia-to-enhance-counter-terror-cooperation/217197.html (accessed 15 December 2016).

Tully, Mark and Satish Jacob. 1985. *Amritsar: Mrs. Gandhi's Last Battle*. London: Jonathan Cape.

US Department of State. n.d. 'Anti-Terrorism Assistance Program'. Available at: http://www.state.gov/m/ds/terrorism/c8583.htm (accessed 16 December 2016).

————. 2013. *Office of Antiterrorism Assistance: 2012 Fiscal Year in Review*. U.S. Department of State, Bureau of Diplomatic Security. Available at: https://www.state.gov/anti-terrorism-assistance-ata-program-summary/ (accessed 21 October 2019).

————. 2015. 'US–India Joint Declaration on Combatting Terrorism'. Media Note, Office of the Spokesperson, US Department of State, September. Available at: https://2009-2017.state.gov/r/pa/prs/ps/2015/09/247201.htm (accessed 21 October 2019).

Wallace, Paul. 1995. 'Terrorism and Political Violence in India: The Crisis of Identity', in Martha Crenshaw (ed.), *Terrorism in Context*, pp. 352–409. University Park: University of Pennsylvania Press.

3 Maritime Security and the Indian Ocean

INDIA HAS TRADITIONALLY NEGLECTED MARITIME SECURITY and until recently, its policy towards the Indian Ocean has been of low priority. The marginal status of maritime security was a result of several factors. The navy, for long, has received the least share of a limited defence budget among the armed services. This is due to British India's deliberate neglect of the navy in contrast to the army for internal security and expeditionary purposes, independent India's consequent focus on the army—and therefore landward threats first from Pakistan and then China—and the dominant role of the army and air force in India's security policy. This was exacerbated by the absence of a naval role in the first India–Pakistan war over Kashmir in 1948 as well as the 1962 war with China, along with a peripheral naval role in the second India–Pakistan war in 1965. By contrast, the navy's active role in the blockade of East Pakistan (now Bangladesh) and its daring exploit in the Arabian Sea during the 1971 India–Pakistan war greatly contributed to its status.

Yet, it was only in the late 1980s and on the basis of the defence of India's growing maritime interests that the navy was given a larger role in India's security policy. This was the result of its additional roles and responsibilities in ensuring the security of Sea Lines of Communication (SLOC) for trade and energy resources. With over 90 per cent of the volume of Indian trade being seaborne and with it 70 per cent of India's energy requirements being met by oil imports, as well as the changes in the international law of the sea and the consequent provision of the Exclusive Economic Zone (EEZ) (following the UN Convention on the Law of the Sea [UNCLOS] in 1982), maritime security issues came to the fore. The navy acquired its second aircraft carrier in 1986, leased a nuclear submarine from the erstwhile Soviet Union in 1987, and the construction of German submarines began at an Indian shipyard in 1981. The navy's share of defence expenditure rose from 8.93 per cent in 1980–81 to 14.14 per cent in 1995–96 (Roy-Chaudhury 1995, 185; 2000, 146).

Nonetheless, maritime security remained relatively neglected. In January 2001, India's Defence Minister George Fernandes publicly stated that the national leadership had been negligent of the maritime dimensions of security and that threats from the sea had simply not figured in New Delhi's perceptions (Fernandes 2000). A month later in February 2001, in a damning indictment on coastal security, the first Bharatiya Janata Party (BJP)-led National Democratic Alliance (NDA) government's Group of Ministers' (GoM) report, *Reforming the National Security System*, stated that 'India's long coastline and coastal areas have remained largely unprotected and unguarded' (GoM 2001, 61). It went on to say that 'little has been done over the years to understand or take action to create the infrastructure for the protection of India's vast coastal areas' (70). It noted the need for greater clarity in the role of state governments vis-à-vis the coastguard for 'shallow water surveillance of the coasts' (61). As a result, the GoM report recommended the strengthening of the coastguard and the establishment of a specialized Marine Police in all coastal states and island territories (PIB 2001). Yet, implementation was mixed. Following the election of the new Congress-led United Progressive Alliance (UPA) government three years later in May 2004, these reforms did not appear to have the requisite political support until a major reform of coastal and maritime security was undertaken by the UPA government after the November 2008 Mumbai terror attacks.

At the same time, the Indian Ocean remained a low priority for India's foreign policy and defence diplomacy. Within the Ministry of External Affairs (MEA), the Indian Ocean region was divided among six geographic and at least three thematic divisions, with little coordination and considerable bureaucratic tussles. There was a marked lack of leadership on policy perspectives towards the region; it was only in January 2016 that a separate division was created in the MEA for the Indian Ocean region, focusing on India's relationships with Sri Lanka, Maldives, Seychelles, and Mauritius. There was no significant Indian foreign policy initiative towards the Indian Ocean with the exception of the UN 'Zone of Peace' resolution in the 1970s and 1980s. There was no Indian prime ministerial speech on Indian Ocean policy until 2015.

Also, until the late 1980s, the Indian Navy's exercises with foreign navies was virtually non-existent since the end of the Joint Exercises off Trincomalee (JET) in 1962 (notwithstanding close defence ties with the erstwhile Soviet Union). In a significant development, this changed with the first set of bilateral naval exercises with Indonesia in 1989, followed by Australia in 1991, and the following year with Australia, the UK, and the USA. It has only been since the early 1990s that the Indian Navy began carrying out a regular series of bilateral exercises with several foreign navies (Roy-Chaudhury 2000, 178). These exercises were subsequently intensified and expanded—the latter including trilateral exercises with the USA and Japan, and a quadrilateral exercise (only once in 2007) with the addition of Australia (along with Singapore's participation). The US and Japan have now emerged as India's key strategic partners in the Indian Ocean/Indo-Pacific region, along with Australia, albeit to a lesser extent.

In the following sections, the analytical framework of this volume will be applied to the analysis of India's maritime security policies. The first section will connect the ideational foundations of India's policies with its actual activities on the ground across three levels of analysis: the domestic, regional, and global. The following sections will focus on the main domestic, regional, and global interests that drive India's maritime policy as well as on the core institutions at the three levels of analysis. The application of this analytical framework will allow us to disentangle some of the complexities of India's maritime policy and to find explanations for India's increased contributions to maritime governance.

Ideas

India as a 'Leading Power' in the Indian Ocean

India as a 'Leading Power'

In a departure from the attitudes of past governments, since May 2014, the BJP government, led by Prime Minister Narendra Modi, is developing a robust new maritime strategy. This perceives the Indian Ocean as an essential part of India's 'immediate and extended neighbourhood' and, therefore, as a foreign- and security-policy priority emanating from its 'neighbourhood first' policy. The Modi government aspires to become a 'leading' rather than a 'balancing' power in the Indian Ocean. Instead of trying to limit Western or erstwhile Soviet (Russian) or Chinese power in the Indian Ocean, India now seeks to leverage its growing national capabilities to take on greater roles and responsibilities, with the apparent goal of maritime dominance.

India's policy towards the Indian Ocean had been conditioned by its support for the UN resolution to declare the Indian Ocean as a 'Zone of Peace' in December 1971. This resolution called upon the great powers to enter into immediate consultations with littoral states to 'halt the further escalation and expansion of their military presence in the Indian Ocean ... eliminate from the Indian Ocean all bases, military installations, logistical supply facilities, the disposition of nuclear weapons and weapons of mass destruction and any manifestation of great power military presence in the Indian Ocean conceived in the context of great power rivalry' (Roy-Chaudhury 1995, 79). India advocated the elimination of the superpowers' military facilities in the Indian Ocean, but this was mainly directed towards the USA, not the erstwhile Soviet Union, due to the American naval intrusion in the Bay of Bengal during the 1971 India–Pakistan war.

India also feared that a naval arms race would bring about client–state relations in the area; give rise to a Chinese naval presence in the Indian Ocean; and encourage superpower intervention against littoral states (Roy-Chaudhury 1995, 80). India was, therefore, more concerned with the perceived vulnerability of its maritime assets than any direct hostile intention towards them. India's dominant position in the South Asian region, moreover, could only be maintained in the absence of the superpower naval presence in the Indian Ocean (Roy-Chaudhury 1995, 80).

Even until the early 2000s, India remained concerned over the implications of US nuclear-powered submarines in the Indian Ocean. The GoM (2001) report noted: 'The heavily militarized Indian Ocean will continue to adversely affect India's economic, political, and military interests in the area. ... US nuclear-powered submarines armed with long-range land-attack missiles continue to operate in the Indian Ocean, with increased emphasis on base facilities in Diego Garcia adjacent to India's own seabed mining area.'

In contrast, two decades later, largely in relation to its transformed relationship with the USA (as its single most important strategic partner instead of the erstwhile Soviet Union/Russia), alongside anxiety over an expanding Chinese naval presence in the Indian Ocean, it encourages US military presence in the Indian Ocean. Even though in June 2017 India voted against the UK and the USA and in favour of a Mauritius-backed UN resolution (on whether the British occupation of the Chagos Archipelago was valid under international law), India reportedly made clear informally that it still supported US naval presence in the Indian Ocean (*The Wire* 2017).

Accordingly, New Delhi also appears to have abandoned its position of non-alignment. Indeed, Modi skipped the April 2015 Asia–Africa Summit held in Indonesia, which marked the 60th anniversary of the Bandung Conference that led to the Non-Aligned Movement; and non-alignment has not been mentioned in any foreign policy statement of the Modi government. Modi was also the first Indian prime minister since 1979 not to attend the Non-Aligned Movement summit, the 17th edition of which was held in September 2016 in Venezuela.

Yet, New Delhi strongly continues to maintain its foreign policy objective of 'strategic autonomy', the term Modi deliberately highlighted during his keynote address at the International Institute for Strategic Studies (IISS) Shangri-La dialogue in Singapore in June 2018. Modi used this term to describe India's simultaneous 'special and privileged' strategic partnership with Russia, the 'global strategic partnership' with the USA, and its uniquely 'multilayered' relationship with China. Significantly, Modi deliberately did not mention the word 'quad'—the security-based quadrilateral grouping of the USA, India, Japan and Australia—in a gesture of reassurance towards China; while emphasizing the freedom of navigation and overflights, and criticizing infrastructure projects that placed countries under a 'debt burden', in a thinly veiled criticism of China (Government of India, MEA 2018). In effect, instead of 'non-alignment', India's foreign policy under Modi has variously been described as 'multi-aligned' (Narayanan 2016) or, more recently, by India's Foreign Secretary Vijay Gokhale in January 2019, as having moved beyond non-alignment to being 'aligned with different countries and groups', with alignment being 'issue-based not on ideology' (Basu 2019).

Modi Government's Policy

In March 2015, on the first prime ministerial visit to the island states of the Indian Ocean, Modi visited Seychelles, Mauritius, and Sri Lanka (a scheduled visit to the Maldives was cancelled due to its domestic political developments). Modi became the first Indian prime minister to conduct a bilateral visit to Seychelles in 34 years and to Sri Lanka in 28 years. In Mauritius, Modi unveiled a five-pronged vision towards the future of the Indian Ocean, the first by an Indian prime minister in decades, called 'Security and Growth for All in the Region' (Sagar, meaning 'sea' or 'lake' in Hindi).

This comprised:

(i) safeguarding India's mainland and islands, defending its interests, ensuring a safe, secure, and stable Indian Ocean, and making available India's capabilities to others;

(ii) deepening economic and security cooperation with India's maritime neighbours and island states, and strengthening their maritime security capacities and economic strength;

(iii) envisaging collective action and cooperation to advance peace and security and respond to emergencies;

(iv) seeking a more integrated and cooperative future for the region that enhanced sustainable development; and

(v) seeking a climate of trust and transparency; respect for international maritime rules and norms by all countries; and peaceful resolution of maritime issues (Modi 2015).

Subsequently, India's then foreign secretary, S. Jaishankar, stated that India was keen on 'reviving the Indian Ocean as a geo-political concept' and that India, which was the 'centre of gravity' of the Indian Ocean, should be a 'facilitator rather than an obstruction' for the Indian Ocean to attain its true potential (Government of India, MEA 2016a). At the IISS Shangri-La dialogue in June 2018, Modi made it clear that the Indian Ocean had not only shaped much of India's history but held 'the key to our future': it carries 90 per cent of India's trade and energy sources; is the life line of global commerce; connects regions of diverse cultures and different levels of peace and prosperity; and bears ships of major powers raising concern over stability and contest (Government of India, MEA 2018).

Since March 2015, India has made considerable progress in formulating a new proactive policy on the Indian Ocean. This provides significant economic, transportation, and energy development incentives to selected South Asian coastal and island states; ensures that India will be among the first contributors to humanitarian and disaster-relief operations in its neighbourhood; expands bilateral maritime security and defence cooperation with island states beyond that of a 'net security provider'; and facilitates a diplomatic and political push into the south-western and eastern areas of the Indian Ocean.

Growing Influence in the Indian Ocean

As a result, India further developed its role in the four key sub-regions of the Indian Ocean. In the Gulf, India moved from a relationship based on energy, trade, and expatriates to one with political and financial investments and security dimensions, covering maritime security, defence cooperation, and counterterrorism. This region accounts for nearly two-thirds of India's oil imports and an estimated 8.5 million expatriate Indians living and working in the Gulf, who send back almost USD 20 billion a year of remittances annually. In November 2008, India for the first time signed a maritime-focused defence cooperation agreement with Qatar. A maritime agreement has been signed with Saudi Arabia. And there are close security links with Oman, which have been significantly enhanced since February 2018 with the Indian Navy being provided access to Oman's new strategic port of Duqm for port facilities and the use of the dry dock for maintenance. Regular Indian naval ship deployments also take place in this region.

Modi visited the UAE in August 2015, marking the first visit by an Indian prime minister in 34 years, followed by subsequent visits in February 2018 and August 2019. He also visited Saudi Arabia (April 2016 and October 2019), Qatar (June 2016), Oman (February 2018), and Bahrain (August 2019) (marking the first-ever visit by an Indian prime minister). The Crown Prince of Abu Dhabi was the chief guest at India's Republic Day parade in January 2016. These bilateral visits significantly upgraded the strategic and economic content of the relationship with the UAE—with which India aims to increase bilateral trade by 60 per cent over the next five years and seeks USD 75 billion investment into its own infrastructure projects (Hokayem and Roy-Chaudhury 2017).

New Delhi also provided economic and financial aid, including defence-related lines of credit, and undertook port and energy projects in littoral states throughout the region, with the exception of Pakistan. During a visit to India in April 2017, Bangladeshi Prime Minister Sheikh Hasina identified 17 new infrastructure projects in her country that would be funded with a USD 4.5 billion Indian line of credit (New Delhi had extended Dhaka two other lines of credit, worth USD 2.8 billion collectively, since 2010). These projects included upgrades to the ports of Chittagong, Mongla, and Payra, as well as of an airport in Bangladesh. New Delhi and Dhaka also signed 13 other agreements collectively involving USD 9 billion of Indian investment, most of them in the energy sector. Sri Lankan President Maithripala Sirisena's first official foreign visit was to India in February 2016. India appeared willing to invest USD 2 billion in Sri Lanka over four years. Apart from developing the port, oil terminals, and refinery at Trincomalee in north-eastern Sri Lanka, India, along with Japan, is setting up a liquefied natural gas (LNG) plant and terminal on Sri Lanka's western coast, along with partnerships on transportation projects. This followed the signing of a bilateral memorandum of understanding (MoU) in April 2017, which stated that India, Japan, and Sri Lanka would develop the second foreign-operated container terminal at Colombo port in a joint venture (China currently operates the first terminal). In January 2018, India provided Sri Lanka USD 45.3 million to upgrade the northern harbour at Kankesanthurai into a commercial port. In addition, India agreed to provide Bangladesh and Sri Lanka defence-related lines of credit for USD 500 million and USD 100 million, respectively.

The Indian Navy has become the first responder for humanitarian and disaster-relief operations in Bangladesh, Sri Lanka, and the Maldives. India has provided the Maldives with basic assistance, including providing drinking water at times of emergency. In 2013, India gifted the Maldives two advanced light helicopters—operated by the Indian naval and coastguard crew and support staff stationed in the Maldives; in November 2018, the Maldives announced the renewal of the lease for these helicopters, as well as visas for the Indian personnel stationed in the country. During Maldivian President Abdulla Yameen's visit to New Delhi in April 2016, six agreements were signed, including a defence action plan that established an institutional mechanism for cooperation, focused on discussions between the countries' top defence officials. The other accords related to the development of port facilities in the Maldives; training and capacity-building programmes for the country's security forces; increased intelligence sharing on maritime affairs; and Indian military aid to Malé, which would include maritime surveillance capabilities. The first India–Maldives defence cooperation dialogue at the level of defence secretary took place in July 2016. During Maldives' newly elected President Ibrahim Solih's first official foreign visit to India in December 2018, Modi announced the provision of a USD 1.4 billion line of credit as financial assistance to the Maldives.

Significantly, India, Sri Lanka, and the Maldives signed a trilateral agreement on maritime security cooperation in July 2013. Focusing on counterterrorism, it significantly enhances cooperation in Maritime Domain Awareness (MDA), strengthens mechanisms for EEZ surveillance, and enhances the sharing of intelligence on illegal maritime activities. India is to share its Long Range Identification and Tracking (LRIT) data services with Sri Lanka and the Maldives to monitor and track their own flagged merchant vessels, along with the provision of MDA training and Merchant Ship Information System (MSIS) software. At the same time, both Sri Lanka and the Maldives have agreed to share intelligence on illegal maritime activities on a regular basis (Government of India, MEA 2014). India, Sri Lanka, and the Maldives maintained their trilateral maritime-security and intelligence-sharing initiatives, conducting their 14th trilateral coastguard exercise in November 2018.

The Modi government has also significantly expanded its predecessor's policy by acting as a provider of 'net security' to Indian Ocean island states. It has provided patrol boats and helicopters to Mauritius. In March 2015, India gave a 1,350-tonne *Barracuda*-class offshore patrol vessel to Mauritius; provided the third Dornier aircraft in July 2016; commissioned two Indian-built patrol vessels into the Mauritius Coast Guard in December 2016 and August 2017; and delivered another offshore patrol vessel to Mauritius in March 2018.

The first Indian defence ministerial visit to Mauritius, the world's third-largest Hindu-majority state, took place in December 2016. The new Mauritian Prime Minister Pravind Jugnauth made his first trip to India in May 2017, when a maritime security agreement was signed. At the same time, India provided USD 500 million for the purchase of Indian small patrol boats, followed by a USD 100 million line of credit for defence procurement during the visit of Indian President Ram Nath Kovind to Mauritius in March 2018. India is also building an airstrip and jetty on the Mauritian island of Agaléga for surveillance purposes. In the meantime, New Delhi has provided consistent support to the Mauritian government in attempts to reassert its sovereignty over the British-controlled Chagos Islands, including Diego Garcia, the site of a US military base. Significantly, the Mauritian national security advisor and commander of the Mauritian Coast Guard are Indian officials supplied by the Indian government (Brewster 2014, 74).

In March 2015, India announced the transfer of a second Dornier maritime patrol aircraft and a coastguard ship to the Seychelles (the latter delivered in June 2018). India also launched a coastal surveillance radar project in the Seychelles in 2016, and is upgrading the jetty and airstrip on Assumption Island for surveillance purposes. Indian naval ships and aircraft regularly carried out joint surveillance, patrols, and hydrographic surveys of the EEZ of Mauritius, the Seychelles, and the Maldives. India has deployed a P-8I maritime reconnaissance aircraft to the Seychelles for surveillance. In June 2018, during Seychelles President Danny Faure's visit to New Delhi, the Modi government announced a line of credit for USD 100 million for the purchase of defence equipment to build its maritime capacity.

However, India faces difficulties in these bilateral partnerships, with some notable recent setbacks. Under the Maldives' previous president, Abdulla Yameen, India's three existing radar stations in the Maldives connected to India's coastal radar network were unlikely to have been operational, with plans for the construction of seven additional Indian radars in the Maldives on hold. The trilateral India, Sri Lanka, and the Maldives coastguard exercise was delayed by a year until November 2018 and the Maldives had temporarily urged the return of India's helicopters and repatriation of its naval personnel. In the Seychelles, there is concern over the Indian construction of a surveillance facility on Assumption Island, with a leak in March 2018 of the secret revised India–Seychelles agreement stalling its ratification by the Seychelles Parliament (Roy-Chaudhury and Sullivan de Estrada 2018, 187–8). In Mauritius, an USD 87 million contract, signed in March 2015, for the Indian construction and upgrading of an airstrip and jetty on Agaléga Island has been delayed by the country's opposition leaders, as well as protests from the local population; completion of the project has been delayed to 2021.

A key aspect of India's Sagar policy (March 2015) was respect for international maritime rules and norms, and the peaceful resolution of maritime issues. In a landmark ruling, India accepted international arbitration over its maritime dispute with Bangladesh in July 2014. A UN tribunal awarded Bangladesh almost four-fifths—19,467 sq km of the 25,602 sq km sea area—of the Bay of Bengal under dispute. The verdict was binding on both countries and was welcomed by both Bangladesh and India. Bangladesh had started the arbitration process in October 2009 over the delimitation of the maritime boundary under UNCLOS (Paul 2014). This means that all of India's maritime boundaries are now demarcated, with the exception of the India–Pakistan maritime boundary in Kutch (although there continue to be issues between India and Sri Lanka over fishing rights).

As half of India's trade passed through the disputed areas of the South China Sea, the country also maintained its diplomatic efforts to promote a rules-based order and freedom of navigation and overflight there. As a consequence, New Delhi supported the July 2016 ruling on the dispute in the South China Sea by the Permanent Court of Arbitration at The Hague, which rejected almost all of China's territorial claims. At the IISS Shangri-La dialogue, Modi emphasized the promotion of a 'democratic and rules-based international order' to keep 'our seas, space and airways free and open; our nations secure from terrorism; and our cyber space free from disruption and conflict' (Government of India, MEA 2018). This would require, he noted, 'freedom of navigation, unimpeded commerce and peaceful settlement of disputes in accordance with international law'.

Interestingly, this was only the second time that Modi had used the term 'rules-based international order' in a speech/statement. He first used it in a press statement during the India–EU Summit in October 2017; it had also been used in joint declarations with Japan, Australia, the EU, the UK, and the Netherlands. However, at the first revived meeting of senior foreign ministry officials of the 'quad' group of countries in November 2017, India was the only country that did not formally state its commitment to 'uphold the rules-based order in the Indo-Pacific'. Instead, it highlighted the need for 'cooperation based on their converging vision and values for promotion of peace'. However, India did use this term in the second meeting of 'quad' officials in June 2018, pledging to 'promote a rules-based order in the Indo-Pacific'; and in the third meeting in November 2018, pledged to 'promote a free, open, rules-based and inclusive order in the Indo-Pacific'. Equally, in June 2016, the Indian Navy had conducted another iteration of its trilateral Malabar exercise with the USA and Japan, close to the South China Sea, and carried out port calls in the area. The July 2017 Malabar exercise was held in the Bay of Bengal, while the June 2018 exercise was held off the coast of Guam in the Philippine Sea (in the Pacific Ocean).

Indian Naval Influence

Meanwhile, the Indian Navy's operational footprint in the Indian Ocean has increased in recent years. This has included non-combatant Evacuation operations in Kuwait (2014) and Yemen (2015), as well as humanitarian assistance and disaster relief operations such as cyclone relief (in 2007, 2008, 2013, and 2014). Navy-to-navy staff talks now take place with over 20 countries and institutional bilateral/trilateral exercises with 11 countries. In August 2013, a dedicated communications satellite for the navy, GSAT-7, was launched for surveillance purposes.

India has played an active role in enhancing the stability and security of the Arabian Gulf's sea lanes through its participation in anti-piracy patrols off the coast of Somalia. Since October 2008, the Indian Navy has continuously deployed one ship in the Gulf of Aden for anti-piracy duties, with active engagement at times, along with operational turnarounds at Salalah, Oman. Although India is not engaged in Combined Task Force 151 on counter-piracy efforts in the Gulf of Aden, it has begun coordinating patrols with warships of China, Japan, and South Korea.

Following the devastating tsunami of 2004, the Indian Navy worked closely with those of the USA, Japan, and Australia to deliver relief and assistance. With the disappearance of Malaysian Airlines flight MH370 in March 2014, India was involved in the search in the Bay of Bengal, the Andaman Sea, and west of the Andaman Islands.

In October 2015, India revised its official maritime security strategy, 'Ensuring Secure Seas', to provide a proactive and expanded outlook towards the navy's roles and responsibilities in the Indian Ocean over the following ten years. The strategy was updated in the following ways.

(i) It was a contrast to the 2007 'Freedom to Use the Seas: India's Maritime Military Strategy' that it replaced, which was relatively conservative in its approach. This shift was reflected in the new title, from 'using' to 'securing' the seas, and from a 'military' to a broader 'security' perspective.

(ii) It expands India's areas of national interest based on a new consideration of 'political reasons', along with earlier considerations of 'Indian diaspora, overseas investments'.

(iii) It pointedly advances the former Manmohan Singh government's policy of becoming a provider of 'net security' to island states in the Indian Ocean by seeking to 'shape a favourable and positive maritime environment' for enhancing net security in India's areas of maritime interest. It essentially aims to 'prevent insecurity' by exercising naval presence and capacity-building, and to 'counter insecurity' through 'stabilising the maritime environment' as well as the 'conduct of maritime security operations, both independently and in coordination with other maritime forces in the region'. (Roy-Chaudhury 2015).

Although the revised strategy was not the result of Modi's initiative, it serves to complement it.

Yet, few states in South Asia shared India's concerns about growing Chinese influence and assertiveness in the region. India opposes China's Belt and Road Initiative (BRI), whose first summit in Beijing in May 2017 it refused to attend. The reason for this is that the Modi government regards projects of China's flagship China–Pakistan Economic Corridor (CPEC) in Gilgit–Baltistan—which it claims as part of Jammu and Kashmir—as a violation of Indian sovereignty. Also, it considers the BRI, with a focus on the development of Gwadar port in Pakistan's southern Baluchistan province, as not simply an economic initiative but a strategic one of seeking to encircle India. In contrast, the leaders of Pakistan and Sri Lanka participated in the event, as did ministers from Bangladesh, the Maldives, and Afghanistan. China has sold two diesel-electric submarines to Bangladesh and is constructing eight submarines for Pakistan. Neither Mauritius nor the Seychelles joined the agreement on maritime security cooperation between India, Sri Lanka, and the Maldives due to political differences between the Maldives and Mauritius. India's initiative to develop the Iranian port city of Chabahar, less than 100 km west of Gwadar port, as a transportation corridor for landlocked Afghanistan suffered delays, but was unaffected by the re-imposition of US sanctions against Iran in November 2018. In December 2018, India took over the operations of a part of Chabahar port, resulting in the start of commercial operations.

Regional: Expanding India's Sphere of Influence from the Indian Ocean towards the Indo-Pacific

Since Independence, the Indian Navy has aspired for a powerful multidimensional naval force in view of the dominance of seaborne trade and India's strategic location in the Indian Ocean. In 1951, the first British chief of the independent Indian Navy went so far as to state that India was 'to all intents and purposes an island, in that she is nearly inaccessible across her land frontiers' (Roy-Chaudhury 1995, 29). However, in view of the perception of the navy's limited role in security policy, the navy's ambitious expansion plans were not implemented. As a result, it largely remained a coastal force until the mid-1980s, focusing on the defence of the coastal peninsula, island territories, merchant shipping, and coastal and offshore installations, despite the commissioning of its first aircraft carrier in 1961.

In 2004, the Indian Navy's first published maritime doctrine confidently stated that 'the Indian maritime vision for the first quarter of the twenty-first century must look at the arc from the Persian Gulf to the Straits of Malacca as a legitimate area of interest' (Ministry of Defence 2004, 56). Clearly, the Indian Navy's primary area of influence and operations was the Indian Ocean. Traditionally, this has included the Arabian Sea and the Bay of Bengal, with focus on the Arabian Sea/Arabian Gulf due to threat perceptions from Pakistan as well as the dependence on energy imports through the Strait of Hormuz. But the Indian Navy's rising profile, India's 'Act East Policy', and the rise of the Chinese navy had shifted the navy's focus eastwards to the Bay of Bengal and the eastern Indian Ocean (west of the Malacca Strait).

In the past few years, this has begun to include areas east of the Malacca Strait and the South China Sea as well. Not surprisingly, the navy's 2009 updated doctrine categorized for the first time India's 'secondary areas' of maritime interest as including the 'South China Sea, other areas of West Pacific Ocean and friendly littoral countries located herein', along with 'other areas of national interest based on considerations of diaspora and overseas investments' (Ministry of Defence 2009, 68), although none of this was elaborated upon. In October 2015, India's revised and updated official maritime security strategy also expanded its 'primary' areas of maritime interests to include the south-western Indian Ocean and the Red Sea (formerly a 'secondary' area of interest); and the 'secondary' area of interest was also expanded to include the western coast of Africa and the Mediterranean Sea. Notably, two additional choke points are now included as 'primary' 'areas of interest'—the Mozambique Channel and the Ombai and Wetar Straits in the south-western and south-eastern Indian Ocean respectively (Ministry of Defence 2015, 32).

Until June 2018, India was hesitant to use the term Indo-Pacific in its official discourse. This expanded regional concept, based on the increasing interdependence of the Indian and Pacific Oceans, was first suggested by Japanese Prime Minister Shinzo Abe in his speech to the Indian Parliament in August 2007 when he talked of the confluence of the two oceans. Yet, the then ruling Congress party–led government in India used the term sparingly. The then prime minister, Manmohan Singh, first used the term only in May 2013 in an address to the Japan–India Association in Tokyo. The Ministry of Defence (MoD) used the term only once in its official annual report (in 2016); the MEA only occasionally referred to it from 2016 onwards. This ambivalence was due largely to the uncertainty over whether the USA would prefer this term instead of the Asia-Pacific or the Indo-Asia-Pacific. This was finally resolved in November 2017, when US President Donald Trump used the term Indo-Pacific ten times during his address to the Asia-Pacific Economic Cooperation (APEC) Summit in Vietnam. This indicated that the USA was keen to ensure India's inclusion, participation, and role within the expanded regional concept of the Indo-Pacific.

Finally, on 1 June 2018, at the IISS Shangri-La dialogue, Modi used the term Indo- Pacific eleven times, and strongly articulated, for the first time, India's vision towards this expansive region. Modi defined this essentially maritime region as stretching 'from the shores of Africa to that of the Americas', thereby incorporating the Arabian Sea/Gulf region and Indian Ocean island states left out of the USA and Australian definitions of the region, but closest to the Japanese definition.

In essence, India's approach to the region is governed by three broad principles:

(i) that the Indo-Pacific region is 'free, open and inclusive', thereby giving equal importance to the term 'inclusive', along with those of 'free and open' in terms of regional prosperity. In effect, it includes all countries in this geographical region and 'others beyond who have a stake in it'; it does not see the region as a strategy or as a club of limited members; and it does not consider such a geographical definition as directed against any country, nor as a grouping that seeks to dominate;

(ii) that partnerships on the basis of shared values and interests 'must equally apply to all individually as well as to the global commons'.

These rules and norms are to be based on 'the consent of all, not on the power of the few'; and

(iii) that the Association of South East Asian Nations (ASEAN) lies at the core of India's engagement with the Indo-Pacific (Government of India, MEA 2018).

Yet, India's engagement with the Indo-Pacific will remain largely diplomatic, economic, and rhetorical, with its core operational and strategic focus located to the west of the Straits of Malacca–Singapore within the Indian Ocean. The reasons for this are threefold:

(i) In comparison to the Indian Ocean, India has limited defence or security leverages east of the Straits of Malacca–Singapore.

(ii) The Indian Navy has clear incentives for a strong operational role in the Indian Ocean and little such incentive for a role that extends to the South China Sea or broader Pacific Ocean. It is also highly unlikely that an Indian government would order the navy to operationally deploy in the South China Sea to protect India's commercial interests in the region. India is also unlikely to carry out freedom of navigation operations (FONOPS) in the South China Sea, especially as it itself remains a target of US FONOPS in terms of prior consent required for military exercises or manoeuvres in India's EEZ or operations at sea.

(iii) Even for the vast expanse of the Indian Ocean, India has relatively limited military and naval capabilities and capacities. Although India has a hugely ambitious warship-building programme, virtually all of this is based on domestic warship construction, with some 40 ships currently being built in India. However, the reality is that India's warship construction projects continue to suffer from innumerable delays and increases in cost. Only a quarter of the warships currently being built are principal combatants. The Indian Navy's overstretched force levels and manpower have already compromised its operational effectiveness amidst a recent spate of warship accidents. India's total number of submarines is in decline with no follow-on acquisition programme in place. This situation is compounded by the lack of an adequate number of multi-role helicopters and minesweepers. India's defence budget for 2018–19 indicates a nominal increase of 9.5 per cent for the capital side of the armed forces, just about covering 5 per cent inflation/rupee depreciation, resulting in a real increase of less than 5 per cent, with much of it to be spent to cover payments for ongoing acquisitions.

Global: Intensified Naval Interactions with the USA, Japan, Australia, and Vietnam

Significantly, to counter China's naval influence in the Indian Ocean, the Modi government continues to build strategic networks with the USA, Japan, and Australia (including that on weapon systems operability such as the P-8 maritime surveillance aircraft, while ramping up the scope and nature of their bilateral/trilateral naval exercises); ensures the provision of reciprocal logistical access with both the USA and France; and deepens engagement with Vietnam. Following the April–September 2002 escort of 24 US-flagged high-value vessels through the Straits of Malacca–Singapore in support of the US-led 'war on terror', the Indian Navy worked closely with those of the USA, Japan, and Australia to deliver relief and assistance following the 2004 tsunami. Of these relationships, the most important has been the expanded India–US naval and maritime ties.

During then President Obama's visit to India in January 2015, the two countries published a document that outlined their joint strategic vision for the Asia-Pacific and the Indian Ocean. It included a paragraph affirming 'the importance of safeguarding maritime security and ensuring freedom of navigation and overflight throughout the region, especially in the South China Sea'. This was widely perceived as implying that the two parties had reached a consensus on the need to counter Beijing's assertive approach to territorial disputes in the region. In May 2016, the first India–US Maritime Security Dialogue took place. In August 2016, India signed the bilateral logistics exchange memorandum of agreement (LEMOA) with the USA, which facilitates additional opportunities for practical engagement and exchanges. In December 2016, India was accorded the status of a 'major defence partner' by the USA. In September 2018, India signed the much delayed Communications, Compatibility and Security Agreement (COMCASA) with the USA, which facilitates the sharing of high-end encrypted communication and satellite data. And in September 2018, the first India–US 2+2 ministerial dialogue took place between their defence and foreign ministers in New Delhi.

The first meeting between Modi and Trump, in Washington on 26 June 2017, was dominated by counterterrorism and trade. There, the Indian prime minister also met with US Secretary of Defence James Mattis, who complimented 'India's long-term efforts to promote stability in the Indian Ocean region'. Similarly, at the IISS Shangri-La dialogue earlier that month, Mattis had publicly stated that India's recognition as a 'major defence partner' of the USA was partly due to its 'indispensable role in maintaining stability in the Indian Ocean region'. Indeed, in a signal to China, the 2017 iteration of the Malabar exercise (India, US, and Japan) took place in the Bay of Bengal during 10–17 July, with India providing its largest ever contribution of nine ships; all three navies deployed aircraft or helicopter carriers. The Indian and Chinese navies had engaged in no joint exercises, but their warships had exchanged calls.

During the 2016 Indo-Japanese defence ministerial meeting, both countries agreed to explore the setting up of a Maritime Strategic Dialogue between the two defence ministries. In 2012, the first Japanese India Maritime Exercise (JIMEX) took place, followed by the second a year later; the third JIMEX was delayed by five years (even as annual trilateral naval exercises with the USA were taking place) and only took place in October 2018 off India's eastern coast of Vishakapatnam. The fifth meeting of the foreign and defence secretaries (2+2) took place in June 2018.

The annual India-Australia Maritime Dialogue was agreed upon in November 2014 under the Framework for Security Cooperation. It was held for the first time in November 2015 in New Delhi and again in Canberra in October 2016. The second edition of the India–Australia bilateral maritime exercise, AUSINDEX, was held in June 2017. The second meeting of the foreign and defence secretaries (2+2) took place in October 2018 to enhance foreign policy and security cooperation. In 2016, India also signed the White Shipping Agreement with Australia.

As it is no coincidence that the resumption of a meeting of the 'quad' took place alongside President Trump's formal enunciation of the term 'Indo-Pacific', it is perceived that whereas the Indo-Pacific is the new regional 'geo-strategic concept', the 'quad' is the 'operating concept' of a revived partnership between the four countries seeking to both counter China as well as offer options other than China.

However, India is currently not keen on 'operationalizing' or militarizing the quad in this respect. Modi's refusal to mention the 'quad' in his IISS Shangri-La dialogue speech was a blow to the concept and disappointing to the defence ministers of the other three countries in the audience. This was compounded by India's reluctance to include Australia in the annual Malabar series of joint trilateral naval exercises with Japan and the USA, which would, most certainly, look and feel like the resumption of the 'quad' naval exercise. It is, perhaps, no coincidence that this decision took place following the 'informal summit' between Modi and Chinese President Xi Jinping in April 2018 in Wuhan, China, to ease tensions between the two Asian giants.

Clearly, the 'quad' will take time to evolve as a security partnership. This will be driven largely by the actions of China and the USA; with India instead currently seeking, in the interim, to focus the 'quad' on economic and infrastructural projects and partnerships. Eager to avoid antagonizing China, India will also continue to reject formal invitations to join the USA in joint patrols in the South China Sea.

However, India has actively participated in joint trilateral naval exercises within the Indian Ocean and the Indo-Pacific, and has strongly encouraged trilateral/quadrilateral security meetings. The first joint trilateral naval exercise with the USA and Japan took place in 2009 as part of the annual Malabar series of exercises with the US Navy, in which the Japanese Navy participated as an observer; in 2015, Japan became a permanent member of the annual Malabar naval exercise.

In April 2018, the 9th US–India–Japan foreign ministry senior official–level meeting took place; the second foreign minister–level meeting was held in September 2017; and in November 2018 the leaders of the three countries—Trump, Modi, and Abe—met on the sidelines of the G20 summit in Argentina. The fourth round of the Japan–India–Australia dialogue at the foreign secretary–level took place in New Delhi in December 2017. The first meeting of the India–Australia–Indonesia foreign ministry senior official–level dialogue was held in November 2017, and the second summit-level meeting of the leaders of India–Russia–China was held in November 2018 on the sidelines of the G20 Summit, after an interval of 12 years. The third revived meeting of foreign ministry senior officials of the 'quad' took place in November 2018. In July 2018, the 10th BRICS (Brazil–Russia–India–China–South Africa) Summit also took place.

Vietnam emerged as another important partner in maritime security. India provided Vietnam with patrol boats; a USD 500-million line of credit for defence spending, boosting an earlier USD 100-million credit line; access to satellite data for monitoring its waters; and submarine and combat-aircraft training. In July 2017, Vietnam granted an Indian oil firm a two-year extension to explore an offshore oil block, part of which is in the South China Sea.

Interests

Domestic: Economy and Energy for SLOC Security as well as Countering Maritime Terrorism

The Modi government's primary interests in maritime security and the Indian Ocean are based on energy and economic dependence as well as countering maritime terrorism. With higher economic growth fuelled by greater energy consumption, India is dependent on the Indian Ocean for both trade and energy. Over 90 per cent of India's foreign trade by volume and 70 per cent in value terms is seaborne, accounting for 42 per cent of India's GDP. Its oil imports have increased to nearly 80 per cent of total demand, with nearly 66 per cent of imports originating from the Gulf, thereby accounting for over 50 per cent of India's total oil demand. Most major international shipping lanes in the Indian Ocean are located close to India's island territories. Some 66 per cent of the world's maritime oil trade, 50 per cent of the global container traffic, and 33 per cent of global cargo trade flows through the Indian Ocean.

India's vulnerability to maritime terrorism was marked by the terror attack on Mumbai in November 2008, which killed 166 people when 10 Pakistan-based Lashkar-e-Taiba (LeT) terrorists used the sea route to travel from Karachi to Mumbai. This took place despite India's first and deadliest maritime terror attack taking place in Mumbai on 12 March 1993, with the smuggling of arms and explosives by sea from Pakistan to the Indian coast (resulting in 257 people getting killed and 713 injured).

As a result of the 2008 Mumbai terror attack, the UPA government undertook a major overhaul of India's coastal and maritime security. These included

(a) significantly, the navy being designated as the nodal authority responsible for overall maritime security, both coastal and offshore;
(b) the coastguard being additionally responsible for security in the areas patrolled by the marine police, from the shoreline to 12 nautical miles;

(c) joint operation centres being set up to coordinate navy–coastguard functions better;

(d) the strengthening and expansion of coastguard and marine police; and

(e) the establishment of a national command, control, communication, and intelligence network for real-time maritime domain awareness between the operations rooms of the navy and the coastguard. (Roy-Chaudhury and Levesques 2012, 129–30)

In August 2009, the Indian Navy's official maritime doctrine incorporated new constabulary missions for the navy, including counterterrorism and anti-piracy operations (IISS 2010, 336).

A key aspect of the Modi government's focus on countering maritime terrorism is greater MDA, the development of a comprehensive operational picture in near-real time to allow the control of surveillance and response assets and rapid response to events. In late 2014, the Indian Navy set up the Information Management and Analysis Centre (IMAC) with the coastguard to function under the National Security Advisor (NSA). This joint operations facility is the nodal centre of the National Command Control Communications and Intelligence Network (NC3I Network), which links 20 Indian Navy and 31 coastguard stations, located along the coast and on island territories, providing coastal surveillance information (Peri 2014). In December 2018, the Indian Navy inaugurated the Information Fusion Centre (IFC) for the Indian Ocean Region. The IFC, based in Gurgaon (adjacent to New Delhi), aims at developing comprehensive maritime domain awareness and will host liaison officers from partner countries, including the USA, the UK, and France (Government of India, MoD 2018).

Regional: Countering China's Expansion in the Indian Ocean

A key driver of Indian naval activism is China's assertive policy towards India and the expansion of Chinese influence in the Indian Ocean since 2008, which India perceives as an attempt—for the first time—to gain permanent access to the Indian Ocean and to 'encircle' India strategically. India remains suspicious of Chinese activities in Pakistan (where it is perceived to be developing refuelling facilities for Chinese warships at the recently commissioned Chinese-built Gwadar port), Myanmar (where China is helping to develop ports and pipelines), Sri Lanka (through the control of Hambantota port and infrastructure), and Bangladesh (through the development of Chittagong port and the supply of its first two submarines).

In view of the Chinese navy's participation in counter-piracy operations off the Somalia coast since 2008, it has used a network of commercial ports—built, financed, operated, or owned by Chinese companies—to rest and resupply. These include ports in Oman, Yemen, and Pakistan as well as in Kenya, Tanzania, and Mozambique. This has hardened New Delhi's attitude towards China, which is India's largest trading partner, with bilateral trade at USD 89.7 billion in 2017–18.

India seeks to offset the growing influence that Beijing has acquired in South Asia through sponsorship of the CPEC/BRI, in particular, CPEC's linkage to the Indian Ocean through the development of Gwadar port; the establishment of China's first overseas military base in Djibouti in 2017; and the significant increase in deployments of Chinese naval vessels in the Indian Ocean (from 3–4 in 2014 to an estimated 14 in mid-2017). The visit of a Chinese diesel-electric submarine to Karachi in May 2017 alongside Chinese diesel-electric submarines at Colombo port in the past and China's resumed work on the Colombo port city project exacerbated this anxiety, as did the lease of the Chinese-financed and -built Hambantota port to Chinese companies for commercial and security operations. A revised agreement for Hambantota port, cleared by Sri Lanka's cabinet in late July 2017, has been reported to include one Chinese company holding an 85 per cent stake in running Hambantota's ports and terminals, whilst a second Chinese company is expected to hold a 49 per cent in security operations in the port.

While the Indian Navy now regularly exercises and trains with the USA and Southeast Asian navies, the Chinese navy further builds its relations with the Pakistan Navy. In September 2007 the Indian Navy participated in the largest multilateral naval exercise in the Bay of Bengal with the USA, Australia, and Japan, along with Singapore. This 'quadrilateral' exercise involved three aircraft carriers (two of which were nuclear-powered), a nuclear submarine, several frigates and destroyers, and over three dozen fighter aircraft. China was deliberately excluded. The tendency for each to be excluded from the international engagements of the other has raised concerns over an emerging naval rivalry in the Indian Ocean.

Global: Emphasizing UNCLOS and 'Freedom of Navigation'

Following the India–US joint vision statement on the Indian Ocean in January 2015, India has subsequently publicly affirmed 'the importance of safeguarding maritime security and ensuring freedom of navigation and over flight throughout the region', whether or not it has directly referred to the South China Sea. India's maritime strategy of October 2015 also emphasized the importance of maintaining freedom of navigation and strengthening the international legal regime at sea, particularly UNCLOS.

In September 2016, Indian Foreign Secretary S. Jaishankar stated:

> Recognising the growing importance of maritime trade in an increasingly globalized world, India supports freedom of navigation and over flight, and unimpeded commerce, based on the principles of international law, as reflected notably in the UNCLOS. … As a State Party to the UNCLOS, India urges all parties to show utmost respect for the UNCLOS, which establishes the international legal order of the seas and oceans. In that connection, the authority of Annex VII Tribunal and its awards is recognized in Part XV of the UNCLOS itself. India's own record in this regard is also well known. (Government of India, MEA 2016a)

However, at times, India has issued contradictory statements. In April 2016, for example, the foreign ministers of India, Russia, and China issued a joint communique, which stated that 'Russia, India and China are committed to maintaining a legal order for the seas and oceans based on the principles of international law, as reflected notably in UNCLOS). All related disputes should be addressed through negotiations and agreements between the parties concerned' (Government of India, MEA 2016b). Some observers viewed the latter sentence as a departure from its earlier position with the USA.

Institutions

Domestic: Navy, Ministry of External Affairs, Prime Minister's Office, Centre–State Relations

An intrinsic problem for the government had been that it lacked a top-level institutionalized mechanism to facilitate coordination among India's multiple domestic stakeholders on maritime security. India's 2015 maritime strategy had been published at a time when there is greater civil–military consensus on the growing importance of the sea for India's prosperity and security. This was marked by the release of the strategy by the defence minister at the Naval Commanders Conference in New Delhi on 26 October 2015—the first time a defence minister had formally released such an official navy document.

Additionally, there is now certainly much greater clarity in decision-making and coordination on maritime security in three areas: (*i*) within the central government; (*ii*) between the centre and the maritime states; and (*iii*) between the central government and the navy and coastguard.

First (in the central government), the Prime Minister's Office (PMO) has a key role on security issues with the NSA to the prime minister in the lead, along with the Foreign Secretary. The cabinet secretary chairs meetings of the National Committee for Strengthening Maritime and Coastal Security (NCSMCS), to coordinate all inter-ministerial and inter-agency matters related to maritime and coastal security. This consists of representatives of all the concerned government ministries and departments and the nine coastal states and four union territories (UTs). But the frequency of these meetings, just once every six months, is not sufficient.

Second (between the centre and the nine coastal states), the union home minister chairs the meeting of coastal states/UTs to ensure coordination among one another. To enhance coordination, over 100 'exercises' have been conducted by the navy in all the coastal states since 2008; registration of over 200,000 fishing vessels has been made compulsory, along with the issue of identity cards to all fishermen with a single centralized database; and fishermen are also involved in navy–coastguard counterterrorism exercises. A Central Marine Police Force is being set up with a mandate to police waters up to 12 nautical miles from the coast, operating without any jurisdiction limitations faced by the state police.

Third (in relation to the centre and the navy), in the aftermath of the November 2008 Mumbai terror attacks, the Manmohan Singh government in February 2009 formally gave the navy an expanded responsibility for the overall maritime security of the country, including coastal and offshore security. This additional mandate was significant as it was the first time that any of the armed services had formally been given such overall responsibility, having been limited in the past, in relation to the government, as assistance to the civilian authority. To enhance MDA, the NC3I Network was inaugurated in 2014. This coastal security network collates data about all ships and boats operating near the Indian coast, from multiple technical sources including the Automatic Identification System (AIS) and radar chains. There is now greater coordination also between the navy, the MoD, and the MEA. A naval officer serves as director (military affairs) in the MEA's Disarmament and International Security Affairs (DISA) division and a foreign service officer is posted in the MoD as the joint secretary, planning and international cooperation (PIC). For the first time, in March 2016, the director general of the coastguard was a regular coastguard officer and not a senior naval officer.

Regional: Indian Ocean Rim Association and the Indian Ocean Naval Symposium

Rhetorically, India looks towards a more cooperative and integrated future for the Indian Ocean region, seeking to strengthen the single Indian Ocean–wide regional body, the 21-member Indian Ocean Rim Association (IORA). The IORA was formed in 1997 with the aim of nurturing economic cooperation and development. At an IORA council of ministers' meeting in Bangalore in 2011, six priority areas for cooperation were agreed upon, including maritime safety and security. India could seek to promote this multilateral forum as the key Indian Ocean body for collective action and cooperation.

Yet, there is little prospect of bolstering the IORA's role on maritime security cooperation, given India's preference for dealing with other states bilaterally rather than in multilateral forums. Nonetheless, India aims to follow China in gaining observer status in the five-member Indian Ocean Commission.

Parallel to this, the Indian Ocean Naval Symposium (IONS) will continue working to strengthen maritime security cooperation among the navies of the 35 littoral and island states in the Indian Ocean. Having conceived of the IONS and hosted its inaugural meeting, India actively seeks to consolidate maritime security and anti-piracy institutional mechanisms. The IONS has been envisaged for primarily fostering informal navy-to-navy interactions.

Global: United Nations

India and the UN work at a global level on maritime security. India is a participant in the Contact Group on Piracy off the Coast of Somalia

(CGPCS), pursuant to UN Security Council Resolution 1851, which has contributed significantly in controlling piracy in the Western Indian Ocean. In its 2015 maritime security strategy, the Indian Navy stated that it will 'remain prepared to contribute to Peace Support Operations mandated by the United Nations, and as directed by the Government of India'.

India is also party to UNCLOS, the agreement relating to the implementation of Part XI of the UNCLOS, and the 1995 United Nations Fish Stocks Agreement. India has been a member of the Council of the International Seabed Authority and its experts are elected to its finance committee and the legal and technical commission. Also, an Indian scientist is regularly elected to the commission on the Limits of the Continental Shelf established under the UNCLOS. Further, an Indian jurist has been an elected judge of the International Tribunal for the Law of the Sea since its establishment in 1996.

***

Unlike in the past, the Modi government is developing a robust new maritime strategy, aspiring to become a 'leading' rather than a 'balancing' power in the Indian Ocean. Instead of trying to limit Western or erstwhile Soviet (Russian) or Chinese power in the Indian Ocean, India now seeks to leverage India's growing national capabilities to take on greater roles and responsibilities, with maritime dominance apparently the goal. This perceives the Indian Ocean as an essential part of India's 'immediate and extended neighbourhood' and, therefore, as a foreign- and security-policy priority emanating from its 'neighbourhood first' policy.

Significantly, this focuses on bolstering India's economic, political, diplomatic, and security initiatives in the Indian Ocean, especially with coastal and island states. India's naval influence seeks to move beyond the arc from the Persian Gulf, to the Strait of Malacca, to areas further east, including the South China Sea. With the Indian Ocean and the South China Sea intrinsically connected, India's interest in the Indo-Pacific region has risen recently. At the same time, the Modi government is continuing to build strategic networks with the USA, France, Japan, Australia, and Vietnam to counter Chinese naval influence in the Indian Ocean.

The Modi government's primary interests in maritime security and the Indian Ocean are based on energy and economic dependence as well as countering maritime terrorism, the latter a result of the terror attacks on Mumbai in November 2008 in which terrorists used the sea route to travel from Karachi to Mumbai. At the same time, it seeks to challenge expanded Chinese influence in the region and provide a counter narrative to the strategic impact of BRI/CPEC.

There is also now certainly much greater clarity in decision-making and coordination on maritime security within the central government, between the central government and the maritime states, and between the central government and the navy and coastguard, which illustrates the greater importance attached to maritime security by the political leadership. Although, rhetorically, India seeks to boost the IORA, it still prefers to deal with other states bilaterally rather than in multilateral forums. The only exception may well be India's policies in relation to the UN and global maritime security.

References

Basu, Nayanima. 2019. 'India Is No Longer "Non-aligned"', Says Foreign Secretary Vijay Gokhale', *The Print*, 10 January. Available at https://theprint.in/diplomacy/india-is-no-longer-non-aligned-says-foreign-secretary-vijay-gokhale/176222/ (accessed on 21 January 2019).

Brewster, David. 2014. *India's Ocean: The Story of India's Bid for Regional Leadership*. London: Routledge.

Fernandes, George. 2000. 'Maritime Dimensions of India's Security'. *Indian Defence Review*, 15 (4), October–December.

Government of India, MEA (Ministry of External Affairs). 2014. 'NSA Level Meeting on Trilateral Maritime Security Cooperation between India, Sri Lanka and Maldives', 6 March. Available at: http://www.mea.gov.in/in-focus-article.htm?23037/NSA+level+meeting+on+trilateral+Maritime+Security+Cooperation+between+India+Sri+Lanka+and+Maldives (accessed 29 November 2017).

———. 2016a. 'Remarks by Foreign Secretary at Indian Ocean Conference', 1 September. Available at: http://mea.gov.in/Speeches-Statements.htm?dtl/27356/Remarks+by+Foreign+Secretary+at+Indian+Ocean+Conference+September+01+2016 (accessed 29 November 2017).

———. 2016b. 'Joint Communiqué of the 14th Meeting of the Foreign Ministers of the Russian Federation, the Republic of India and the People's Republic of China', 18 April. Available at: http://mea.gov.in/bilateral-documents.htm?dtl/26628/Joint_Communiqu_of_the_14th_Meeting_ of_the_Foreign_Ministers_of_the_Russian_Federation_the_Republic_of_ India_and_the_Peoples_Republic_of_China (accessed 29 November 2017).

———. 2018. 'Prime Minister's Keynote Address at Shangri La Dialogue', 1 June. Available at: https://www.mea.gov.in/Speeches-Statements. htm?dtl/29943/Prime+Ministers+Keynote+Address+at+Shangri+La+ Dialogue+June+01+2018 (accessed 18 January 2019).

Government of India, MoD (Ministry of Defence). 2018. 'Raksha Mantri Inaugurates Information Fusion Centre—Indian Ocean Region (IFC-IOR)', 22 December. Available at http://pib.nic.in/newsite/PrintRelease. aspx?relid=186757 (accessed 22 January 2019).

Group of Ministers (GoM). 2001. *Recommendations of the Group of Ministers: Reforming the National Security System*, February 2001, Declassified Version.

Hokayem, Emile and Rahul Roy-Chaudhury. 2017. 'India and the UAE: Towards Strategic Cooperation', *IISS Voices*, 23 January. Available at: https://www.iiss.org/en/iiss%20voices/blogsections/iiss-voices-2017-adeb/january-850b/india-and-the-uae-towards-strategic-cooperation-82af (accessed 29 November 2017).

Ministry of Defence (Integrated Headquarters, Navy). 2004. *Indian Maritime Doctrine 2004*.

———. 2009. *Indian Maritime Doctrine 2009*.

———. 2015. *Ensuring Secure Seas: Indian Maritime Security Strategy 2015*.

IISS (International Institute for Strategic Studies). 2010. *The Military Balance*, 110 (1), Chapter Seven, 'South and Central Asia', pp. 335–76.

Modi, Narendra. 2015. Speech delivered at Joint Commissioning of Offshore Patrol Vessel Barracuda in Mauritius, 13 March. Available at: http://www. narendramodi.in/prime-minister-narendra-modis-visit-to-mauritius-7319 (accessed 29 November 2017).

Narayanan, M.K. 2016. 'Non-alignment to Multi-alignment', *The Hindu*, 5 January. Available at: https://www.thehindu.com/opinion/lead/Non-alignment-to-multi-alignment/article13982580.ece (accessed 21 January 2019).

Paul, Ruma. 2014. 'U.N. Tribunal Rules for Bangladesh in Sea Border Dispute with India', *Reuters*, 8 July. Available at: https://uk.reuters.com/ article/uk-bangladesh-india-seaborder-idUKKBN0FD15N20140708 (accessed 22 January 2019).

Peri, Dinakar. 2014. 'IMAC Will Help Navy Step Up Coastal Surveillance', *The Hindu*, 22 November. Available at: http://www.thehindu.com/news/ national/imac-will-help-navy-step-up-coastal-surveillance/article6622612. ece (accessed 29 November 2017).

PIB (Press Information Bureau). 2001. 'Group of Ministers' Report on "Reforming the National Security System"', 23 May. Available at: http://pib.nic.in/archieve/lreleng/lyr2001/rmay2001/23052001/r2305200110.html (accessed 29 November 2017).

Roy-Chaudhury, Rahul. 1995. *Sea Power and Indian Security*. London: Brassey's.

———. 2000. *India's Maritime Security*. New Delhi: Knowledge World in association with the Institute for Defence Studies and Analyses.

———. 2015. 'India's Official Maritime Security Strategy', *IISS Voices*, 14 December. Available at: https://www.iiss.org/en/iiss%20voices/blogsections/iiss-voices-2015-dda3/december-5c5a/indias-official-maritime-security-strategy-e6a0 (accessed 29 November 2017).

Roy-Chaudhury, Rahul and Antoine Levesques. 2012. 'India's Concerns and Responses to the "War on Terror"', in Rachel E. Utley (ed.), *9/11 Ten Years After: Problems and Perspectives*, pp. 119–38. Farnham: Ashgate.

Roy-Chaudhury, Rahul and Kate Sullivan de Estrada. 2018. 'India, the Indo-Pacific and the Quad', *Survival: Global Politics and Strategy*, 60 (3), June–July.

Wire, The. 2017. 'India Backs ICJ Opinion on Chagos Islands, Indian Ocean Territory That UK Refuses to Leave', 23 June. Available at: https://thewire.in/150536/un-icj-indian-ocean/ (accessed 29 November 2017).

4   Rising Digital Power

India's Global Internet Governance Policy

HANNES EBERT

INDIA'S ECONOMIC TRANSFORMATION SINCE THE EARLY 1990s has become inextricably linked to the rapid growth of its Internet software industry and its trademark as a global leader of information technology (IT) services.[1] Following extensive computerization of services in the late 1980s under then Prime Minister Rajiv Gandhi, the IT sector's contribution to the Indian gross domestic product (GDP) rose from 1.2 per cent in 1998 to 9.5 in 2015 (IBEF 2017). Banking on its high cost competitiveness in providing IT services, India emerged as the world's largest sourcing destination for the global IT industry, accounting for approximately two thirds of the market, as well as the fastest growing e-commerce market (*The Economist* 2016). As a result, the Indian IT sector managed to attract increasing foreign investments and produce a surplus of skilled IT workers, becoming the world's third-largest hub for technology start-ups and employing a workforce of an estimated 3.7 million directly and 10 million indirectly in 2016

[1] The author is grateful for comments on earlier drafts of this chapter by the editors, the anonymous reviewers, Cherian Samuel, Jayadev Parida, and the participants of the 2018 Annual Indian Security Studies Workshop at the Center for the Advanced Study of India, University of Pennsylvania, U.S., in particular Michael Horowitz and Rohan Mukherjee.

(*The Hindu* 2016; IBEF 2017).[2] Consequently, the sector's value is expected to grow from USD 150 billion in 2016 to USD 350 billion in 2025 (*The Times of India* 2016). As the fastest-growing large economy with the largest population of 'millennials', India will likely be able to attract increasing investments into its IT market.

Parallel to the rise of India as a proclaimed 'IT superpower' (Joshi 2013), access of Indians to information and communication technologies (ICT) grew exponentially in the past 15 years. In 2000, 5.5 million people or 0.5 per cent of the population had access to the Internet at home, rising to 93.3 million or 7.5 per cent in 2010; by 2015, a downward trend in costs of mobile devices and Internet access led to an Internet boom that enabled India to replace the United States (U.S.) as the second-largest Internet user base after China with 354.1 million Internet users or 27 per cent of the population, expected to grow to an estimated 462.1 million or 34.8 per cent in 2016 (see Figure 4.1).[3] While in 2016 penetration rates were still low compared to other emerging economies and Internet usage remained highly concentrated in urban areas, India had the world's highest Internet usage growth rate

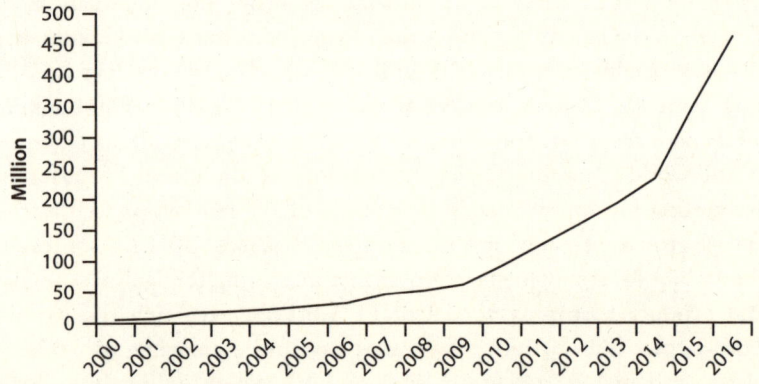

Figure 4.1 Internet users in India

Source: Internet Live Stats (2016); data for 2015 and 2016 are estimated.

[2] Rajaraman (2012) provides the most comprehensive account of the evolution of computing in India.

[3] For a discussion of the Internet boom's impact on India's economy, see McKinsey and Company (2012).

and is expected to reach the one billion mark by 2030 (*Internet Live Stats* 2016; *The Economist* 2016). To ensure greater connectivity and develop e-governance services, the Indian government under Prime Minister Narendra Modi made constructing and upgrading high-speed Internet networks in rural areas across India a top priority under its 'Digital India' campaign launched in July 2015 (Government of India 2016a). However, India's rapid digital transformation made its networks highly vulnerable to threats (Ebert 2018).

Growing stakes and vulnerabilities have compelled the Indian state not only to step up its institutional, legislative, and policy efforts to secure its domestic networked infrastructure, but also to considerably enhance its role in international negotiations on norms and rules on Internet governance. Until now, New Delhi has been perceived as a 'swing state' between the different poles of the global Internet governance debate. Only recently has the Indian government under Prime Minister Modi taken steps to transform India's role as a 'norm taker' into a 'norm shaper' by promoting a 'middle way' of global Internet governance. The sources of this shift are so far contested.

This chapter, therefore, examines whether rising India's global-level Internet governance policy is primarily driven by interests, institutions, or ideas. To address this question, the chapter is divided into three parts. The first part illustrates how India's global-level Internet governance policy evolved. While focusing on policy making under Modi, who came into office in 2014, it takes into account changes of India's Internet governance policy since 2000, when the Indian Parliament passed the Information Technology Act in the context of growing stakes in ICT governance, the key policy guideline for ensuing legislation. The second part inquires to what extent and in what ways interests, institutions, and ideas have shaped this approach and if these three factors originated predominantly from the domestic, regional, or global level of politics. Finally, this chapter discusses the likely prospects of India's Internet governance policy.

India's Evolving Approach to Global Internet Governance Policy

India has placed growing importance on Internet governance negotiations in global multilateral institutions. With the Internet connecting half of the world's population and contributing an estimated USD 4 trillion to the global economy in 2016, the question of who governs the Internet has become one of the most contested disputes in contemporary global governance (cf. Nye 2017).[4] The status quo of Internet governance is best described as a multistakeholder regime complex of organically developed Internet institutions, which assigns a policy making role to business and civil society actors and an advisory role to governments. This model was originally put in place by and still tends to favour the USA. Rising sovereignty-oriented, authoritarian cyber powers such as Russia and (to a lesser extent) China have challenged this status quo by promoting a more hierarchical, top-down approach based on greater authority by states and international organizations such as the International Telecommunication Union (ITU), a United Nations (UN) specialized agency, in global cyber governance under the pretext of national security concerns (Ebert and Maurer 2013).

Swinging Digital Power

With growing stakes in a secure and efficient cyberspace, the Indian government has increasingly sought to position itself in this polarized debate, engaging in a balancing act of not taking sides on the one hand and enhancing its leverage on the other—a diplomatic conduct for which it was perceived as a 'swing state' (for example, Maurer and Morgus 2014). At the 66th session of the UN General Assembly (UNGA) in October 2011, the Indian delegation submitted a proposal for the establishment of a new 50-member UN Committee on Internet Related Policies (CIRP) based on equitable geographic representation, a multilateral mechanism to manage global public policy concerns on Internet governance by providing non-binding recommendations to the UNGA (Government of India 2011).[5]

---

[4] Choucri, Madnick, and Ferwerda (2014) analyse the evolving institutional architecture managing global cyber activities.

[5] The proposal was originally drafted as a joint initiative by the IBSA (India–Brazil–South Africa) Dialogue Forum member states, including India, Brazil, and South Africa, in September 2011, but India's vested interests and considerable opposition to the IBSA draft led it to submit a revised version unilaterally. For a discussion of IBSA's cyber policy cooperation, see Ebert and Maurer (2013).

The proposal suggested to invert the hierarchy between state and non-state actors in the existing transnational multistakeholder institutions by assigning to governments a policy making role and business and civil society groups an advisory and assisting role (Mueller 2011). It expressed India's concerns about the US dominance over critical governance issues within the existing multistakeholder regime institutions, in particular its control over the Domain Name System (DNS) overseen by the Internet Assigned Numbers Authority (IANA), a department of the California-based private non-profit Internet Corporation for Assigned Names and Numbers (ICANN), and their failure to account for many developing countries' concerns about their digital networks' security and international jurisdiction over national data flows (Kovacs 2015a). New Delhi sought to mitigate US dominance and increase its influence by shifting parts of Internet governance to a new multilateral international organization. At the same time, while the proposal put governments firmly on top of the Internet governance hierarchy, the CIRP was reportedly intended to serve as an addition to (not a substitute of) the Internet Governance Forum (IGF) and thus establish a government-centred but overall inclusive governance process.

Yet, the proposal triggered rising opposition from the USA and other Western governments as well as business and civil society groups in India who feared that the numerous ambiguities in the text, including with regard to the latter's specific roles, would leave room for effectively establishing exclusive state control over the Internet and greater censorship of the ICT. In 2012, this opposition eventually compelled the Indian government to back down from the proposal and shift away from its global-level promotion of sovereigntist Internet governance approaches, with the then Union Telecom Secretary R. Chandrashekhar admitting that his government is 'yet to take a final position' (cited in Singh 2012a). In two Internet governance meetings in New Delhi in September 2012, Telecom Minister Kapil Sibal similarly confirmed that India opposes government control of the Internet and seeks multistakeholder consultations on reforming the ICANN-led system (Singh 2012b). In October 2012, India hosted the first multistakeholder India Internet Governance Conference in New Delhi, a platform for domestic stakeholder consultations, and participated in the Budapest Cyber Space Conference, where then Minister of State for Telecom Sachin Pilot opted to promote the developing countries' representation in, instead of promoting opposition to, the ICANN, noting that 'the extreme views being floated by some countries on Internet governance could lead to the Balkanization of the Internet and we are against any such move, including control of Internet by government or inter-governmental bodies' and that 'while the existing system certainly needs to be changed, India's position will include multistakeholder involvement and not inter-governmental bodies that may have been proposed in the past' (cited in Singh 2012b). Finally, Sibal publicly reiterated his stance in favour of multistakeholderism at the IGF in Baku, Azerbaijan, in November 2012. According to one observer, India had 'reinvented its position on Internet governance, hoping to become a new voice of reason in what has so far been a deeply polarised global debate', a change that 'intended to distance India from any model propagating governments taking "charge" or "balkanising" the Internet' (Singh 2012b).

As another precursor of India's cautious, gradual embrace of multistakeholderism, India put forward more nuanced positions accounting for business and civil society concerns at the World Conference on Information Technology (WCIT) hosted by the ITU in Dubai in December 2012 to renegotiate a 1988 treaty governing cross-border telecommunications traffic, the International Telecommunication Regulations (ITRs). A group of states led by China and Russia proposed revisions to the ITRs that aimed at expanding the ITU's role to also include Internet governance functions, which were blatantly rejected by the USA and its allies. India stated that while it principally backed efforts to expand the ITU's role, it insisted that this role should be limited to aspects related to the physical layer of ICT and not to content, and underlined the need to incorporate multistakeholder mechanisms and human rights standards in the text (Kovacs 2013). Eventually, India as the only one among the IBSA Dialogue Forum members, along with the USA and most Organisation for Economic Cooperation and Development (OECD) governments, refused to sign the final text, citing the need for prior domestic consultations to account for the resolutions' wider ramifications (Government of India 2012).

However, India's reservations about the ITRs did not reflect unconditional support to the existing multistakeholder model either. In April 2014, the Indian delegation refused to sign the final document of the Global Multistakeholder Meeting on the Future of Internet Governance NetMundial in Brazil. In October, the new Indian government submitted a draft proposal on the ITU's role in realizing a secure information society at the ITU's Plenipotentiary Conference in Busan, South Korea, suggesting that the ITU should incorporate the Internet in its portfolio and be formally responsible for address resolution, naming and numbering, network architecture standardization, and routing (ITU 2014a). The proposal again triggered opposition by business and civil society groups anxious about its implications for privacy and freedom of expression, compelling India to withdraw.[6]

Endorsing and Reforming Multistakeholderism

The most far-reaching change in India's position on global Internet governance occurred when India's Minister for Communications and IT Ravi Shankar Prasad announced the new Indian government's official embrace of the multistakeholder approach in a video address at the opening ceremony of the ICANN's 53rd public meeting (ICANN53) in Buenos Aires in June 2015, stating that 'India recognizes that all stakeholders are key and multistakeholderism is perhaps the only way to keep the system integrated, growing and expanding' (Prasad 2015). While the overture to multistakeholderism had commenced with Sibal's endorsements in 2012, Prasad's statement was a critical juncture in India's approach to global Internet governance because it signalled the first unequivocal endorsement of this approach from the highest level of government, notably the Prime Minister's Office (PMO). In fact, it laid out for the first time a comprehensive outlook of India's policy on Internet governance, framed by Prasad as the 'Indian vision for the Internet' (Kovacs 2015a), setting straight India's vacillating position expressed in the NetMundial and ITU Plenipotentiary Conference statements in 2014. Announcing the policy shift at the ICANN53 in itself indicated that India sought a deeper engagement with multistakeholder institutions it had hitherto distanced itself from (Saran and Kaul 2015).

While the statement expressed India's new appreciation of the multistakeholder model as the best mechanism to manage cross-border cyber activities, it also underlined that the government planned to use its deeper engagement to reform and decentralize the existing institutions to become more equitable, geographically representative,

---

[6] For a discussion of India's ITU proposal, see Kovacs (2015b).

plural, and democratic. More specifically, New Delhi sought to reduce the US monopoly not only on management but also on oversight, rebalance control toward Asia and the developing world to ensure greater involvement in commercial policies related to top-level domains and the development of technical protocols and standards, and increase Indian voice within these institutions' boardrooms (Sukumar 2015b). Prasad's statement outlined India's vision of how the global Internet governance system should function to account for these goals, suggesting a 'multi-layered' system of multilateral and multistakeholder institutions in which the various stakeholders' policy making competence depends on the specific issue area (Kovacs 2015a). He acknowledged that solutions for cyber security should be increasingly addressed at the global level, and that governments should 'continue to shoulder the central responsibility to secure [digital] networks' (Prasad 2015). India's insistence on the pre-eminent role of states in security combined with openness toward decentralized multistakeholder governance reflected New Delhi's continuous attempt to promote an Indian 'middle way', 'third path', or 'exceptionalism' in cyberspace (cf. Kovacs 2015a, 2015b).

Modi's government reiterated its embrace of multistakeholderism in the framework with the USA agreeing on it in the same month and during the first UNGA Governmental Preparatory meeting for the Ten-Year Review of the World Summit on the Information Society (WSIS) (WSIS+10 Review) in July 2015 and the 10th annual IGF meeting in Brazil in November 2015, as well as by hosting the 57th ICANN meeting in November 2016 in Hyderabad (Alawadhi 2016). The shift coincided with the deepening of bilateral cyber security cooperation with the US government, which expressed great relief (CFR 2015, 43), and was widely acknowledged as a potential 'game changer' (Sukumar 2015b) given India's influence on developing nations and other 'swing states' in the Internet governance debate.[7] In fact, during the 7th BRICS (Brazil, Russia, India, China, and South Africa) summit in Ufa, Russia, in July 2015, India reportedly played a mediatory role and managed to include a language of compromise in the declaration's references to Internet governance, acknowledging the need to involve multiple stakeholders, listing multilateralism as one among other principles, and granting the

---

[7] ICANN's president and CEO, Fadi Chehadé, praised the statement as a 'significant decision' (ICANN 2015).

UN a facilitating rather than a decision-making role (Kovacs 2015a).
Since then, India reportedly encouraged China and Russia to support
multistakeholderism. At subsequent BRICS summits in India in 2016,
China in 2017, and South Africa in 2018, BRICS member states
continued to refer to the need to involve multiple stakeholders in
governing cyberspace. Similarly, at the 14th foreign ministers' meeting
between China, India, and Russia in Moscow in April 2016, India
successfully pushed to include a reference to multistakeholderism in
the final communiqué, which otherwise highlighted the primary role
of states in cyber security, according to some observers a testament to
its 'role as the bridge between the liberal international regime and its
counter-construct' (Sukumar and Saran 2016).[8] The shift was also
facilitated by the successful transfer of IANA stewardship from the US
National Telecommunications and Information Administration (NTIA)
to ICANN by September 2016, a transition that was supported by all
BRICS member states and which constituted a key concern of the Indian
government.

These developments indicated that India has turned from a 'norm
taker' to a 'norm shaper' in global Internet governance. Beyond the
question of authority, India has become increasingly active in debates
about specific governance aspects, such as the applicability of existing
international law to cyberspace. In this context, India has been the only
state except the permanent members of the UN Security Council and
Germany with a membership of at least five years in the UN Group of
Governmental Experts (UNGGE), a governmental advisory body that
has drafted groundbreaking reports outlining how existing international
laws, including the UN Charter, apply to cyberspace in 2013 and 2015
(Digital Watch 2017). India embraced both reports, and participated in
all of the five UNGGE meetings since 2004 except the one in 2014–15,
from which it was reportedly omitted due to its refusal to sign the
NetMundial outcome document (Sukumar 2016d). Following its 2015
endorsement of multistakeholderism, India became a member of the
fifth UNGGE meeting in 2016–17. With the goal of delegitimizing the
use of non-state cyber proxies by China and Pakistan, India's delegation
emphasized the disruptive role of non-state actors in cyberspace and
the need to attribute their activities to states. Following the failure of

[8] For the joint communiqué, see Government of India (2016c).

the 2016–17 UNGGE to produce a consensus report, India established a working group led by its former permanent representative to the UN, Asoke Mukerji, to develop a national position on norms and international law in cyberspace. Moreover, India endorsed the norm against ICT-enabled theft by states proposed in the 2015 G20 communiqué. Finally, India participated in the discussions around the Estonian Government–sponsored group of non-governmental legal experts' work on how international law applies to cyberspace. In 2013, the group published the 'Tallinn Manual on the International Law Applicable to Cyber Warfare', assessing which laws of armed conflict apply how to cyberspace. In 2017, the expanded version called 'Tallinn Manual 2.0 on the International Law Applicable to Cyber Operations' was published; it examined peacetime principles such as sovereignty, non-intervention, and due diligence. While the group has been comprised exclusively of European and North American experts, Indian legal advisors contributed to consultations in the preparation for the 2017 Tallinn Manual during the Global Conference on Cyberspace (GCCS) in The Hague in 2015, the third in a series of conferences since 2011 under the 'London Process'. In February 2016, India's Deputy National Security Advisor (NSA) Arvind Gupta noted that 'while being a useful exercise, [the Tallinn Manual] does not reflect the existing law on the subject because of the absence of state practice which is critical for [the] development of customary international law' (Gupta 2016). Despite this reservation, India expressed its commitment to contribute to developing cyber norms for times of war and peace.[9] In November 2017, India hosted the fifth GCCS as the first non-OECD country, signalling that it is 'casting away its image as a reluctant digital power' (Saran 2016a).

India's official support of the multistakeholder model—notwithstanding its nuanced interpretation—signalled that it joined the US bandwagon in the Internet governance debate. In contrast, New Delhi withstood Washington's pressure to join the Convention on Cybercrime which was adopted by the Council of Europe in 2001, known as the Budapest Convention, the first and only binding international

[9] As, for example, stated in the U.S.–India framework (The White House 2016b). India also became a founding member of the Global Forum on Cyber Expertise, a multistakeholder platform for exchange, launched during the GCCS in 2015 (Samuel 2017).

treaty on the issue. Similarly, New Delhi opposed US and French efforts to incorporate cyber security technologies under the Wassenaar Arrangement, an international arms export control regime that India joined only in December 2017.

What factors have driven India's global Internet governance policy? More specifically, why has the Indian government increased its engagement at the global level, and why has it shifted from a preference of multilateralism to its official support of multistakeholderism while insisting on a focus on security as an ultimate state responsibility? The following sections examine the relative impact of interests, institutions, and ideas at the domestic, regional, and global levels on this evolving policy.

Interests

Managing cyber security concerns at the domestic, regional, and global levels constitutes the primary interest driving India's more active and security-focused global Internet governance policy and the concomitant traditional preference for multilateralism.[10]

Domestic Interests: Securing the Digital Transformation via Global Internet Governance

At the domestic level, the growth of vulnerabilities of India's critical information infrastructure accommodating its rapid digital transformation have foremost driven its more active engagement in global Internet governance, the emphasis on security as a state responsibility, and the concomitant traditional preference for multilateralism in global Internet governance debates. The rapid pace of growth of its IT industry, Internet population, and digitized social and governmental services compelled India to construct a low-cost software and hardware infrastructure vulnerable to cyber threats. While Indian corporations deliver high-technology software and services globally, public and private institutions increasingly dependent on ICT continue to rely on outdated low-technology practices, and individual users remain insufficiently aware

---

[10] For an extensive discussion of cyber security threats to India, see Ebert (2018). For a similar argument, see Datta (2016).

of risks by criminals, hackers, and phishers (Saran 2015, 2016a; Sukumar 2016c).[11] India, according to a leading strategic analyst, has become 'an inviting laboratory for anyone wanting to test out cyber warfare techniques' (Mohan 2012).

As a result, cyber security incidents reported by system administrators and monitored and analysed by Computer Emergency Response Team-India (CERT-In) rose exponentially from 23 in 2004 to 130,338 in 2014 (see Table 4.1). According to a survey by the IT security company McAfee, India replaced China and Russia as the most targeted state already by 2009, with almost eighty per cent of IT executives in India reporting large-scale distributed denial-of-service (DDoS) attacks, while their companies exhibited one of the lowest security adoption rates (Baker, Waterman, and Ivanov 2010). India's rate of malware infection thus exceeded global average. Between 2012 and 2014, it was the third worst affected among G20 countries and the worst affected of all BRICS member states, and has developed into the major source of global spam and future waves of DDoS attacks as well as the target with the highest probability of future data breach since

Table 4.1 Cyber security incidents handled by CERT-In

Year	Number of incidents	Annual growth rate
2004	23	—
2005	254	11.04
2006	552	2.17
2007	1,237	2.24
2008	2,565	2.07
2009	8,266	3.22
2010	10,315	1.25
2011	13,301	1.29
2012	22,060	1.66
2013	71,780	3.25
2014	130,338	1.88
2015	49,455	0.38

Source: Author's compilation based on CERT-In (2016).

[11] The tension between development and security is common to many developing countries (Saran 2015).

then (English and Kleiner 2015). This is particularly troubling given the increasing dependence of multiple institutions and the growing online population on ICT as well as the need to maintain trust in India's global IT trademark. The Unique Identification Authority of India (UIDAI)'s Aadhaar project, established in 2009 to store biometric and demographic data of all Indian residents in a centralized database, and Modi's November 2016 decision to demonetize higher denominations of the rupee and to further digitize India's payment system substantiated these concerns (PTI 2017). Evidently, India's more assertive global Internet governance policy reflected its internal transformation and politicization, and the need to promote affordable access and infrastructure investment drove its vacillating search for the best global governance structure to guarantee this domestic agenda.

Regional Interests: Securing the Next Billion

The pervasive vulnerabilities of India's networked systems have been exploited by nation states, terrorist networks, and criminal hackers in India's regional neighbourhood and beyond. As a result, increasing Indian fears of cyber conflict, terrorism, or crime further contributed to India's more active and security-focused global Internet governance approach.

First, India's enduring conflicts with its rivals China and Pakistan have become increasingly 'cybered', as the involved parties made use of cyber instruments that are less attributable and technologically more sophisticated than conventional means of sabotage, espionage, or subversion (cf. Dombrowski and Demchak 2014). China, with whom India has unresolved territorial disputes that regularly escalated since their border war in 1962, is one of the world's leading cyber powers. Its People's Liberation Army has made controlling information a strategic priority for future conflicts, established an offensive cyber command, and built up sophisticated offensive cyber capabilities (IISS 2016b, 249). While sources of cyber attacks are difficult to attribute, numerous intrusions and infiltrations of sensitive Indian governmental, military, and commercial information networks have been traced back to Chinese IP addresses or were publicly exploited for foreign policy purposes by the Chinese government. Moreover, Pakistan's military and intelligence agencies have also engaged in increasingly sophisticated cyber espionage activities against Indian targets, allegedly including the networks of the

Central Bureau of Investigation in 2010, Indian government websites in 2012–13, and military personnel in the context of the militant attack on the Pathankot airbase and army brigade headquarters in Uri in 2016. Confronted with the gradual 'cyberization' of its enduring rivalries, the Indian government felt compelled to increase its voice in shaping international norms that regulate state behaviour in cyberspace and address cyber threats.

Second, terrorist groups targeting India have increasingly used ICT to propagate, finance, train, plan, and execute their activities. While a series of cyber-enabled terrorist incidents between 2006 and 2008 remained under the central government's radar (Datta 2016), Indian authorities paid more attention to cyber terrorism when, to their surprise, the Pakistan-based armed Jihadi group Lashkar-e-Taiba (LeT) used sophisticated modern technologies, including self-produced devices, for preparing, launching, and propagating its attacks against sites in Mumbai in November 2008 (Sharma 2016). The LeT had recruited IT engineers, executives, and technicians since the early 2000s (Singh 2012), becoming one of the 'world's most technologically sophisticated terror organizations' (Glanz, Rotella, and Sanger 2014).[12]

The Mumbai attacks catalysed the political will to not only enhance domestic cyber capabilities but also to revise domestic cyber jurisdiction, which laid the groundwork for India's approach to global Internet governance. Until then, cyber jurisdiction was based on the IT Act, passed by the Indian Parliament in June 2000, the first law in India to secure commercial IT industry interests (Ministry of Law, Justice and Company Affairs 2000). The 2000 IT Act, however, did not yet incorporate cyber security concerns as a broader political issue. In December 2008, only one month after the attacks in Mumbai, the Indian Parliament passed a major amendment to the IT Act with provisions related to cyber terrorism, for the first time officially mentioning cyber security and acknowledging the rise of cyber threats to India (Ministry of Law, Justice and Company Affairs 2008). The Mumbai attacks, thus, marked a transition of India's

---

[12] Terrorist organizations also used ICT to more effectively exploit internal political instabilities, as was the case in August 2012 when Pakistan- and Bangladesh-based groups used social media to escalate a communal conflict between Muslim settlers and indigenous Bodo tribe members in Assam (Yardley 2012).

cyber policy from a focus on commerce to one on national security objectives, particularly terrorism, which New Delhi traditionally saw as state responsibility (Singh and Krupakar 2014, 710). Protecting its critical information infrastructure through national and international policy making gradually became a primary state interest.

Finally, India's security-oriented approach to global Internet governance was informed by a growing number of reported cases of cybercrime, rising from only 142 in 2006 to 11,592 in 2015 (see Table 4.2). In 2016, India ranked among the five states most affected by cybercrime according to a report by the IT security company Sophos (Das 2016), and is expected to become the key target following demonetization and the concomitant growing use of mobile web- and wallet-based transactions according to IT security company F-Secure (PTI 2017). Already in 2015, cybercrime caused an estimated loss of USD 28 billion for the Indian economy (Norton 2016). Most crimes originated abroad, including from Bangladesh, China and Pakistan (Business Standard 2015). While cybercrime entails activities such as fraud, identity theft, and Internet scams that are foremost commercially driven, its dramatic proliferation and the trend that criminals disproportionately often target government institutions resulted in increasing political ramifications (cp. Kshetri 2013) and pressures on the Indian state to become more active both nationally and internationally to protect India's digitized society and cashless economy.

Table 4.2   Cyber crime in India, 2006–15

Year	Number of cyber-related crimes	Annual growth rate
2006	142	—
2007	217	1.53
2008	288	1.33
2009	420	1.46
2010	966	2.30
2011	1,791	1.85
2012	2,876	1.61
2013	5,963	2.07
2014	9,622	1.61
2015	11,592	1.2

Source: NCRB (2016, 2017).

Global Interests: Hedging US Cyber Hegemony

Global-level interests have played a secondary role in India's global Internet governance policy. On the one hand, India's traditional suspicion of US hegemony, dating back to Indo-US divergences during the Cold War, also translated into opposition to US dominance of the multistakeholder model and the location of most root servers in the U.S., and was expressed collectively through the BRICS, the Shanghai Cooperation Organization (SCO), or the Group of 77 (G77), an informal cooperation mechanism among developing nations in the UN in which India has played a leading role (Kovacs 2015c).

Two incidents affirmed India's general interest in curbing U.S. dominance in cyberspace. First, India had to upgrade its systems after the 'Stuxnet' worm—a malware against Iran's nuclear programme identified in 2010 and allegedly built with US involvement—that affected eight per cent of computers in India as an unintended consequence (Saran 2015). Second, in 2013, top-secret documents leaked by Edward Snowden disclosed that India was the fifth most targeted state (and the most targeted one among BRICS member states and only behind Iran, Pakistan, Jordan, and Egypt) by the US National Security Agency's data mining tool 'Boundless Informant' and by the 'PRISM' programme intercepting and collecting network content, and served as a special collection site for targeting Third-World countries (Greenwald and Saxena 2013). The Snowden revelations drove the Ministry of Communications and IT to promulgate a new national strategy, the National Cyber Security Policy (NCSP), published in June 2013. The NCSP outlined an integrated vision 'to build a secure and resilient cyberspace for citizens, businesses and government' (Ministry of Communications and Information Technology 2013, 3) by creating early warning systems, strengthening cyber security awareness, public–private partnerships and the indigenous cyber security industry, and helping to recruit an additional workforce of 500,000 private sector cyber security professionals within five years. It also had a provision 'to enhance global cooperation by promoting shared understanding and leveraging relationships for furthering the cause of security of cyberspace' (Ministry of Communications and Information Technology 2013, 4). Cyber security was thus ultimately elevated to the highest level of governmental priorities. Concerns over US cyber hegemony contributed to the Indian state's urge to have a greater voice in global Internet governance.

On the other hand, the broader global interest to continue rapprochement with the USA and to gain access to the U.S.-dominated regime also arguably contributed to India's decisions to succumb to US pressure to shelve the 2011 CIRP and 2014 ITU proposals and to endorse multistakeholderism in 2015. It signalled a strategic reassessment that this shift would be a more effective way to protect its security rather than insisting on pure multilateralism and emphasizing the principles of non-interference and sovereignty, as it would create goodwill in Washington for concessions in other areas, such as opening a multi-track dialogue on cyber security and data protection, enabling Indian presence in top-level regional and global multistakeholder fora such as ICANN, and supporting India's bid for a root server located in India (Datta 2016). Growing ties between ICT industries of India and the USA and shared concerns about Chinese espionage further substantiated this strategy.

Institutions

Since the early 2000s, a security-oriented, state-centred institutional cyber regime has evolved in India. Security-focused institutions dominated national and international policy making; but turf wars between departments contributed to India's vacillating positions and outside perception as a 'swing state'. It was only until the end of this institutional competition that, driven by increasing domestic civil society pressures and the need to gain regional and global institutionalized support to mitigate lack of domestic cyber capacities, the Indian state took a whole-of-government decision to endorse multistakeholderism in 2015.

Domestic Institutions: Turf Wars, Undercapacities, and Civil Society Pressure

The institutional cyber policy landscape that evolved in India since the early 2000s initially conceded only limited space to domestic and—by extension—global multistakeholder governance. Overlapping mandates resulted in inter-ministerial and inter-agency turf wars and a lack of governmental unity. As a reaction to intelligence failures in the Kargil War of 1999, the Indian government established the National Technical Facilities Organization (NTFO), later called National Technical Research Organization (NTRO), a specialized agency mandated to improve coordination by creating secure digital networks for inter-agency information sharing, in 2004. Nevertheless, turf wars between the Ministry of External Affairs (MEA) and the NTRO on one side against the Department of Telecommunications and IT on the other erupted, with the former institutions advocating a 'traditional, inter-governmental diplomacy on Internet concerns, with UN forums being [the] preferred forum for dialogue' (Sukumar 2015b) and the latter focusing on technical aspects and inviting multistakeholder involvement.[13] Their divergent views translated into the vacillating positions India took between 2011 and 2014, when the MEA promoted its stance in the 2011 CIRP and the 2014 NetMundial and ITU proposals, while the then Minister of Telecommunications and IT Kapil Sibal publicly supported multistakeholderism at Internet governance forums in 2012 (Sukumar 2015a). Gradually, a three-layered cyber regime evolved whose overlapping competencies resulted in diverging policies. The first layer consists of institutions entrusted with cyber security management, such as the National Security Council Secretariat (NSCS) and the NTRO; the second layer consists of institutions fulfilling governance functions and includes the ministries of communications, electronics and IT, defence, external affairs, and home affairs; and the third layer consists of non-governmental stakeholders such as academia, critical infrastructure providers, and businesses.[14] Overall, security-focused institutions became the majority in this 'multilayered' structure and thus set the tone in the Internet governance debate, although the cacophony of voices also resulted in India's vacillating positions.

Modi's 2015 decision to endorse multistakeholderism reflected the end of these turf wars. The NCSP of 2013 had already designated the national-level CERT-In to act as the nodal agency for coordinating cyber security response activities among departments and sectoral CERTs and created the role of a National Cyber Security Coordinator, but it was not until March 2015 that the PMO designated Gulshan Rai, who as the former head of the CERT at the Department of Electronics and IT (DeitY) leaned toward the technical community to fill this position inside the PMO (Aggarwal 2015). Modi had commenced inter-ministerial

---

[13] This is also confirmed by former NSA, Narayanan (2016).

[14] See Sukumar and Sharma (2016, 6–7). The Internet Democracy Project (2016) provides an interactive overview of institutional linkages.

consultations in late 2014, and filled in the MEA before directing IT minister Ravi Shankar Prasad to announce India's policy shift at the ICANN53 (Sukumar 2015b). At the WSIS+10 Review conference in New York in 2015, the MEA reaffirmed the ICANN53 position, thus signalling governmental unity on Internet governance (Government of India 2015). Finally, Modi's government also took steps to engage more with third-layer non-governmental actors and domestic multistakeholder mechanisms (Stevens 2016).

In part, Modi's decision was also driven by undercapacities of India's cyber security infrastructure and the concomitant need to gain US support in this area. A report by the NSCS leaked in 2013 revealed that India deployed a mere 556 official cyber security experts in various government institutions, a 'grossly inadequate' workforce compared to an estimated 7,300 in Russia, 91,080 in the U.S., and 125,000 in China (Joshi 2013). In early 2013, India had announced the plan to recruit over 4,000 additional experts, but the Modi government realized it would require external support in this ambitious endeavour.

Pressures exerted by civil society and business organizations constituted a final key domestic driver of India's 2015 endorsement of multistakeholderism. This was most apparent in the withdrawal from the 2011 CIRP proposal and the refusal to sign the ITRs in 2012 following concerted non-governmental opposition. Civil society and business organizations—including NGOs such as the Centre for Internet Society and the Internet Democracy Project and India's largest mobile operators—sceptical of the threat of content control and censorship and the ability of the state to govern the cyberspace, called on the Indian government to withdraw from the CIRP and not sign the ITRs, pointing to insufficient multistakeholder consultation (Ebert and Maurer 2013, 1064–5). Strong domestic opposition, thus, contributed to the withdrawal of the CIRP and the refusal to sign the ITRs, and strengthened domestic multistakeholder consultations. The MEA's increasing engagement with multiple stakeholders reportedly facilitated its renewed membership at the 2016–17 GGE (Sukumar 2016d).

Regional Institutions: Ambiguous Engagement

Although regional institutions played a subordinate role in India's global Internet governance policies, New Delhi's engagement at this level reflects its growing aspirations and effort to position itself as a mediator in the polarized debates. India's attempt to balance its strong military ties with Russia and economic links with China and a commitment to US and Western values in cyberspace was tangible in its engagement with regional multilateral institutions entrusted with cyber security issues. Regional organizations such as the SCO, the Association of Southeast Asian Nations (ASEAN), the ASEAN Regional Forum (ARF), and the Asia-Pacific Economic Cooperation (APEC) all initiated coordination efforts on cyber security, and the Modi government used its participation to shape regional norms of cyber security. It hosted the ASEAN–India Cyber Security Conference on coordinating efforts against cyber threats to Southeast Asia in January 2015 (ASEAN–India Centre 2015) and co-founded the cyber security working group with the ASEAN Defence Ministers' Meeting-Plus platform. Furthermore, at the 14th ASEAN–India summit in September 2016 in Vientiane, Laos, Modi announced that India was 'willing to take concrete steps to enhance cooperation in cyber security' (Ministry of External Affairs 2016). Finally, CERT-In joined the annual drills by the Asia-Pacific Computer Emergency Response Team (APCERT) from 2010.

Global Institutions: Preference for Bilateralism

Finally, India's global Internet governance policy evolved in the context of a proliferation of its bilateral cyber policy agreements and dialogues, the majority of which was security-oriented. The proliferation reflected India's initial preference for bilateralism in this area, with little oversight for non-governmental actors, as well as efforts to formulate a 'middle way' in the governance debates. Prior to Modi's election, India had entered bilateral cyber agreements mostly focused on capacity- and confidence-building, joint training and information sharing. Already in 2001, India and the USA established a joint cyber terrorism initiative and the India–US Cyber Security Forum, which continued despite setbacks triggered by revelations of the USA spying in India in 2006 and the Snowden revelations in 2013.[15] In 2012, New Delhi concluded an agreement with Israel, whose companies have been leading providers of cyber security solutions (*The Economic Times* 2016), and established a cyber security

---

[15] For a concise history of Indo-US cyber cooperation, see Ranganathan (2015).

mechanism with Japan that guarantees the acquisition of technology against cybercrime (*The Times of India* 2012). Moreover, India entered into cyber dialogues with South Korea and France in 2013.

The agenda of India's cyber policy bilateralism broadened significantly after Modi's election. In 2015, India launched dialogues with Australia, the EU, Germany, Malaysia, Mongolia, Singapore, and the UK (Kovacs 2015d); CERT-In signed MoUs with counterparts in Australia, Japan, Malaysia, and Singapore; and India's Ministry of Home Affairs established a mechanism for joint anti-cybercrime efforts with its Chinese counterpart. India signed further agreements with the U.S., Russia, Qatar, and the United Arab Emirates in 2016 and with Vietnam in early 2017. Most importantly, Modi revitalized Indo-US cyber cooperation. During his first visit to the USA in September 2014 and Obama's visit to India in January 2015, both governments agreed to enhance cooperation on cybercrime, terrorism, and the development of norms for responsible state behaviour (The White House 2014, 2015), elevating the issue to a priority concern of future bilateral relations and paving the way for India's endorsement at the ICANN53.[16] On Modi's second visit to Washington in June 2016, the guidelines for a future 'Framework for the U.S.–India Cyber Relationship' were outlined (The White House 2016a).

At the same time, the fact that India entered into a far-reaching agreement on cooperation in international information security with Russia—signed on the sidelines of the BRICS summit in Goa only four months after the U.S.–India framework agreement and in the midst of allegations against Russia using cyber means to influence the outcome of the US elections—best illustrates the hedging diplomacy characterizing India's global-level cyber policy. As one observer noted, India is 'the only major power to have concluded formal negotiations with both Moscow and Washington D.C.', which 'opens up a unique opportunity for India, not only to prevent the rise of exclusionary non-proliferation regimes, but also emerge as a crucial interlocutor and indeed, the convenor of important conversations on the stability of digital spaces' (Sukumar 2016a).

---

[16] On Modi's second visit to Washington in June 2016, the guidelines for a future 'Framework for the U.S.–India Cyber Relationship' were outlined (The White House 2016a). In January 2017, CERT-In and US-CERT renewed their 2011 MoU to promote mechanisms for information sharing.

While India signalled its embrace of the U.S.-favoured multistakeholder approach to global Internet governance and the applicability of international law to cyberspace in its framework agreement with the U.S., the comprehensive agreement with Russia reportedly emphasized cooperation on security-related issues. This suggests that the 2015 endorsement reflects a tactical shift in how to best achieve what otherwise remains India's primary interest, namely cyber security.

Ideas

In 2015, the *People's Liberation Army Daily*, China's military newspaper, called the Internet 'the primary battlefield for ideological struggle' (cited in Tiezzi 2015). Contested political ideas in the evolving global Internet governance structure primarily include the mix of norms and world views commonly associated with the multistakeholder and the multilateral model. India's attempt to position its exceptional approach between both ideal–typical variants is ultimately an outcome of how it reconciles competing ideas of security, access, and privacy domestically, but also of how it projects its aspired status as an IT great power regionally and globally.

Domestic Ideas: Transformed Sovereignty in Cyberspace and Belief in Technology

India's vacillating position on global Internet governance also derives from its complex domestic balancing between security, privacy, and access. As outlined earlier, India's view on cyberspace became heavily securitized following the 2008 Mumbai attacks and the 2013 Snowden revelations. India's conviction that security is the exclusive responsibility of the state—and by extension its call for a stronger role of the state and intergovernmental institutions in cyberspace—has been based on its traditional emphasis on principles of domestic and Westphalian sovereignty and strategic autonomy and the conviction that these principles best guarantee national and international security. To address increasing vulnerabilities of the rapidly growing information networks, the Indian state—as other developing countries—introduced fierce measures of surveillance and selective filtering of ICT, infringing on Indian citizens' privacy rights (Saran 2015) (and was thus categorized as only 'partly free' in Freedom House's Freedom on the Net Status index [see Table 4A.1 in the Appendix of this chapter]). Against this background, the 2011 CIRP and the 2014 ITU plenipotentiary proposals reflect the Indian state's reflex to align with sovereignty-oriented states such as Russia and China to strengthen what Chinese President Xi Jinping called 'cyber sovereignty', arguably rooted in a shared interpretation of strong, centralized sovereignty entailing hierarchical state–society relations and limited stakeholder consultation, in a space in which the authority of governments was limited by design (*BBC* 2015). Similarly, India's concerns over the infringement of its sovereignty also contributed to its refusal to sign the Budapest Convention.

Yet, the failure of India's 2011 and 2014 proposals also reflects the impact of democratic forces rallying behind the idea of privacy. Even in these proposals, while highlighting its legitimate security concerns, the government felt compelled to acknowledge the importance of maintaining the Internet as a free, unrestricted, and open medium instrumental for the freedom of expression, innovation, and access to information. The successful opposition against both proposals by civil society and business organizations exemplified the limits of the Indian state's unilateral efforts to control the Internet. In his 2015 endorsement of multistakeholderism, Prasad thus conceded that 'security cannot be for the sake of security', but constitutes a 'means to offer unfettered liberty, limitless collaboration in the new age of ideas', and that 'pluralism is the only ecosystem that can manage the dynamism [the Internet] demonstrates' (Prasad 2015). Santosh Jha, the MEA's then joint secretary for counterterrorism and global cyber issues, also concluded that 'democratic norms, openness of [the] Internet, inter-operability' (cited in IISS 2016a) were key drivers of the 2015 decision. At the behest of the Indian government, finally, the BRICS Goa declaration of 2016 not only highlighted the principles of sovereignty, non-interference, and territorial integrity in cyberspace, but also included the 'respect for human rights and fundamental freedoms, including the right to privacy' (Government of India 2016b).

The belief of technology as an enabler of economic and political progress in Modi's development model and governance style constitutes a final domestic ideological factor driving the 2015 endorsement. Indian policy makers since Independence perceived technology as a means 'to not only make up for lost time on economic and political progress, but also to arrive on the world stage as a major power' (Datta 2016). As chief minister of Gujarat, Modi pushed for greater Internet access and digitized government services, and as prime minister he continued to pursue a technology-enabled development model in his Digital India initiative, of which seeking greater access to ICT and bridging digital divides nationally and internationally became key components. His business-friendly approach to development further contributed to increasing openness toward the private sector and the multistakeholder approach both domestically and globally.

Regional Ideas: South Asian Connectivity

Regional ideas played only a minor role in driving India's global Internet governance policy. While Modi's policy to revitalize India's regional neighbourhood policy was also based on the idea of enhancing regional connectivity, this has not yet included information infrastructure investments. However, given the fast growth of ICT in other countries of South Asia, India is evolving as a key provider for mid-priced cyber security solutions to governments and corporations in the region. Separately, the way India will use its membership within the SCO—which has served as a key vehicle for promoting sovereigntist interpretations of Internet governance and increased content control, most prominently in its International Code of Conduct for Information Security submitted to the UN General Assembly in 2011 and in a revised form in 2015—will reveal the viability of its aspired role as mediator between competing global Internet governance models.

Global Ideas: Autonomy and Status

Corresponding with its efforts to maintain domestic and Westphalian notions of governance domestically, India's traditional emphasis on autonomy in its foreign policy also informed the sovereigntist components of its Internet governance policy. Building on the principle of non-alignment and a commitment to anti-imperialism and decolonization, India's post-1991 foreign policy promotion of autonomy and related principles such as equality, fairness, justice, non-discrimination, and ownership had entered into the language of its Internet governance proposals. In a concluding statement at the 2014 ITU plenipotentiary, the Indian delegation highlighted that increasing broadband penetration and connectivity 'can only be built on the principles of fairness, justice, and equality', and that 'respecting the principle of sovereignty of information through network functionality and global norms' would increase trust and confidence in the use of ICT (ITU 2014b).

In 2015, Prasad reiterated that Internet governance 'must be fair, it must be equitable' (Prasad 2015), and future multistakeholder Internet governance should therefore be decentralized. According to Sukumar (2016b), India's 2015 endorsement did not undermine its strategic autonomy, because 'both sides traded bargains evenly', a sign of India's flexible practice of autonomy. The urge to be recognized as an autonomous and equal sovereign in cyberspace has been motivated by the 2013 Snowden revelations, feeding into a long-held anti-hegemonic foreign-policy orientation, but also by the perception of discriminatory treatment of technology denial regimes, an underlying motive that explains India's opposition to include cyber-related items under the Wassenaar Arrangement. Similarly, India refused to sign the Budapest Convention or join the Wassenaar export control regime (before its entry in December 2017) on the basis that it has not been party to the treaties' drawing process, and thus lacked ownership (Datta 2016).

Finally, the decision to endorse the multistakeholder approach in 2015 despite the urge to maintain autonomy was also driven by status-seeking considerations. It reflected the Indian government's novel understanding that maintaining India's trademark as a global leader in providing IT services and its aspiration to represent the developing nations' demands in cyberspace required it to enter the widely accepted multistakeholder regime and shape norms of responsible state behaviour from a position of power in the existing institutions. By crafting a 'third path' with a dual emphasis on multistakeholderism and state responsibility on security issues, India sought to underline its ambition to serve as a global 'norm shaper' without compromising its autonomy.

***

India's role in global Internet governance has evolved from a reluctant and hedging 'swing state' promoting diverging institutional interests and ideas to a core interlocutor between entrenched positions advocating a dual emphasis of multistakeholder governance and state responsibility in security affairs. This shift was tactical in nature and primarily driven by

India's commitment to actively shape a governance system that can best accommodate the security and development demands of its domestic digital transformation.

This calculus will also determine India's positions in future bilateral, multilateral, and multistakeholder negotiations on developing norms and standards for times of war and peace. With Prime Minister Modi's decision to tie India's future rise closely to the success of its ICT-enabled transformation, India's engagement in these negotiations is likely to increase. At the same time, governments across the world will pay even closer attention to how India, the world's largest democracy with the fastest growing economy and the fastest growing Internet user base, will position itself in the increasingly polarized debates. India will remain not only 'a bellwether country in the world's march towards ubiquitous connectivity' (English and Kleiner 2015, 8), but will also have the potential to tip the scales during future negotiations. If it can unleash this potential, the rising digital power will have the opportunity to become a leading voice for shaping a governance system sensitive to the claims of a growing number of governments, Internet corporations, and users with increasing stakes in cyberspace.

Appendix

Table 4A.1 Comparison of cyber security indicators

	India	China	Russia	Pakistan	USA
Internet usage (%)[a]	34.8	52.2	71.3	17.8	88.5
IDI (rank)[b]	131	82	45	143	15
Internet censorship[c]	Selective filtering	Substantive and pervasive filtering	Selective filtering	Selective and substantial filtering	—
Freedom on the Internet[d]	Partly free	Not free	Not free	Not free	Free
Cyber Power Index[e]	17/28.3	13/34.6	14/31.7	—	2/75.4
Cyber Maturity Score[f]	50.0	30.7	—	—	90.7

| NTI Index[g] | 3 | 0 | 4 | 1 | 4 |
| Budapest Convention[h] | No | No | No | No | Yes |

Source: Author's compilation from the following sources.

[a]Percentage of total population with access to the Internet, estimated for 2016 (*Internet Live Stats* 2016).

[b]IDI = ICT development indicator ranking (out of 167 countries) for 2015, aggregating 11 ICT indicators on access, use, and skills (ITU 2015).

[c]Data obtained from OpenNet Initiative (2016).

[d]Freedom House's Freedom on the Net Status index distinguishes between the categories 'free', 'partly free', and 'not free' to measure Internet freedom (Freedom House 2016).

[e]Cyber Power Index rank (among G20) and weighted sum of category scores (0–100 where 100 = most favourable) for 2010 (EIU 2011).

[f]Rates countries against 10 factors of cyber maturity on a scale of 0 to 10 (10 being the highest level of maturity) (ASPI 2017).

[g]Nuclear Threat Initiative (NTI) Nuclear Security Index includes indicators on states' ability to protect their nuclear facilities against cyber threats, ranked by 0–4 points (with 4 as the maximum protection ability and 0 indicating a lack of basic requirement to protect nuclear facilities from a cyber attack) (NTI 2016).

[h]Budapest Convention on Cyber Crime (Council of Europe 2016).

References

Aggarwal, Varun. 2015. 'Gulshan Rai Becomes First Chief of Cyber Security', *The Economic Times*, 4 March. Available at: http://economictimes.indiatimes.com/news/politics-and-nation/gulshan-rai-becomes-first-chief-of-cyber-security-post-created-to-tackle-growing-e-threats/articleshow/46449780.cms (accessed 15 December 2016).

Alawadhi, Neha. 2016. 'India's Cybersecurity Doors are Left Wide Open', *The Economic Times*, 5 April. Available at: https://m.economictimes.com/tech/internet/indias-cybersecurity-doors-are-left-wide-open/articleshow/51693705.cms (accessed 3 November 2019).

ASEAN–India Centre. 2015. 'India–ASEAN Conference on Cyber Security', 19 January, New Delhi'. Available at: http://ris.org.in/india-asean-conference-cyber-security (accessed 3 November 2019).

ASPI (Australian Strategic Policy Institute). 2017. *Cyber Maturity in the Asia-Pacific Region 2017.* Barton: ASPI.

Baker, Stewart, Shaun Waterman, and George Ivanov. 2010. *In the Crossfire. Critical Infrastructure in the Age of Cyber War.* London: McAfee. Available at:

http://img.en25.com/Web/McAfee/CIP_report_final_uk_fnl_lores.pdf (accessed 15 December 2016).

BBC. 2015.'China Internet: Xi Jinping Calls for "Cyber Sovereignty"', 16 December. Available at: http://www.bbc.com/news/world-asia-china-35109453 (accessed 15 December 2016).

Business Standard. 2015.'India among the Top-10 Countries Hit by Ransomware Cybercrime', 7 August. Available at: http://www.business-standard. com/article/technology/india-among-the-top-ten-countries-hit-by-ransomware-cybercrime-115080700567_1.html (accessed 15 December 2016).

CERT-In (Computer Emergency Response Team-India). 2016. *Indian Computer Emergency Response Team: Annual Report.* Available at: http://www.cert-in. org.in/ (accessed 15 December 2016).

CFR (Council on Foreign Relations). 2015. *Working with a Rising India,* Independent Task Force Report 73. New York: Council on Foreign Relations.

Choucri, Nazli, Stuart Madnick, and Jeremy Ferwerda. 2014. 'Institutions for Cyber Security: International Responses and Global Imperatives', *Information Technology for Development,* 20 (2): 96–121.

Council of Europe. 2016. 'Convention on Cybercrime', Treaty Office. Available at: https://www.coe.int/en/web/conventions/full-list/-/conventions/treaty/ 185/signatures?p_auth=khgo43mn (accessed 3 November 2019).

Das, Poulomi. 2016. 'India Ranks among the Top 5 Countries at Risk for Cyber Attacks in 2016', *Business Insider,* 20 May. Available at: http://www. businessinsider.in/India-ranks-among-the-top-5-countries-at-risk-for-cyber-attacks-in-2016/articleshow/52364243.cms (accessed 15 December 2016).

Datta, Saikat. 2016. *Cybersecurity, Internet Governance and India's Foreign Policy: Historical Antecedents.* New Delhi: Internet Democracy Project.

Digital Watch. 2017. 'UN GGE', Tableau Software. Available at: https:// public.tableau.com/views/UNGGE/GGEMembers?:embed=y&:show VizHome=no&:host_url=https%3A%2F%2Fpublic.tableau.com%2F &:tabs=no&:toolbar=yes&:animate_transition=yes&:display_static_ image=no&:display_spinner=no&:display_overlay=yes&:display_ count=yes&:loadOrderID=0 (accessed 15 December 2016).

Dombrowski, Peter, and Chris Demchak. 2014. 'Cyber War, Cybered Conflict, and the Maritime Domain', *Naval War College Review,* 67 (2): 71–96.

Ebert, Hannes. 2018.'Building Resilience: India's Cyber Security, 2000-2016', in Sumit Ganguly, Nicolas Blarel, and Manjeet Pardesi (eds), *Oxford Handbook on India's National Security,* pp. 341–68. New Delhi: Oxford University Press.

Ebert, Hannes, and Tim Maurer. 2013. 'Cyberspace and Rising Powers', *Third World Quarterly*, 34 (5): 1054–74.

Economic Times, The. 2016. 'Israel Ready to Assist India with a Comprehensive and Effective Cyber Security Plan', 7 October. Available at: http://economictimes.indiatimes.com/news/politics-and-nation/israel-ready-to-assist-india-with-a-comprehensive-and-effective-cyber-security-plan/articleshow/54741404.cms (accessed on 3 November 2019).

Economist, The. 2016. 'India Online', 5 March. Available at: http://www.economist.com/news/leaders/21693925-battle-indias-e-commerce-market-about-much-more-retailing-india-online?fsrc=scn/fb/te/pe/ed/indiaonline (accessed 15 December 2016).

English, Erin, and Aaron Kleiner. 2015. 'Today's Decisions, Tomorrow's Terrain: Strategic Directions for India in Shaping the Future of Cyberspace', in Samir Saran (ed.), *Digital Debates: CyFy Journal*, pp. 12–19. London: Global Policy Journal.

EIU (Economist Intelligence Unit). 2011. *Cyber Power Index: Findings and Methodology*. London: Economist Intelligence Unit. Available at: https://www.boozallen.com/content/dam/boozallen/media/file/Cyber_Power_Index_Findings_and_Methodology.pdf (accessed 3 November 2019).

Freedom House. 2016. *Freedom on the Net 2016, Silencing the Messenger: Communication Apps under Pressure*. Available at https://freedomhouse.org/report/freedom-net/freedom-net-2016 (accessed 3 November 2019).

Glanz, James, Sebastian Rotella, and David Sanger. 2014. 'In 2008 Mumbai Attacks, Piles of Spy Data, but an Uncompleted Puzzle', *The New York Times*, 21 December. Available at: http://www.nytimes.com/2014/12/22/world/asia/in-2008-mumbai-attacks-piles-of-spy-data-but-an-uncompleted-puzzle.html (accessed 15 December 2016).

Government of India. 2011. 'India's Proposal for a United Nations Committee for Internet-Related Policies (CIRP)', Proposal, Sixty-Sixth Session of the UNGA, 26 October. Available at: http://itforchange.net/sites/default/files/ITfC/india_un_cirp_proposal_20111026.pdf (accessed 15 December 2016).

———. 2012. 'India's Officially Submitted Stand on ITRs at WCIT-2012', 14 December. Available at: http://pib.nic.in/newsite/mbErel.aspx?relid=90748 (accessed 15 December 2016).

———. 2015. 'Inputs for the United Nations General Assembly Review of Tunis Agenda for the Information Society'. Available at: http://workspace.unpan.org/sites/Internet/Documents/UNPAN95026.pdf (accessed 15 December 2016).

———. 2016a. 'Digital India Programme'. Available at: http://www.digitalindia.gov.in/ (accessed 15 December 2016).

————. 2016b. 'Goa Declaration at 8th BRICS Summit', 16 October. Available at: https://www.mea.gov.in/bilateral-documents.htm?dtl/27491/Goa+Declaration+at+8th+BRICS+Summit (accessed 3 November 2019).

————. 2016c. 'Joint Communiqué of the 14th Meeting of the Foreign Ministers of the Russian Federation, the Republic of India and the People's Republic of China', 18 April. Available at: http://mea.gov.in/bilateral-documents.htm?dtl/26628/Joint_Communiqu_of_the_14th_Meeting_of_the_Foreign_Ministers_of_the_Russian_Federation_the_Republic_of_India_and_the_Peoples_Republic_of_China (accessed 15 December 2016).

Greenwald, Glenn, and Shobhan Saxena. 2013. 'India among Top Targets of Spying by NSA', *The Hindu*, 23 September.

Gupta, Arvind. 2016. 'Keynote Address at the 18th Asian Security Conference on "Securing Cyberspace: Asian and International Perspectives"'. Available at: http://www.idsa.in/keyspeeches/18asc-securing-cyberspace-asian-and-international-perspectives_deputy-nsa (accessed 15 December 2016).

Hansen, Lene, and Helen Nissenbaum. 2009. 'Digital Disaster, Cyber Security, and the Copenhagen School', *International Studies Quarterly*, 53 (4): 1155–75.

Hindu, The. 2016. 'India Has 3rd Largest Base of Start-up Firms', 27 February. Available at: http://www.thehindu.com/business/Industry/india-has-3rd-largest-base-of-startup-firms/article8286284.ece (accessed 15 December 2016).

IBEF (India Brand Equity Foundation). 2017. 'IT Industry in India, Indian Information Technology, ITeS Sector, Services'. Available at: http://www.ibef.org/industry/information-technology-india.aspx (accessed 15 December 2016).

ICANN (Internet Corporation for Assigned Names and Numbers). 2015. 'Indian Government Declares Support for Multistakeholder Model of Internet Governance at ICANN53'. Available at: https://www.icann.org/resources/press-material/release-2015-06-22-en (accessed 15 December 2016).

IISS (International Institute for Strategic Studies). 2016a. *Identifying Common Security Interests in the Cyber-Domain*, report published at 15th Asia Security Summit, IISS Shangri-La Dialogue, 4 June. London: International Institute for Strategic Studies.

————. 2016b. *Military Balance 2016*. London: International Institute for Strategic Studies.

Internet Democracy Project. 2016. 'Watchtower: Mapping the Indian Government's Cybersecurity Institutions'. Available at: https://internetdemocracy.in/watchtower/ (accessed 15 December 2016).

Internet Live Stats. 2016. 'Internet Users'. Available at: http://www.internetlivestats. com/internet-users/ (accessed 15 December 2016).

ITU (International Telecommunication Union).

2014a. 'India: Draft New Resolution on ITU's Role in Realising Secure Information Society', Plenipotentiary Conference (PP-14), Busan, 20 October 2014, Document 98-E, International Telecommunication Union. Available at: http://cis-india.org/internet-governance/blog/india-draft-resolution-itus-role-in-securing-information-security/at_download/file (accessed 15 December 2016).

———. 2014b. 'Statement 1: Made at the 12th Session of Working Group, ITU Plenipotentiary Conference, Busan, 20 October–7 November 2014, by Ram Narain, India, in Relation to the Approval of the Revision of Resolution 101, 102, 133 and 180'. Available at: http://files.wcitleaks.org/public/S14-PP-C-0164!!MSW-E.pdf (accessed 15 December 2016).

———. 2015. 'ITU Releases 2015 ICT Figures'. Available at: https://www.itu. int/net/pressoffice/press_releases/2015/17.aspx (accessed 15 December 2016).

Joshi, Sandeep. 2013. 'An IT Superpower, India Has Just 556 Cyber Security Experts', *The Hindu*, 19 June. Available at: http://www.thehindu.com/news/national/an-it-superpower-india-has-just-556-cyber-security-experts/article4827644.ece (accessed 15 December 2016).

Kovacs, Anja. 2013. 'WCIT 2012: India Sets an Example', The Internet Democracy Project, 4 January. Available at: https://internetdemocracy. in/2013/01/india-sets-an-example/ (accessed 15 December 2016).

———. 2015a. 'Opportunism or Glasnost? India's Embrace of Multistakeholderism in Internet Governance'. New Delhi: The Internet Democracy Project. Available at: https://internetdemocracy.in/2015/09/opportunism-or-glasnost/ (accessed 15 December 2016).

———. 2015b. 'Re-Interpreting Document 98: India's Proposals at the ITU Plenipot 2014 and the Evolution of Internet Governance'. New Delhi: Internet Democracy Project. Available at: https://internetdemocracy.in/wp-content/uploads/2015/08/Anja-Kovacs-Internet-Democracy-Project-Reinterpreting-Document-98.pdf (accessed 15 December 2016).

———. 2015c. 'The Road to WSIS+10: Key Perspectives from India'. New Delhi: The Internet Democracy Project. Available at: https://internetdemocracy. in/reports/the-road-to-wsis10/ (accessed 15 December 2016).

———. 2015d. 'With or without Us: Bilateralism and India's Cybersecurity Policies'. New Delhi: The Internet Democracy Project. Available at: https:// internetdemocracy.in/2015/12/with-or-without-us-bilateralism-india-cybersecurity-policies/ (accessed on 3 November 2019).

Kshetri, Nir. 2013. *Cybercrime and Cybersecurity in the Global South*. Basingstoke: Palgrave.

Maurer, Tim, and Robert Morgus. 2014. 'Tipping the Scale: An Analysis of Global Swing States in the Internet Governance Debate', *Internet Governance Papers* 7. Waterloo: CIGI.

McKinsey and Company. 2012. *Technology, Media and Telecom Practice: Online and Upcoming; The Internet's Impact on India*. Mc Kinsey and Company. Available at: http://1icz9g2sdfe31jz0lglwdu48.wpengine.netdna-cdn.com/wp-content/uploads/2014/02/Impact-of-Internet-on-India-McKinsey.pdf (accessed 15 December 2016).

Ministry of External Affairs. 2016. 'Main Remarks by Prime Minister at the 14th ASEAN-India Summit Held on 8 September 2016 in Vientiane, Laos', 8 September. Available at: http://www.mea.gov.in/aseanindia/SpeechStatementEAS.htm?dtl/22612/Main+Remarks+by+Prime+Minister+at+the+14th+ASEANIndia+Summit+held+on+8+September+2016+in+Vientiane+Lao+PDR (accessed 15 December 2016).

Ministry of Communications and Information Technology. 2013. *National Cyber Security Policy—2013*. Available at: http://deity.gov.in/sites/upload_files/dit/files/National%20Cyber%20Security%20Policy%20(1).pdf (accessed 15 December 2016).

Ministry of Law, Justice and Company Affairs. 2000. 'The Information Technology Act, 2000'. Available at: http://www.dot.gov.in/sites/default/files/itbill2000_0.pdf (accessed 15 December 2016).

———. 2008. 'The Information Technology Act, 2008'. Available at: http://www.tifrh.res.in/tcis/events/facilities/IT_act_2008.pdf (accessed 15 December 2016).

Mohan, Raja. 2012. 'Cyber War: Blaming Pakistan Is Not Enough', *Indian Express*, 20 August. Available at: http://archive.indianexpress.com/news/cyber-war-blaming-pakistan-is-not-enough/990637/ (accessed 15 December 2016).

Mueller, Milton. 2011. 'A United Nations Committee for Internet-Related Policies? A Fair Assessment', 29 October. Internet Governance Forum. Available at: http://www.internetgovernance.org/2011/10/29/a-united-nations-committee-for-internet-related-policies-a-fair-assessment/ (accessed 15 December 2016).

Narayanan, M.K. 2016. 'The Cyberthreat Is Very Real', *The Hindu*, 14 March. Available at: http://www.thehindu.com/opinion/lead/lead-article-by-mk-narayanan-on-aadhaar-bill-the-cyberthreat-is-very-real/article8371335.ece (accessed 15 December 2016).

NCRB (National Crime Records Bureau). 2016. *Annual Reports Crime in India, 1953–2014*. New Delhi: National Crime Records Bureau. Available at: http://ncrb.gov.in/ (accessed 3 November 2019).

———. 2017. *Crime in India: 2016*. New Delhi: National Crime Records Bureau.

Norton. 2016. 'Norton Cybersecurity Insights Report. Global Comparisons'. Available at: http://us.norton.com/norton-cybersecurity-insights-report-india (accessed 15 December 2016).

NTI (Nuclear Threats Initiative). 2016. *NTI Nuclear Security Index: Building a Framework for Assurance, Accountability, and Action*. Washington, DC: Nuclear Threats Initiative. Available at: http://2016.ntiindex.org/wp-content/uploads/2013/12/NTI_2016-Index_FINAL.pdf (accessed 3 November 2019).

Nye, Joseph. 2017. 'Deterrence and Dissuasion in Cyberspace', *International Security*, 41 (3): 44–71. Available at : doi:10.1162/ISEC_a_00266 (accessed on 3 November 2019).

OpenNet Initiative. 2016. *Country Profiles*. Available at: https://opennet.net/research/profiles (accessed 3 November 2019).

Prasad, Ravi. 2015. 'India Internet Governance' (video), 22 June. Available at: http://indiaig.in/blog/ (accessed 15 December 2016).

PTI. 2017. 'India Has Become Key Target for Cybercrime after Demonetization: Report', *Zee News*, 20 January. Available at: http://zeenews.india.com/technology/india-has-become-key-target-for-cybercrime-after-demonetization-report_1968950.html (accessed 15 December 2016).

Rajaraman, V. 2012. *History of Computing in India (1955–2010)*. Bangalore: Indian Institute of Science. Available at: http://www.cbi.umn.edu/hostedpublications/pdf/Rajaraman_HistComputingIndia.pdf (accessed 15 December 2016).

Ranganathan, Nayantara. 2015. 'Cybersecurity and Bilateral Ties of India and the United States: A Very Brief History', 30 September. New Delhi: The Internet Democracy Project. Available at: https://internetdemocracy.in/reports/cybersecurity-and-india-us-bilateral-ties-a-very-brief-history/ (accessed 15 December 2016).

Samuel, Cherian. 2017. 'Destination India for Global Conference on Cyberspace 2017'. Issue Brief. Delhi: Institute for Defence Studies and Analyses. Available at: http://www.idsa.in/issuebrief/destination-india-global-conference-cyberspace-2017_csamuel_160117 (accessed 15 December 2016).

Saran, Samir. 2015. 'Securing Digital Terrain', 17 March. Observer Research Foundation. Available at: http://www.orfonline.org/research/securing-digital-terrain/ (accessed 15 December 2016).

————. 2016a. 'A Reluctant Digital Power Emerges from the Shadows', *The Wire*, 22 December. Available at: https://thewire.in/88698/emergence-reluctant-digital-power/ (accessed 15 December 2016).

————. 2016b. 'Net Politics' (audio). Available at: https://www.cfr.org/podcasts/net-politics-podcast-samir-saran (accessed 15 December 2016).

Saran, Samir, and Mahima Kaul. 2015. 'The "I" in the Internet Must Also Stand for India', *The Wire*, 24 June. Available at: https://thewire.in/4688/the-i-in-the-internet-must-also-stand-for-india/ (accessed 15 December 2016).

Sharma, Munish. 2016. 'Lashkar-e-Cyber of Hafiz Saeed', IDSA Comment, 21 March. Institute for Defence Studies and Analyses. Available at: http://www.idsa.in/idsacomments/lashkar-e-cyber-of-hafiz-saeed_msharma_310316 (accessed 15 December 2016).

Singh, Aarti. 2012. 'Lashkar's Own Skype Frazzles Indian Intelligence', *The Times of India*, 30 April. Available at: http://timesofindia.indiatimes.com/india/Lashkars-own-Skype-frazzles-Indian-intelligence/articleshow/12934037.cms (accessed 15 December 2016).

Singh, Shalini. 2012a. 'Civil Society and Industry Oppose India's Plans to Modify ITRs', *The Hindu*, 23 November.

————. 2012b. 'On Internet Rules, India Now More Willing to Say ICANN', *The Hindu*, 13 October. Available at: http://www.thehindu.com/news/national/On-Internet-rules-India-now-more-willing-to-say-ICANN/article12557693.ece (accessed 15 December 2016).

Singh, Swaran, and Jayanna Krupakar. 2014. 'Indo–US Cooperation in Countering Cyber Terrorism: Challenges and Limitations', *Strategic Analysis*, 38 (5): 703–16.

Statista. 2016. 'India: Number of Cyber Crimes under IT Act 2014 | Statistic'. Available at: http://www.statista.com/statistics/309435/india-cyber-crime-it-act/ (accessed 15 December 2016).

————. 2017. 'India: Number of Cyber Crimes 2015'. Available at: https://www.statista.com/statistics/309435/india-cyber-crime-it-act/ (accessed 15 December 2016).

Stevens, Tim. 2016. 'India's Cybersecurity Challenges', *Sovereign Data*, 2 (4): 1–4.

Sukumar, Arun. 2015a. 'India's Internet Diplomacy: Reading the Tea Leaves'. Council on Foreign Relations—Net Politics, 14 July. Available at: http://blogs.cfr.org/cyber/2015/07/14/indias-internet-diplomacy-reading-the-tea-leaves/ (accessed 15 December 2016).

————. 2015b. 'India's New "Multistakeholder" Line Could Be a Gamechanger in Global Cyberpolitics'. *The Wire*, 22 June. Available at: https://thewire.in/4585/indias-new-multistakeholder-line-could-be-a-gamechanger-in-global-cyberpolitics/ (accessed 15 December 2016).

———. 2016a. 'India and Russia Sign Cyber Agreement, Pushing the Frontier for Strategic Cooperation'. ORF—Observer Research Foundation, 15 October. Available at: http://www.orfonline.org/expert-speaks/india-and-russia-cyber-agreement/ (accessed 15 December 2016).

———. 2016b. 'No Threat to Strategic Autonomy, Yet'. *The Hindu*, 14 June.

———. 2016c. 'The Case for Cyber and Cyber-Physical Weapons: India's Grand Strategy and Diplomatic Goals'. *ORF Special Report* 15. New Delhi: Observer Research Foundation.

———. 2016d. 'UN Reconstitutes Its Top Cyber Body, This Time with India at the High Table'. *The Wire*, 22 June. Available at: https://thewire.in/44696/un-reconstitutes-its-top-cyber-body-this-time-with-india-at-the-high-table/ (accessed 15 December 2016).

Sukumar, Arun and Samir Saran. 2016. 'What the Moscow Communique on Internet Governance Says about India's Role in the Global Order', *The Wire*, 19 April. Available at: http://thewire.in/2016/04/19/what-the-moscow-communique-says-about-indias-role-in-the-global-order-30364/ (accessed 15 December 2016).

Sukumar, Arun, and R.K. Sharma. 2016. *The Cyber Command: Upgrading India's National Security Architecture*, ORF Special Report 9. New Delhi: Observer Research Foundation. Available at: http://www.orfonline.org/wp-content/uploads/2016/03/SR_9_Arun-Mohan-Sukumar-and-RK-sharma.pdf (accessed 15 December 2016).

White House, The. 2014. 'U.S.–India Joint Statement', 30 September. Available at: https://www.whitehouse.gov/the-press-office/2014/09/30/us-india-joint-statement (accessed 15 December 2016).

———. 2015. 'U.S.–India Joint Statement: Shared Effort; Progress for All', 25 January. Available at: https://obamawhitehouse.archives.gov/the-press-office/2015/01/25/us-india-joint-statement-shared-effort-progress-all (accessed 15 December 2016).

———. 2016a. 'Fact Sheet on U.S.–India Strengthening Cooperation on Cybersecurity'. Available at: https://www.whitehouse.gov/sites/default/files/india-factsheets/Fact_Sheet_on_Cybersecurity_Cooperation.pdf (accessed 15 December 2016).

———. 2016b. 'Joint Statement: The United States and India: Enduring Global Partners in the 21st Century', 7 June. Available at: https://www.whitehouse.gov/the-press-office/2016/06/07/joint-statement-united-states-and-india-enduring-global-partners-21st (accessed 15 December 2016).

Tiezzi, Shannon. 2015. 'Chinese Military Declares the Internet an Ideological "Battleground"', *The Diplomat*, 21 May. Available at: http://thediplomat.com/2015/05/chinese-military-declares-the-internet-an-ideological-battleground/ (accessed 15 December 2016).

Times of India, The. 2012. 'India and Japan Agree to Boost Maritime, Cyber Security', 2 May. Available at: http://timesofindia.indiatimes.com/india/India-and-Japan-agree-to-boost-maritime-cyber-security/articleshow/12944684.cms (accessed 15 December 2016).

———. 2016. 'Cybersecurity to Create 1 Million Jobs: Nasscom', 18 April. Available at: http://timesofindia.indiatimes.com/tech/tech-news/Cybersecurity-to-create-1million-jobs-Nasscom/articleshow/51884133.cms (accessed 15 December 2016).

Yardley, Jim. 2012. 'India Asks Pakistan to Investigate Panic Tied to Assam', *The New York Times*, 19 August. Available at: http://www.nytimes.com/2012/08/20/world/asia/india-asks-pakistan-to-help-investigate-root-of-panic.html (accessed 15 December 2016).

5 Political Economy of India's Trade Liberalization

BISWAJIT DHAR

Trade Liberalization Agenda: A Synoptic View

A QUARTER OF A CENTURY BACK, INDIA officially embarked on the policy of economic reforms, a key element of which was to bring about a degree of market orientation that India had not seen since it attained political independence in 1947. After pursuing a state-controlled economic model, where the state sector was controlling 'the commanding heights of the economy' (Government of India 1991), India joined the global trend of economic liberalization in the beginning of the 1990s, the ideational lynchpin of which lay in the 'Washington Consensus.'[1]

One of the central pillars of the new policy stance of the government, which blossomed over time after being nurtured by successive governments since the early 1990s, was an accelerated pace of global integration of the Indian economy. The most prominent plank of this new policy stance was the unilateral reduction of the high levels of tariff protection that India had provided till then. Simple average applied (or actual) tariff rate for all products, which was 82 per cent in 1990, immediately preceding the launch of economic reforms, was brought

[1] According to the originator of the term, John Williamson, the 'Washington Consensus' is a 'list of ten specific policy reforms, which ... were widely agreed in Washington to be desirable in just about all the countries of Latin America, as of 1989'. For details, see Williamson (2004).

down to 32 per cent in 2001. The subsequent decade saw a sharp decline in the average tariff to 12 per cent in 2010, but it went up marginally to 13.2 per cent in 2016.[2] It may be pointed out that in 2013, India's average tariffs were only slightly lower than that of South Korea, but were considerably higher than those in Japan or in the member countries of the Association of South East Asian Nations (ASEAN).

The reduction in average tariffs over the two decades since the adoption of trade liberalization policies was a result of an interesting pattern protection provided to agriculture and industry. As can be seen in Figure 5.1, until the end of the 1990s, average tariffs on products in both the sectors were lowered in tandem. In other words, the levels of protection provided to both sectors were quite comparable. Thus, while

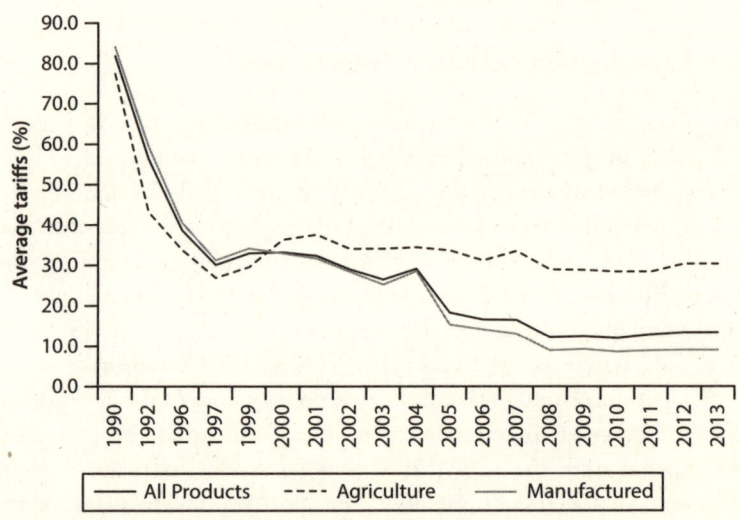

Figure 5.1   India's tariff reduction trend since 1990
Source: TRAINS database (UNCTAD).

---

[2] Data from WTO's Tariff Analysis Online facility for all years, except 1990. Data for 1990 from the TRAINS (Trade Analysis Information System) database of the UNCTAD (United Nations Conference on Trade and Development), available at https://databank.worldbank.org/reports.aspx?source=UNCTAD-~-Trade-Analysis-Information-System-%28TRAINS%29 (accessed on accessed 25 August 2016).

the average tariff for agriculture was 36 per cent in 2000 (down from 78 per cent in 1990), the corresponding figure for manufacturing was 33 per cent (declining from 84 per cent in 1990). However, in the subsequent years, tariff protection enjoyed by the manufacturing sector is rapidly reduced, which happened at an accelerated pace since 2005. Thus, average tariffs on manufacturing sector declined from 32 per cent in 2001 to 15 per cent in 2005 and thereafter to 9 per cent in 2013.

In sharp contrast to the manufacturing products, average tariffs on agricultural products were lowered only very slightly in relative terms after 2000. By the year 2010, average applied tariff on agricultural products had declined to 28 per cent, and was increased slightly thereafter.

As we have seen earlier, in 2013, the average tariffs on agricultural products as a whole was more than three times of that on manufactures in 2013. But the overall levels of tariff protection provided to the agricultural sector do not show the true picture of the tariff protection that different product groups within the sector have enjoyed. The average tariffs on agricultural raw materials have always been much lower than those for the sector as a whole (Figure 5.2). In fact in 2013, the average tariff on agricultural raw materials was only slightly higher than those applied on the manufactured products. This implies that India imposed very high tariffs on food grains, animal and dairy products, and other primary products, and these levels of tariffs have consistently been maintained since the 1990s.

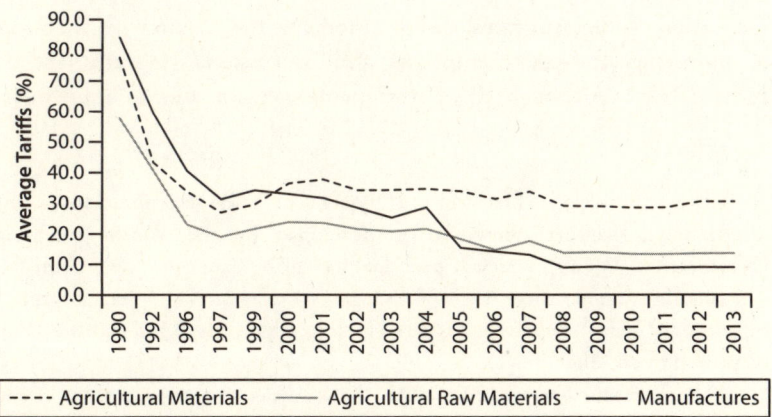

Figure 5.2 Reduction of tariffs on groups of products
Source: TRAINS database (UNCTAD).

The preceding phenomenon can be presented in a slightly different manner using the World Trade Organization (WTO) Integrated Data Base (IDB) on tariffs, which provides data for India until 2015. Using this database, the levels of tariff protection can be obtained for broad groups of products, captured by HS chapters.[3] In 2015, average levels of tariffs were 20 per cent or more for 25 HS chapters (out of a total of 96), and these chapters (excluding one), covered the agricultural sector in totality. The only exception was the automobile sector, which has consistently enjoyed high levels of tariff protection. It may be pointed out that the maximum tariffs imposed in all these HS chapters, including automobiles, were all more than 50 per cent.

The extent of tariff liberalization that India has brought about over the past decade can be gauged from the fact that in 2015, 65 HS chapters had average tariff levels of 10 per cent or less. On the contrary, in 2005 only 2 HS chapters had average levels of tariffs of 10 per cent or less.

There was an interesting mix of three dimensions through which India's tariff liberalization programme must be seen. The first was the unilateral decision of the Government of India to reduce import tariffs, which, as mentioned previously, was one of the key objectives of the economic reforms programme initiated in 1991.[4] Immediately after the initiation of economic reforms, the government was advised by the 'Tax Reforms Committee' (better known as the 'Chelliah Committee' after its chairperson, Raja J. Chelliah) to reduce the 'general level of tariffs' and 'dispersion of the tariff rates', and to rationalize the 'system with abolition of numerous end-use exemptions and concessions' (Government of India 1992a). Although the government was not able to implement

---

[3] The HS, or the Harmonized System of trade classification, is an international product nomenclature developed by the World Customs Organization (WCO), which is used for presenting data on trade and tariffs. The classification has three levels of disaggregation, namely chapters (captured by two-digit codes), headings (captured by four-digit codes), and sub-headings (captured by six-digit codes).

[4] The *Economic Survey 1992–1993* (the annual economic statement of the government) argued that 'the policy of progressively reducing customs tariffs is an essential element of any strategy for making the Indian economy internationally competitive' (Government of India 1993, 12).

the recommendations of the Chelliah Committee in the first decade of the economic reforms programme, it was able to embark on the trade liberalization agenda from the mid-2000s onwards.

It was not just the Government of India and agencies that favoured reduction of tariffs from the levels existing in the late 1990s; international agencies, especially the International Monetary Fund (IMF), sought to reinforce the government's intent. The IMF raised this issue consistently during its Article IV consultations wherein it 'encouraged' the Government of India to embark on a fast-paced tariff reduction, which was seen as the key factor for furthering India's economic reforms programme.[5] Further, the IMF lent support to the objective set by the government to lower its tariffs to ASEAN levels.[6]

The second dimension was India's stance against tariff liberalization in the negotiations in the WTO that were being conducted under the rubric of the Doha Round. India, along with several developing countries, emphasized the importance of tariffs to protect peasant agriculture in developing countries. These countries argued that protecting agriculture was essential for protecting livelihoods as well as food security in developing countries.

The third dimension has been India's engagement with bilateral free trade agreements (FTAs) with a number of countries in the East Asian region. While participating in the negotiations leading to the formation of the FTAs, India had agreed to provide substantial market access to its partners participating in the FTAs. Interestingly, the government was able to pursue a more liberal trade agenda during the phase when it was negotiating the FTAs. There was, therefore, a fair degree of congruity between the unilateral trade liberalization agenda that the government had pursued and its commitment to offer enhanced market access to its FTA partners.

[5] 'Directors were encouraged by signs that trade liberalization had regained momentum, particularly with measures to eliminate quantitative import restrictions in early 2001 and recent tariff reforms. Nonetheless, they noted that the level of protection in India was still high, and they encouraged continued tariff reduction' (IMF 2000).

[6] 'Directors welcomed India's progress in bringing down tariff rates last year and their commitment to further reductions to ASEAN levels over the medium term' (IMF 2005).

In the following sections, we shall discuss each of the dimensions of India's tariff policies as it has evolved over the past 25 years. We will argue that the dynamics in each of the three dimensions of India's trade liberalization experience were conditioned by the challenges that the governments of the day had faced while pursuing the trade liberalization agenda and their responses to these challenges. In particular, we will show how ideas, interests, and institutions originating at the domestic, regional, and global levels underwent an interplay in shaping India's trade liberalization policies.

Understanding India's Stance on Tariff Liberalization: Global and Domestic Influences

Although the process of India's tariff liberalization began with the initiation of economic reforms in 1991, plans for opening India's markets were afoot at least since 1985. The government under Rajiv Gandhi's leadership had proposed a long-term fiscal policy (LTFP), which included 'customs tariff reform'. An important objective of this reform package was to progressively reduce the role of quantitative restrictions[7] to regulate imports and replacing them with tariffs. This measure was suggested to 'moderate unduly high protection provided by quantitative import restrictions to certain industries and reduce the delays and uncertainties associated with the administration of import licensing'. The LTFP also sought to 'reduce the enormous multiplicity of nominal and effective rates of protection' by way of rationalization of the tariff structure through a two-tier tariff structure for capital goods, raw materials and components, and 'an even lower ... rate [of import tariffs] for certain "universal intermediate" used in a large number of industries' (Government of India 1986, 63, paragraph 6.23).

But despite this attempt to break from the past trends of protecting the domestic entities, the customs tariff reforms did not materialize until the early 1990s. In the first place, the quantitative restrictions were never removed by the Indian government of its own volition. In fact, global-level

---

[7] According to the WTO, quantitative restrictions are limits imposed on the volume or value of goods and are typically enforced through quotas, import or export licences, or other measures such as voluntary export restraints.

institutions played an important role in shaping India's policies, since India was obligated to remove quantitative restrictions following its accession to the WTO. Secondly, the rationalization of import tariffs did not take place. The 'tariffs were raised for revenue reasons, and the weighted average rate increased from 38 per cent in 1980–81 to 87 per cent in 1989–90' (Rao and Rao 2006, 74).

The decisive break from the past was announced by the then Finance Minister Manmohan Singh while presenting his first union budget in 1991. One of the key objectives of the reforms programme was to lower the high levels of protection. The Tax Reforms Committee (TRC) that set the tone for tariff liberalization in the subsequent years proposed that the peak level of import tariffs should be brought down from 300 per cent prior to the reforms to 50 per cent by 1997–98. The TRC also recommended that the number of tax rates should also be sharply reduced to 7 from more than 100 rates existing earlier. Alongside the reduction in import tariffs, quantitative restrictions were also removed to some extent (Government of India 1992b, paragraph 4.2.2).

The tariff reforms undertaken by the government were strongly supported by several commentators. Arguments were advanced for moving towards a uniform rate of tariff (Joshi and Little 1993), a move which would have resulted in a much steeper reduction in tariffs. However, the TRC took a more reasoned view while making its recommendations, which it said was made keeping in view the 'inherent disadvantages from which varying types of Indian industrial units suffer because of the general inefficiencies in the economy such as higher interest costs, power cuts, lack of efficient infrastructure, and cascading types of state and local taxes' (Kelkar, Shome, and Chelliah 2003, 592). In other words, the TRC took the reality of economic policies, which were a function of the complex political economy of the Indian democracy, as an important yardstick for making its recommendations on import tariff reform—thereby clearly revealing the importance of domestic interests in shaping India's approach to tariff reforms.

If the government initiating the process of import tariff reforms was unequivocal about its intention of reducing tariffs, the steps taken by the governments that followed to push the trade liberalization agenda were very ambiguous as the following discussion highlights.

The coalition government that took office in 1996 made at least three announcements that gave mixed signals regarding India's trade regime.

The first of these came in the form of a target for reducing import tariffs. In 1997, the then Finance Minister P. Chidambaram expressed his intent to lower India's tariffs and to make them comparable with some of the more open economies in the country's neighbourhood by the turn of the millennium.[8] Considering that the simple average tariff in 1996–97 was still in excess of 30 per cent, bringing this average down to around 5 per cent (the ASEAN level) seemed very ambitious. As a part of this thinking, import tariffs were reduced on 'raw materials and components used in the employment-oriented sectors such as textiles, electronics and metals' (Government of India 1997b, 30).

A second measure that the government took was to accede to the WTO's Information Technology Agreement (better known as ITA-I),[9] a plurilateral agreement which eliminated tariffs on a wide range of electronics products. India was among the 29 original signatories to ITA-I[10] and it agreed to eliminate tariffs on 183 products.[11] From the point of view of India, joining the ITA-I was a 'radical' step for two reasons: first, it broke ranks with its fellow travellers such as Brazil and South Africa to join the agreement and second, evidence on the unilateral reduction of import tariffs available till then showed that the government was more intent on decreasing the 'peak' tariffs, rather than walking down the path of tariff elimination. In other words, there was an element of caution that the Government of India adopted while decreasing tariff protection.

The cautious approach of the government became evident even as it was submitting the schedule of commitments to accede to ITA-I. As briefly alluded earlier, the WTO made it mandatory for its members

---

[8] While presenting the government budget in 1997, the finance minister expressed his intent thus: 'On more than one occasion, I have stated that we would achieve the average levels of tariffs prevalent in ASEAN countries by the turn of the century. This will give time to Indian industry to adjust to these changes' (Government of India 1997a, paragraph 110).

[9] ITA-I was concluded in December 1996.

[10] For details on the products covered in India's schedule of commitments, see WTO (1997).

[11] These were tariff lines at six-digit sub-heading level under the HS classification developed by the World Customs Organization. The WTO uses the HS to classify products. Tariffs on about a third of these tariff lines were to be eliminated by the year 2000 and the remaining between 2002–5.

to discontinue the use of quantitative restrictions that they were using for balance of payments reasons.[12] This was articulated in the Understanding on the Balance of Payments Provisions of the General Agreement on Tariffs and Trade, which forms a part of the discipline that the WTO enforces. This 'Understanding' provided that the WTO members would 'publicly announce, as soon as possible, time-schedules for the removal of restrictive import measures for balance-of-payments purposes'. The quantitative restrictions to manage imports, to 'announce publicly, as soon as possible, time schedules for the removal of restrictive import measures', and to replace such restrictive measures with tariffs (WTO 1994).

Having gone through a serious balance of payments crisis in 1991, India was one of the largest users of the quantitative restrictions when it acceded to the WTO.[13] In 1997 and in compliance with the 'Understanding', India offered to remove the quantitative restrictions on imports over a nine-year period. A longer phase-out period was sought to delay the process of opening the markets for agricultural products. Vulnerabilities in a small-farmer dominated agricultural sector forced the government to adopt this stance, which exemplifies the tensions between multilateral norms and institutions on the one hand and domestic imperatives on the other, as the key drivers of India's policies in the realm of trade.

India's protectionist stance was rejected by most of the country's major trading partners. But after a series of consultations, the phase-out period was reduced to six years. All the major trading partners of the country, with the exception of the United States, agreed to the shortened phase-out period. The disagreement over the period of phase-out as well as the coverage of commodities in each of the phases proposed by India led to the United States moving the WTO's Dispute Settlement Body (DSB). The DSB ruled against India, and India's regime of quantitative restrictions was discontinued in 2001—an interesting case that shows

---

[12] Article XVIII, particularly XVIII(B), was addressed to the developing countries who, in course of their economic development, encountered severe balance of payments strains, and in order to alleviate the problems resulting therefrom the use of quantitative restrictions (QRs) were allowed.

[13] Nearly 3,000 tariff lines at six-digit level were covered by the quantitative restrictions.

the pressures that India was under from the multilateral norms and institutions on India's domestic policies.

India's exertions on the removal of quantitative restrictions exposed the reality of trade liberalization a decade after the economic reforms were initiated. The situation that prevailed in 2002 was summarized by an expert group on indirect tax reforms: 'Customs tariff has continued to remain most complicated even after several years of reforms since 1991. This can be seen from the rates of duty, which are 20 in number. Thirty per cent rate is the median rate, that is, the most common rate' (Ministry of Finance & Corporate Affairs 2002: paragraph 2.2.2). This expert group once again underlined the objective of the government to reduce the level of import tariffs to match those of the ASEAN economies.

The second decade of the economic reforms witnessed steep reduction in import tariffs on industrial products. P. Chidambaram, the finance minister of the government that took office in 2004, pursued his goal of making the 'customs duty structure closer to that of [India's] East Asian neighbours' (Government of India 2005). Within the next four years, the peak rate for non-agricultural products, which was 20 per cent in January 2004, was down to 10 per cent (Government of India, n.d.). The government took the advantage of a rapidly expanding economy whose growth rates had reached historical highs, to carry out the trade liberalization agenda.

This shift in India's policy was mainly driven by regional compulsions. In fact, the objective of the government to reduce import tariffs comparable to those prevailing in East Asia was pursued in this phase when India had begun engaging with its eastern neighbours for formalizing comprehensive economic partnerships agreements (CEPA). This would open up markets in goods and services and encourage free flow of investment resulting in greater economic integration among the CEPA partners. There was, thus, an added impetus to reduce tariff unilaterally, and this was accomplished fairly rapidly for a wide range of industrial products. However, in this phase, too, agriculture was protected from the ambitions of economic integration. We shall dwell on this issue in a subsequent section.

The account of trade liberalization attempted by successive governments since the initiation of economic reforms shows that the progress in realizing the objectives was inadequate, particularly in the first decade. A key factor causing this hiatus between the aspirations and outcomes was that some of the critical realities facing India were not given due credence by those driving the economic policies. We will allude to two of the more important areas in which the inadequacies were most evident.

The first and more significant of these arose in agriculture, where the policy makers involved in the making of the trade regime appear to have glossed over the stark realities of Indian agriculture, especially the declining fortunes of this sector. This was hardly surprising since the economic reforms followed a top-down approach and they, therefore, had little connect with the vast rural population. Thus, the trade liberalization agenda was set in motion without realizing the fact that agriculture would eventually set limits to this agenda. It was only then that the government began pulling back on its ambitions on an across-the-board liberalization. Although, the reasons for pulling back on trade liberalization were never made explicit in the first decade of economic reforms, we would provide two evidences, which indicate that the pull-back happened because agriculture needed the additional dose of protection. The first evidence is provided by Figure 5.2 wherein tariffs on agricultural products as a whole are seen to decline in the initial years of economic reforms and are then moderately increased. The second evidence is from India's proposal to the WTO to remove the quantitative restrictions on imports, which we had discussed in the foregoing. In its proposal, India had offered to remove these restrictions in three phases totalling nine years, from 1997 to 2006, and agricultural products were mostly included in the third three-year phase. In other words, there was a clear objective of providing a longer period of protection to agriculture.

Although the narrative on India's unilateral trade liberalization does not mention the role of the factors explained earlier, the domestic interests and sensitivities (or, according to the framework of this volume, domestic norms and interests) have played out in good measure in India's engagements in trade negotiations during the past decade and a half, both at the multilateral and the bilateral levels. In the WTO, India articulated its position more prominently in three areas—namely, (*i*) agriculture, for protecting the interests of small farmers; (*ii*) intellectual property rights, for ensuring that medicines remain affordable; and (*iii*) services, demanding that its citizens be allowed to seek employment in developed countries, in other words, access under Mode 4 of the General Agreement on Trade in Services (GATS).

In the following sections, we give two examples as to how the aforementioned domestic sensitivities have played out in the tariff negotiations that India participated in. We use India's experience in two forums to make our point about the pre-dominant role that India's domestic norms and economic interests played in its international economic engagements. The first is India's participation in the Doha Round negotiations under the WTO that commenced in 2002. The second is India's engagement in the bilateral FTAs, in which India had to grant preferential market access to its partner countries.

Agriculture Negotiations in the Doha Round and India: The Imprint of Domestic Norms and Interests

In 2001, the Doha Round negotiations were initiated after the ministers of the WTO member states took the decisions of expanding the 'negotiating agenda [of the WTO] and to undertake activities necessary to address the challenges facing the multilateral trading system' (WTO 2001b, paragraph 11). The Doha Round mandate was a compromise between the positions taken by developing countries and the advanced countries. The former group of countries was focused on two sets of issues: one, rebalancing the Uruguay Round agreements to make them more development-friendly, and two, ensuring that these agreements were effectively implemented.[14] On the other hand, the advanced countries led by the United States and the European Union, stuck to a more conventional agenda—namely, expanding the market access opportunities in the goods sector for the business interests that they were home to. Besides, these countries also argued for the introduction of new issues in the WTO, including investment, competition policy, government procurement, and trade facilitation.

---

[14] According to Robert Wolfe, 'implementation' in WTO jargon means that developing countries find it too hard to meet their Uruguay Round commitments quickly, despite the special and differential treatment provisions and that developed countries have been too slow in meeting their obligations to developing countries (Wolfe 2004). See also the preamble to the Doha Ministerial Decision on 'Implementation-Related Issues and Concerns', which states that the decision was adopted as a 'concrete action to address issues and concerns that have been raised by many developing-country Members regarding the implementation of some WTO Agreements and Decisions, including the difficulties and resource constraints that have been encountered in the implementation of obligations in various areas' (WTO 2001a).

The Doha Round was mandated to deal with the substantial issue of reviewing the Agreement on Agriculture (AoA) that had introduced discipline in three areas (referred to as 'pillars' in WTO speak)—namely, subsidies given by the governments to support production (or, domestic support), government support for promoting exports (or export competition), and market access issues, essentially the issue of tariffs. One of the key elements of the negotiating mandate was the recognition that the AoA needed to put in place a framework for protecting the food security and rural livelihood concerns of developing countries.

It must be pointed out that the outcome of the Doha Ministerial Conference, especially the mandate for agriculture negotiations, was a culmination of a systematic process of interventions made by the developing countries. India was a prominent participant in this process, having made a series of interventions to highlight the importance of food security and rural livelihoods for developing countries since 1998. In its first statement on the issue, India argued that it would be 'too simplistic to assume that agricultural liberalization sought to be ushered in by the Agreement would by itself, be able to overcome the problems of food security for developing countries with sizeable rural population' (WTO 1998, 2). India, therefore, opined that it was

> extremely important to provide a certain degree of flexibility to developing countries for the adoption of such domestic policies whose intention is to provide continued employment to the large segment of population dependent on this sector and to improve the general levels of production both with the aim of improving the overall availability of food grains and for enhancing the income levels of the rural poor. (WTO 1998)[15]

India's stance in the Doha negotiations went through an interesting process, which was clearly guided by its domestic compulsion of protecting its small farmers and the country's imperatives of food security and rural livelihoods/development. This was effectively articulated in India's first submission on agriculture in the Doha Round: 'Developing countries can be expected to reciprocate in market access, subject to their economic and social conditions, *development needs, food and livelihood security and*

---

[15] These arguments were further developed in a series of submissions. See, for instance, WTO 1999a, 2000, and 2001c.

rural development requirements, only if they get adequate concessions and commitments by developed countries in all three pillars' (WTO 2002a, paragraph 6; emphasis added).

India made a specific intervention highlighting the centrality of food security and rural development in the agricultural policies of the developing countries. Its position was that 'food and livelihood security and rural development underpin agricultural policies in developing countries. The safeguards to address these concerns of developing countries must encompass flexibility to apply measures suited to the specific needs and situations of the agricultural sector of the developing country concerned' (WTO 2003d, 1).

India went on to spell out the elements that the modalities, or the overall approach to the negotiations on agriculture, must include for meeting the objectives of food security and rural development:

> A core element of food and livelihood security is physical and economic access to sufficient, safe and nutritious food to meet their dietary needs and food preferences for an active and healthy life. Appropriate protection at the border through price based and quantity based measures should be an integral part of the modalities. Products eligible for such special import measures shall include (*i*) food staples which account for a substantial proportion of total domestic production or total domestic consumption, (*ii*) products that play a vital role in the diet of low income consumers, (*iii*) products that are produced by a substantial number of farm households, (*iv*) products that are primarily produced by low-income and resource-poor farmers, and (*v*) products that are important for supporting livelihood in the rural areas such as the numbers of active population engaged in production of the product concerned or products where the proportion of landless agricultural labourers employed is high. (WTO 2003d, 2)

This focus on food security and rural development reveals that not only domestic interests—the desire to not worsen the already precarious condition of small farmers (also an important vote bank)—but domestic norms of high levels of agricultural tariffs also played an important role in shaping India's approach in negotiations on agriculture. India favoured a slow paced liberalization of agricultural markets and while doing so it made common cause with 75 countries (WTO 2002d), covering the entire development spectrum, which came together with the demand that the Uruguay Round approach to tariff cuts in agriculture should be accepted as the basis in the Doha Round. This position challenged the position taken by the Cairns Group, the group of exporters of agricultural commodities. The latter had pitched for an accelerated reduction in agricultural tariffs by both developed and developing countries using the 'Swiss Formula' (WTO 2002c). Besides prompting steep tariff reductions, the 'Swiss Formula' sets an upper bound for tariffs, which implies that countries cannot use higher tariffs on commodities so as to stave-off an imminent threat of imports.

The dynamics of the agriculture negotiations changed completely after the then chairman of the Committee on Agriculture, Stuart Harbinson, made an attempt to provide direction to the agriculture negotiations by proposing the draft modalities.[16] Harbinson's modalities made an attempt to fulfil the negotiating mandate by offering developing countries some space to address their food security and livelihood concerns by introducing two instruments. The first was that developing countries could designate a certain number of products as 'strategic products with respect to food security, rural development and/or livelihood security concerns' (WTO 2003e, paragraph 10). The tariffs on these 'strategic products' would have to be reduced by only 10 per cent (WTO 2003e, paragraph 12). A second proposal by Harbinson was to extend the benefits of 'special safeguards' to all developing countries by introducing the 'special safeguard mechanism'. This instrument could protect producers from developing countries from sudden surge of imports. These proposals completely changed the negotiating dynamics of Doha Round on agriculture.

The Harbinson modalities resulted in a significant realignment of partnerships that had been hitherto witnessed in the Doha Round agriculture negotiations. As mentioned earlier, in the initial phases of the negotiations, the European Union was aligned with a large number of developing countries; they had made a common cause with these countries, favouring modest reduction of tariffs on agricultural products. The other major player, the United States, had a position on tariff reduction similar to that of the Cairns Group—namely, application of the 'Swiss Formula' for effecting deep cuts in agricultural tariffs (WTO 2002b).

The Harbinson modalities triggered a coming-together of the European Union and the United States, the culmination of which was a

---

[16] These modalities were introduced by Harbinson in his personal capacity. For details, see WTO (2003b).

joint paper in the run-up to the Cancun Ministerial Conference in which they tried to find a common ground.[17] The major developing countries too altered their alignments almost completely and orchestrated the formation of strong coalitions, the first of their kind in the multilateral trading system. These coalitions formally emerged at the Cancun Ministerial Conference in 2003, but initiatives for forging at least one of these were taken a few months earlier.[18]

The Cancun Ministerial Conference was marked by the formation of the G-20 grouping. The base document of the grouping emphasized that negotiations in the Doha Round should establish a fair and market-oriented trading system through fundamental reform in agriculture. The interventions made by this group have had two substantive dimensions. One, the market distortions created by the subsidies' regime in some of the more prominent members of the WTO has to be reduced and eventually removed; and two, special and differential treatment for developing countries should be an integral part of the negotiations, and that non-trade concerns should be taken into account.

The latter element, in view of the G-20, was to be addressed in the revised AoA through two mechanisms. First, products that are critical for realizing the objectives of food security, rural livelihoods, and rural development—the so-called Special Products (SPs)—would not be subjected to any tariff cuts. Secondly, there would be introduction of a Special Safeguard Mechanism (SSM) aimed at allowing developing countries to counter anticipated or actual import surges. The SPs and the SSM were seen by the developing countries as measures that

---

[17] On the issue of tariff reductions, the European Union–United States paper spoke of a 'blended formula', which accommodated the extreme positions that the two WTO members had taken. While the United States favoured the 'Swiss Formula', the European Union sought a more moderate approach. For details, see WTO (2003d).

[18] The groundwork for the establishment of G-33 was made by Brazil, India, and South Africa in June 2003 through the Brasilia Declaration. While commenting on some of the more significant developments, the foreign ministers of these countries 'reiterated their expectation that negotiations will gain new political impetus and that it will be possible to overcome deadlocks on issues of fundamental interest to developing countries'. For details, see Ministry of External Affairs (2003). See also Narlikar and Tussie (2004).

would help them in addressing the twin problems of food security and livelihood concerns in the face of mounting pressures to lower agricultural tariffs.

Demand for introduction of SPs and SSM in the AoA was lent by another group of developing countries, the G-33, which has focused solely on the need to include these two mechanisms in the AoA (WTO 2003b). The G-33 argued that developing countries must have the right to designate as SPs 'at least 20 per cent of its agricultural tariff lines' guided by an 'illustrative, non-exhaustive, non-prescriptive, and non-cumulative list of indicators' (WTO 2005, paragraph 3.1). The G-33 argued that one half of the SPs would not be subjected to any tariff cuts, while on the remaining products there would be a nominal reduction in tariffs. As regards SSM, both G-20 and G-33 argued that developing countries must have the right to impose additional duty for guarding against actual or potential surges in imports in respect of any agricultural product, based on volume or price triggers. The G-33 held the view that these mechanisms were essential for meeting the food security and rural livelihoods, the cornerstone of the provisions on special and differential treatment for developing countries included in the Doha mandate on agriculture. Although the G-33 spoke of the SPs and SSM as part of the same framework that it was putting forth, the importance of the former instrument seems to have receded somewhat in recent years. Yet, from the point of view of their domestic sensitivities, the SSM remains an important instrument.[19]

India, which was initially a member of the G-20 grouping alone, played an increasingly important role in the dynamics of the G-33 group, essentially because the demands of this group suited its own domestic imperatives. When implemented, SPs and the SSM would dampen reduction in tariffs proposed in the Doha Round, providing a higher degree of protection to the agricultural products in which India was maintaining relatively high levels of tariffs. India was thus able to delicately balance the domestic pressures against tariff reduction in the major agricultural products, which are critical from the point of view of the country's food and livelihood security.

[19] For a discussion on the importance of the SSM that the G-33 had highlighted in the Nairobi Ministerial Conference in December 2015, see Dhar (2016).

India's Bilateral FTAs: Regional and Domestic Interests

Traditionally, a strong votary of multilateralism in trade,[20] India changed its stance at the turn of the millennium by agreeing to enter into a series of bilateral FTAs. The beginnings were made in 2003 when India and the ASEAN members agreed to initiate negotiations on the Comprehensive Economic Cooperation Agreement. Three years later, India and Japan decided to negotiate the Bilateral Economic Partnership Agreement/Comprehensive Economic Partnership Agreement (EPA/CEPA) (Government of India 2006).[21] Almost simultaneously, the negotiations for a Comprehensive Economic Partnership Agreement (CEPA) with South Korea were launched. The two latter agreements were 'comprehensive' in their coverage for they included investment, services, and a few regulatory issues such as investment and intellectual property rights, besides the traditional area of goods. In all these agreements, India made far-reaching commitments to open its market, which was a reflection of the liberal trade regime that was being ushered in by the then government and of its political interest in strengthening ties with Southeast and East Asian countries.[22] In this section we will dwell on this issue by taking the case of the FTA in goods that India had signed with the ASEAN members.

The mandate for negotiations on market access in goods was provided by the 'Framework Agreement on Comprehensive Economic Cooperation between the Republic of India and the Association of South East Asian

[20] Until 2003, India viewed the emergence of the RTAs and their impact on the multilateral trading system with a degree of concern, which was summed up by its following assertion: 'The multilateral framework for international trade under the rules-based system by the WTO needs to be strengthened by addressing issues of concern emerging on account of formation of such a large number of RTAs including their impact on development' (see WTO 2003a, paragraph 2).

[21] The Comprehensive Economic Partnership Agreements (CEPAs) tend to mimic the WTO in terms of the coverage of the areas. Thus, besides goods, CEPAs include services, investment, intellectual property rights, and the rules compact of the WTO.

[22] India's relations with the ASEAN received a fillip when the neighbours agreed to hold annual summit-level meetings in 2002. India's close political ties with South Korea and Japan began with the establishment of the East Asia Summit process in 2005.

Nations' (henceforth, 'Framework Agreement') in 2003, in which the two partners agreed on 'progressive elimination of tariffs and non-tariff barriers *in substantially all trade in goods*' (Government of India 2003; emphasis added). In fact, by adopting this mandate, India and ASEAN had ensured that the ASEAN–India Free Trade Agreement (AIFTA) would be consistent with Article XXIV of the General Agreement on Tariffs and Trade (GATT), which allows members of the World Trade Organization (WTO) to participate in FTAs and to form free trade areas. Article XXIV 8(b) of the GATT defines a free-trade area as 'a group of two or more customs territories in which the duties and other restrictive regulations of commerce ... are eliminated on *substantially all the trade* between the constituent territories in products originating in such territories' (emphasis added)[23]. But while neither the GATT nor the WTO has given any definition of what is implied by the phrase *substantially all the trade*, the agreement between India and the ASEAN members on 'progressive elimination of tariffs and non-tariff barriers' gave enough indications of their commitment to open their markets in a meaningful manner.

The negotiations between India and the ASEAN initiated after the adoption of the mandate in 2003 culminated in the 'Agreement on Trade in Goods under the Framework Agreement on Comprehensive Economic Cooperation between the Republic of India and the Association of Southeast Asian Nations' in 2009 (Government of India 2009). The results of the negotiations on market access in goods is summarized in Table 5.1,

Table 5.1 Market access commitments in goods of India and ASEAN members (figures are percentage of total tariff lines)

Categories	India	Malaysia	Indonesia	Vietnam	Thailand	Philippines
Tariffs Eliminated	74.2	77.5	46.6	68.1	75.6	75.6
Excluded from Tariff Cuts	10.7	8.6	7.2	19.1	12.6	13.2

Source: Government of India (2009).

[23] Available at https://www.wto.org/english/docs_e/legal_e/gatt47_01_e.htm (accessed 31 October 2019).

where we compare India's commitment to open its market with the major economies in the ASEAN region.

The table shows two key elements of the market access commitments made by India and its ASEAN partners—namely, the share of tariff lines on which tariffs were eliminated after the implementation of the AIFTA and the share of tariff lines on which tariffs were left unaltered. Taken together, India's market access commitment was the most liberal after Malaysia. India had agreed to eliminate tariffs on more than 74 per cent of the total tariff lines and had excluded just over 10 per cent of the tariff lines from tariff cuts. This implies that India did not adhere to the principal of reciprocity, which is usually adopted by most countries in such bilateral trade deals.

There are other indicators to show that India's market access commitments went way beyond those of its ASEAN partners. The first of these is the nature of tariff protection that India provided prior to agreement to reduce tariffs. The market access negotiations used the year 2007 as the benchmark for reducing tariffs. Table 5.2 gives a comparative picture of structure of tariffs in India and major ASEAN economies.

The table shows that in the base year (2007), the level of trade protection provided by India was much higher than those of all major ASEAN economies. And, this was on two counts. First, the share of tariff lines with zero tariffs was the least for India and the share of tariff lines attracting import tariffs of 10 per cent or more was the highest. Given that India's structure of tariffs in the base year (2007) afforded higher degree of protection, the tariff concessions that the country gave under the AIFTA meant that protection was sharply lowered immediately after the coming into force of the FTA. This conclusively proves that India had

Table 5.2 Structure of tariffs of India and ASEAN members in 2007

Base rates of duty (%)	India	Indonesia	Thailand	Malaysia	Philippines	Vietnam
Zero	3.3	23.9	16.3	57.9	3.9	11.0
Less than 10% (including 'zero' tariff lines)	35.9	66.3	52.9	67.6	66.7	34.4
10% or more	64.1	33.7	47.1	32.4	33.3	65.6

Source: TRAINS database (UNCTAD).

reduced its level of protection substantially more than its partners in the ASEAN region through its accession to AIFTA.

The market access commitments made by India across sectors once again bore the imprint of the tariff-cutting exercise that was being carried out domestically. Therefore, the case of India's bilateral FTAs is useful to illustrate the interplay between regional and domestic factors on its policies. Two sensitive sectors—namely, agriculture and allied products and automobiles—accounted for nearly 60 per cent of the total number of tariff lines that were excluded from tariff cuts under AIFTA.

Table 5.3 provides further evidence as to how effectively India protected its agricultural sector. Ten of the twelve HS chapters figuring in the table cover agricultural products. The major products belonging to these HS chapters that figure in the exclusion list are coffee, tea, mate (a South American caffeine-rich drink), and spices; wheat, maize, and rice; all products of cereals; vegetable oils and seeds; and alcoholic beverages. The two remaining HS chapters include dairy products and motor vehicles used for transport, which have traditionally been among the sensitive sectors that India has tried to protect using tariffs. In both

Table 5.3 Prominent sectors figuring in India's 'exclusion list'

Chapter	Share of tariff lines in 'exclusion list' in total tariff lines of the HS chapter
Tobacco and Manufactured Tobacco Substitutes	100.0
Products of the Milling Industry	97.1
Beverages, Spirits, and Vinegar	76.9
Residues and Waste from Food Industries	75.8
Cocoa and Cocoa Preparations	70.4
Cereals	67.6
Dairy Produce; Birds' Eggs; Natural Honey	65.9
Animal or Vegetable Fats and Oil	64.3
Miscellaneous Edible Preparations	62.5
Coffee, Tea, Mate, and Spices	54.8
Preparations of Vegetables, Fruits, Nuts	51.4
Vehicles Other than Railway or Tramway Rolling-Stock	50.8

Source: Government of India (2009).

these product categories, India had put all tariff lines in the exclusion list, thereby retaining the right to impose appropriate levels of tariffs to protect these sectors.

The dynamics of the ASEAN–India FTA showed that India's engagements in the FTAs were closely linked with the autonomous trade liberalization agenda. This pattern was replicated in the two other bilateral economic integration agreements that India had entered into with South Korea and Japan. In its CEPA with South Korea, India had agreed to eliminate tariffs on almost 70 per cent of the tariff lines, while in a similar agreement with Japan, tariff elimination covers more than 86 per cent of its tariff lines. In both these agreements, India had successfully protected the sensitive sectors.

However, nearly a decade after these agreements having come into force, India has not managed to leverage these FTAs to increase its presence in its partner country markets in a sustained manner. India's exports to ASEAN spurted rapidly in the first year after the FTA was signed in 2009, but fell considerably thereafter (Figure 5.3). However, the increase between 2009 and 2010 cannot be attributed to the FTA since most of the opening of markets took place subsequently; and in this

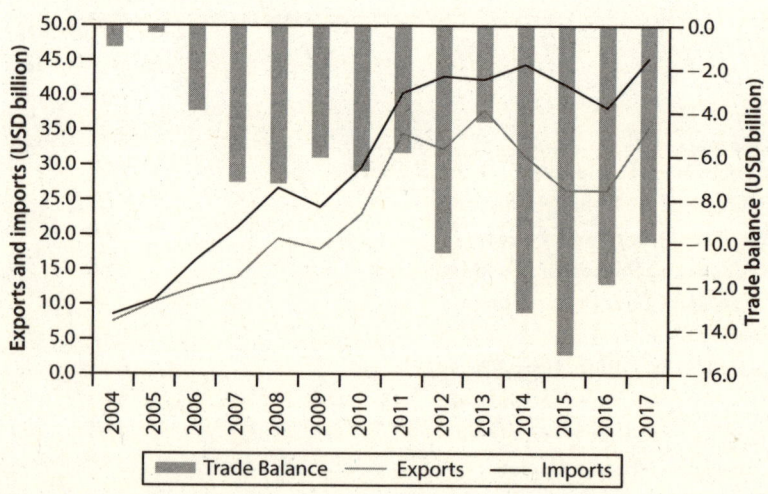

Figure 5.3 India–ASEAN trade (2004–17)

Source: WITS database (2019); available at https://wits.worldbank.org/Default. aspx?lang=en (accessed on 31 October 2019).

latter period, India's exports increased by a quarter. In case of two other agreements—those with South Korea and Japan—the value of India's exports to the countries fell in nominal terms after these agreements came into force (figures 5.4 and 5.5)

The results of these agreements seem to have had a chilling effect on the Indian industry. Over the past few years, some of the major industries have shown marked reluctance to accept tariff liberalization through FTAs[24], largely because of the perceived threat to their interests from growing import competition. More recently, the government seems to have tacitly supported this view of the industry by increasing import tariffs on products across several industries. This was tantamount to a reversal of the policy of import liberalization, according to the finance minister. While presenting the union budget for 2018–19, he declared that he was making a calibrated departure from the underlying policy in the last two decades, wherein the trend largely was to reduce the customs

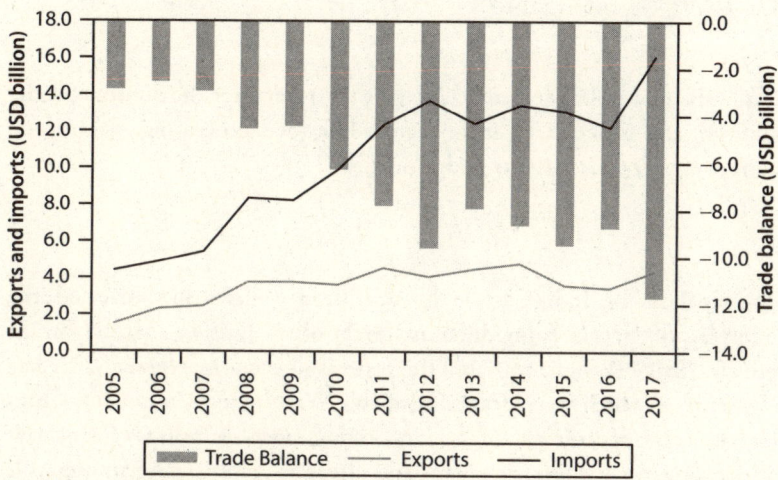

Figure 5.4 India–RoK trade (2005–17)
Source: WITS database (2019).

[24] Among the most coherent positions in this regard has been taken by the Society of Automobile Manufacturers of India (SIAM). In 2013, SIAM produced a 'White Paper' on India's FTAs, which argued its anti-FTA position in considerable detail (see SIAM [2013]).

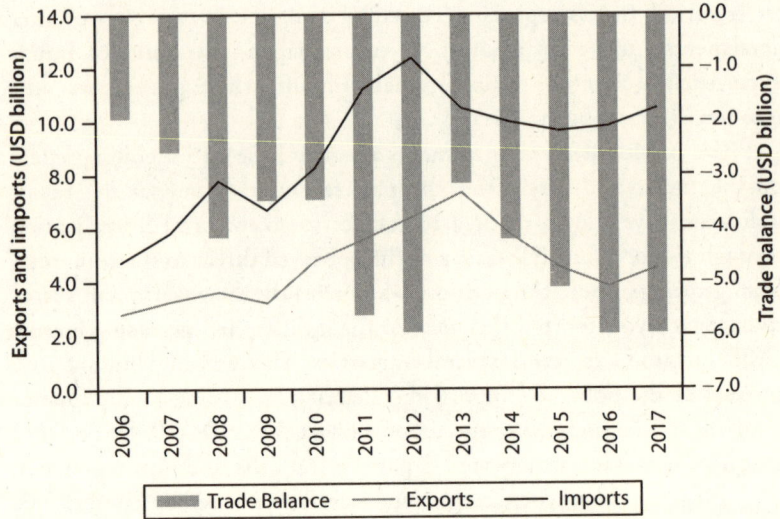

Figure 5.5 India–Japan trade (2006–17)

Source: WITS database (2019).

duty'. The new policy stance 'was to further incentivize the domestic value addition and Make in India' in sectors like 'food processing, electronics, auto components, footwear and furniture.'[25]

***

The analysis of India's trade liberalization policies has revealed the interplay of factors from different levels of analysis in shaping India's policies. In 1991, India initiated the process of economic reforms, the key elements of which were drawn from the 'Washington Consensus'. Thus, global norms became one of the key driving forces of India's reforms. But at the same time, domestic norms and interests played a determining role in shaping India's approach in the negotiations in the WTO and in its bilateral agreements with its East Asian partners, particularly in the area of agriculture.

[25] See Government of India (2018), paragraph 160. This policy pronouncement set the tone for across–the–board tariff increases. See also Dhar (2018).

One of the central pillars of the reforms package was trade liberalization, whereby India's legacy of high walls of protection created through import tariffs and quantitative restrictions on imports were dismantled. Roadmaps for trade liberalization were drawn up by the political system by setting in motion reforms of the customs tariff regime. But, despite the political intent, the process of trade liberalization moved relatively slowly. The implementation of the customs tariff reforms had to face the realities of the Indian economy and the fact that lagging sectors such as agriculture were not in a position to bear the shock of rapid dismantling of tariff protection. Accordingly, the lowering of import tariffs was calibrated to the needs of sectors such as agriculture, which had vulnerable groups such as the small farmers. Interestingly, the narrative on trade liberalization initiated by the government in 1991 never captured this dimension of the opening up of Indian economy.

The sensitivities were, however, articulated by the government in the WTO during the Doha Round negotiations, in which agriculture was a major issue. India's official position was that the small farmers could not be exposed to the market forces and that they needed adequate degree of tariff protection. An additional argument for protecting the small holder agriculture system, according to India, was the imperative of protecting the country's food security.

The domestic compulsions, such as the need to protect agriculture, were also expressed in the bilateral free trade agreements that India has entered into. The explicit intent for participating in the FTAs was to provide preferential market access to the FTA partner countries, and this objective could be realized to a significant extent as the government was able to push the trade liberalization agenda quite considerably in the new millennium. Once again, domestic norms played a dominant part in the shaping of India's position in the FTAs.

Bibliography

Dhar, Biswajit. 2016. 'Prospects of the Nairobi Decision on Special Safeguard Mechanism', in Jonathan Hepburn and Christophe Bellmann (eds), *Evaluating Nairobi: What Does the Outcome Mean for Trade in Food and Farm Goods?* pp. 53–68. Geneva: International Centre for Trade and Sustainable Development (ICTSD).

———. 2018. 'RCEP Deal Can Be Disastrous for India', *The Hindu Business Line*, 13 September.

Government of India. n.d. *Budget 2008–2009: Speech of P. Chidambaram, Minister of Finance, Government of India*. Available at: http://indiabudget. nic.in/ub2008-09/bs/speecha.htm (accessed 18 August 2016).

———. 1986. *Economic Survey 1986–87*.

———. 1991. 'Statement on Industrial Policy', 24 July. Available at: https:// dipp.gov.in/sites/default/files/IndustrialPolicyStatement_1991_15July 2019.pdf (accessed 31 October 2019).

———. 1992a. *Budget 1992–93: Speech of Shri Manmohan Singh, Minister of Finance*, 29 February. Available at: http://indiabudget.nic.in/bspeech/ bs199293.pdf (accessed 18 August 2016).

———. 1992b. *Eighth Five Year Plan*, vol. 1.

———. 1993. *Economic Survey 1992–1993*.

———. 1997a. *Budget 1997–98: Speech of Shri P. Chidambaram, Minister of Finance*, Part A, 28 February; available at: http://indiabudget.nic.in/ bspeech/bs199798.pdf (accessed 18 August 2016).

———. 1997b. *Economic Survey 1996–97*, Chapter 2.

———. 2003. 'Framework Agreement on Comprehensive Economic Cooperation between the Republic Of India and the Association of South East Asian Nations', 8 October. Available at: http://commerce.gov.in/PageContent. aspx?Id=124 (accessed 2 August 2016).

———. 2005. *Budget 2005–2006: Speech of P. Chidambaram, Minister of Finance, Government of India*. Available at: http://indiabudget.nic.in/ub2005-06/ bs/speecha.htm (accessed 18 August 2016).

———. 2006. 'Joint Statement towards India–Japan Strategic and Global Partnership', 15 December. Available at: http://mea.gov.in/bilateral- documents.htm?dtl/6368/Joint+Statement+Towards+IndiaJapan+ Strategic+and+Global+Partnership (accessed 20 August 2016).

———. 2009. 'Agreement on Trade in Goods under the Framework Agreement on Comprehensive Economic Cooperation between the Republic of India and the Association of Southeast Asian Nations', 13 August. Available at: http://commerce.gov.in/writereaddata/UploadedFile/MOC_ 636205354502532516_ASEAN-India_Trade_Goods_Agreement.pdf (accessed 10 August 2016).

———. 2018. *Budget 2018–2019: Speech of Arun Jaitley, Minister of Finance*. Available at https://www.indiabudget.gov.in/budget2018-2019/ub2018- 19/bs/bs.pdf (accessed on 5 February 2019).

IMF (International Monetary Fund). 2000. 'Public Information Notice: IMF Concludes Article IV Consultation with India', Public Information Notice No. 00/47, 30 June. Available at: https://www.imf.org/external/np/sec/ pn/2000/pn0047.htm (accessed 15 August 2016).

———. 2005. 'Public Information Notice: IMF Executive Board Concludes 2004 Article IV Consultation with India', Public Information Notice No. 05/12, 3 February. Available at: https://www.imf.org/external/np/sec/pn/2005/pn0512.htm (accessed 15 August 2016).

Joshi, Vijay and IMD Little. 1993. 'Future Trade and Exchange Rate Policy for India', *Economic and Political Weekly*, 28 (31): 1599–1605.

Kelkar, Vijay, Parthasarathi Shome, and Raja J Chelliah. 2003. *Reports on India's Tax Reforms*. New Delhi: Academic Foundation.

Ministry of External Affairs (Government of India). 2003. 'Brasilia Declaration', 6 June. Available at: http://mea.gov.in/bilateral-documents.htm?dtl/7670/Brasilia+Declaration# (accessed 25 August 2016).

Ministry of Finance & Company Affairs (Government of India). 2002. 'Task Force on Indirect Taxes: Consultation Paper'. Available at: http://www.taxindiaonline.com/RC2/pdfdocs/kelrep/ind/kelreport.pdf (accessed on 25 August 2016).

Narlikar, Amrita and Diana Tussie. 2004. 'The G20 at the Cancun Ministerial: Developing Countries and Their Evolving Coalitions in the WTO', *World Economy*, 27 (7): 947–66.

Rao, Govinda M. and R. Kavita Rao. 2006. 'Trends and Issues in Tax Policy and Reform in India', *India Policy Forum*, pp. 55–122. Available at: https://www.brookings.edu/wp-content/uploads/2016/07/2005_rao.pdf (accessed 10 August 2016).

SIAM (Society of Automobile manufacturers of India). 2013. *India's Free Trade Agreements: SIAM Position and Rationale*. New Delhi.

Williamson, John. 2004. 'The Washington Consensus as Policy Prescription for Development', Lecture for the Series 'Practitioners of Development'. The World Bank, Washington, D.C.. Available at: https://piie.com/sites/default/files/publications/papers/williamson0204.pdf (accessed 15 August 2016).

Wolfe, Robert. 2004. 'Crossing the River by Feeling the Stones: Where the WTO Is Going after Seattle, Doha and Cancun', *Review of International Political Economy*, 11 (3): 574–96.

WTO (World Trade Organization). 1994. 'Understanding on the Balance of Payments Provisions of the General Agreement on Tariffs and Trade 1994'. Available at: https://www.wto.org/english/docs_e/legal_e/09-bops_e.htm (accessed 29 November 2017).

———. 1997. 'Certification of Modifications to Schedule XII – India', WT/Let/181, 2 October.

———. 1998. 'Communication from India', WT/GC/W/114, 18 November.

———. 1999a. 'Preparations for the 1999 Ministerial Conference: Proposals Regarding Food Security in the Context of Paragraph 9(a)(ii) of the Geneva

Ministerial Declaration, Communication from India', WT/GC/W/342, 29 September.

———. 1999b.'Proposals Regarding Food Security in the Context of Paragraph 9(a)(ii) of the Geneva Ministerial Declaration: Communication from India'. WT/GC/W/342, 29 September.

———. 2000.'Second Special Session of the Committee on Agriculture, 29–30 June 2000: Statement by India', G/AG/NG/W/33, 13 July.

———. 2001a. 'Implementation-Related Issues and Concerns: Decision of 14 November 2001', WT/MIN(01)/17, 20 November.

———. 2001b. 'Ministerial Declaration: Adopted on 14 November 2001', WT/MIN(01)/DEC/1, 20 November.

———. 2001c.'Proposals by India in the areas of: (i) Food Security, (ii) Market Access, (iii) Domestic Support, and (iv) Export Competition', G/AG/NG/W/102, 15 January.

———. 2002a. 'Agriculture from a Development Perspective: Special and Differential Treatment for Developing Countries—Specific Input: Contribution by India on Modalities for Negotiations', JOB(02)/175, 18 November.

———. 2002b. 'Market Access, Domestic Support and Export Competition—Specific Drafting Input: United States', JOB(02)/122, 19 September.

———. 2002c. 'Market Access (Further Commitments): Specific Input: Cairns Group Negotiating Proposal on Market Access', JOB(02)/112, 12 September.

———. 2002d. 'WTO Countries in Favour of the Uruguay Round Approach to Tariff Reductions', JOB(03)/53, 11 March.

———. 2003a. 'Discussion Paper on Regional Trading Arrangements: Communication from India'. TN/RL/W/114, 6 June.

———. 2003b. 'Joint EC–US Paper: Agriculture'. JOB(03)/157, 13 August.

———. 2003c. 'Ministers' Communiqué: Alliance for Strategic Products and Special Safeguard Mechanism'. WT/MIN(03)/14, 9 September.

———. 2003d. 'Special and Differential Treatment for Developing Countries: Food and Livelihood Security and Rural Development—Specific Input by India'. JOB(03)/7, 22 January.

———. 2003e. 'Negotiations on Agriculture: First Draft of Modalities for the Further Commitments'. TN/AG/W/1, 17 February.

———. 2005. 'G-33 Proposal on the Modalities for the Designation and Treatment of Any Agricultural Product as a Special Product (SP) by any Developing Country Member', JOB(05)/304, 22 November.

———. 2017. 'Quantitative Restrictions'. Available at: https://www.wto.org/english/tratop_e/markacc_e/qr_e.htm (accessed 25 August 2016).

6 Deciphering India's Foreign Policy on Climate Change

Role of Interests, Institutions, and Ideas

SANDEEP SENGUPTA

F EW ISSUES EPITOMIZE THE NEED FOR effective global governance as much as climate change. Over the past quarter century, the international community has endeavoured, with varying degrees of success, to construct a workable international regime to address this critical global challenge. India has been a major player in this process over this entire period. It has been actively engaged since the very beginning of the intergovernmental climate negotiations in the late 1980s—which culminated in the adoption of the United Nations Framework Convention on Climate Change (UNFCCC) at the Rio Earth Summit (in Brazil) in 1992—right up to the successful adoption, most recently, of the Paris Agreement on climate change in 2015.

Over these two and a half decades, India's engagement has largely been a story of continuity. However, in recent years, significant changes have also been witnessed in India's international positions and engagement on climate change. This chapter aims to chart out some of the major continuities and changes seen in India's foreign policy on climate, and provide an explanation for them using the multilayered analytical framework developed in this book.

The chapter is organized in four parts. The first part presents the traditional positions that India has held on climate change in the international arena. The second part identifies some of the key shifts that have been witnessed in India's foreign policy on climate in recent years. The third part focuses on explaining these continuities and changes by unpacking, in turn, the different roles that interests, institutions, and ideas have played across different spatial scales—domestic, regional, and international—in shaping India's external behaviour on this issue. The fourth section concludes the chapter. Cumulatively, this chapter helps to demonstrate that applying such a multilayered analytical framework can provide a more comprehensive and nuanced understanding of India's foreign policy thinking and engagement on this key global issue.

India's Traditional Position on Climate Change (1988–2007)

The origins of India's international engagement on climate change can be traced back to the late 1980s, when the issue first formally emerged on the agenda of the United Nations (UN). In 1988, the UN General Assembly (UNGA) recognized climate change as a 'common concern of mankind' and endorsed the setting up of the Intergovernmental Panel on Climate Change (IPCC) to examine its scientific basis in greater depth (UNGA 1988). More specifically, in 1989, the UNGA passed a resolution urging its member states to urgently prepare a 'framework convention' to address this global problem (UNGA 1989).

India's earliest positions on this topic were expressed at the Conference of Select Developing Countries on Global Environmental Issues held in New Delhi in 1990. India had convened this conference with the aim of developing a common Southern position ahead of the convention negotiations. At this meeting, India articulated three basic arguments. First, the primary responsibility for reducing greenhouse gas (GHG) emissions that caused the problem of climate change rested with the developed world, since they were the ones responsible for producing the bulk of these emissions. Second, the emissions of developing countries were still very low, and needed to grow to meet their development and poverty-reduction needs, and hence no GHG reduction targets could be prescribed for them. And third, any formal convention on climate change would need to provide for technology transfer to and funds for developing countries to help them address this challenge (MoEF 1990).

In its first official statement within the actual convention negotiations in 1991, India went on to argue that the problem of global warming had been 'caused not by emissions of greenhouse gases as such but by *excessive* levels of per capita emissions' (Dasgupta 1994, 133; emphasis in original). Making 'equity' and 'per capita convergence' a central plank of its negotiating position, it asserted that '[a]n equitable solution can only be found on the basis of significant reductions in levels of per capita emissions of developed countries, so that over a period of years these converge with rising per capita emissions in developing countries' (Dasgupta 1994).

During the entire convention negotiations, India continued to argue, more specifically, that:

1. it could have 'no legal responsibility' for addressing climate change;
2. any voluntary mitigation measures that it took to address it would have to be consistent with its national development plans and priorities;
3. the 'full incremental costs involved' for the same would need to be provided through 'new and additional financial resources' from the developed world; and
4. the latter would also need to provide developing countries with 'assured access to technology on preferential terms'. (Dasgupta 1994)

Together with China, it also strongly opposed the voluntary 'pledge and review' proposal, which had been introduced at this time by the United States (U.S.) and Japan. This was criticized as an alternative to the more rigorous 'targets and timetables' approach, for not only attempting to take the pressure off the North but also for trying to impose legal obligations on developing countries through the back door (Dasgupta 1994, 136–7). Indian negotiators particularly feared that 'pledge and review' could evolve into an intrusive mechanism whereby the North would be able to interfere in the domestic policies of the South, especially in key sectors such as energy and industry (Rajan 1997, 124–5).

Through a mix of strong Southern coalitions and the presence of significant divisions within the North at the time, India was largely successful in securing its core positions in the convention negotiations. This can be seen from the fact that the final text of the UNFCCC that was adopted in June 1992 clearly noted that 'the largest share of historical and current global emissions of greenhouse gases has originated in developed countries' (UNFCCC 1992, Preamble). It also set out that '[p]arties should protect the climate system ... on the basis of equity and in accordance with their common but differentiated responsibilities and respective capabilities', and that '[a]ccordingly, the developed country Parties should take the lead in combating climate change' (UNFCCC 1992, Article 3.1).

Specifically, the UNFCCC called on developed countries to aim to return their GHG emissions to 1990 levels by the year 2000 (UNFCCC 1992, Article 4.2 a and b). It also recognized that the per capita emissions in developing countries were 'still relatively low', and that their future share of global emissions would need to 'grow to meet their social and development needs' (UNFCCC 1992, Preamble). On finance, the convention required developed countries to provide developing countries with 'new and additional financial resources' to meet not only the 'agreed full incremental costs' of implementing climate mitigation and adaptation measures, including for technology transfer, but also the 'agreed full costs' of preparing their national communications and other reporting requirements (UNFCCC 1992, Article 4.3).

On India's insistence, the UNFCCC also confined its review function to conducting individual reviews of only the developed country commitments, while assessing the commitments and communications of developing countries in 'aggregated' terms (UNFCCC 1992, Article 10.2). Most importantly, from India's point of view, the UNFCCC explicitly recognized that 'economic and social development and poverty eradication are the first and overriding priorities of the developing country Parties', and that the extent to which developing countries would be able to effectively implement their commitments under the convention would depend on the extent to which developed countries fulfilled their own commitments with regard to finance and technology transfer (UNFCCC 1992, Article 4.7). The convention moreover created two clearly distinct categories of countries—Annex I and non-Annex I—in the architecture of the regime itself to recognize the differential obligations and treatment of developed and developing countries.

Although India was not able to get everything that it wanted (such as agreement on 'per capita convergence'; concrete emission reduction commitments from the North; and technology transfer on 'preferential' terms), its overall assessment at the end of the UNFCCC negotiations was that 'the outcome was entirely satisfactory' from its point of view (Rajan 1997, 151–2). It noted that its negotiators, working closely with their counterparts in G-77 and China, had 'ensured that the obligations imposed [on India] are minimal and, furthermore, that in all areas there is "differentiation" between developed and developing countries' (Rajan 1997). This notion of 'differentiation' was extremely important to India, and it played a critical role in ensuring that what had been originally sought by the West to be framed as the 'common responsibility' of all countries, was ultimately agreed to be dealt with in accordance with the principle of 'common but differentiated responsibilities and respective capabilities' (CBDRRC)—which then became the core foundational norm of the treaty (Rajan 1997, 108; Rajamani 2012).

Ever since then, India's principal objective in the climate negotiations has been to staunchly defend this sharply 'differentiated' architecture of the climate regime, and to ensure that no fresh legal obligations are placed on it. This was evident at all key junctures of the negotiations that followed. Thus, at the first Conference of the Parties (COP-1) to the UNFCCC, held in Berlin in 1995—when discussions were initiated to consider a more stringent 'protocol' to the convention to ensure legally binding emission reduction 'targets and timetables'—India strongly resisted the proposals of developed country that called for additional commitments from 'certain more advanced developing countries' (cited in Sengupta 2013, 396).

Despite an official agreement under the Berlin Mandate (UNFCCC 1995) that the protocol development process would 'not introduce any new commitments' for non-Annex I parties, such calls—including for the establishment of 'new categories' among the parties and 'voluntary commitments' from developing countries—nevertheless continued to be raised by developed countries at regular intervals (Oberthur and Ott 1999). At COP-3 in Kyoto, Japan, in December 1997, India voiced its strong opposition to these attempts, with its environment minister noting that: 'India categorically rejects ideas suggesting any new commitments for developing countries. Any idea that seeks further to deprive us of our equitable entitlement to grow can never be allowed to take root' (cited in Agarwal, Narain, and Sharma 1999, 59).

In view of this resistance from India and other developing countries, the Kyoto Protocol adopted at the end of COP-3 did not prescribe any additional mitigation commitments for non-Annex I parties. However, it did put in place a more ambitious and legally binding requirement upon Annex I parties to reduce their collective GHG emissions by 5 per cent below 1990 levels over a first commitment period of 2008–12 (UNFCCC 1997). The period between 1997 and 2001 largely focused on developing the modalities and rules for operationalizing this protocol, including for the flexible market-based mechanisms that had been negotiated within the treaty to assist developed countries to meet their assigned mitigation targets.

One of these flexible mechanisms—the Clean Development Mechanism (CDM), which allowed for developed countries to invest in specific emission-reduction projects in developing countries, and use the credits generated from the same to meet their own mitigation target—was of particular interest to India. This was something that India had originally opposed, and accepted only very reluctantly at the end of COP-3, out of concern that it was a Northern ploy to shift emission reduction obligations to the South on the cheap (Agarwal, Narain, and Sharma 1999). However, this was also one of the few issues on which India changed its mind during the post-Kyoto phase, sensing that the CDM offered a valuable opportunity for it to gain foreign investment and clean technology from the West. Indeed, together with China, India became a global leader in hosting CDM projects in the years that followed, capturing a significant share of the global market of such projects (Newell and Bumpus 2012, 54).

Nevertheless, developed countries—especially the U.S.—continued to raise the question of developing countries' participation in the post-Kyoto period as well. These efforts gained particular momentum after President George W. Bush formally withdrew the USA from the Kyoto Protocol in June 2001, arguing that the absence of mitigation commitments for key developing countries such as China and India had made the treaty impossible to ratify for the USA. Although the Kyoto Protocol formally managed to enter into force at COP-11 in Montreal in 2005, with the support of the European Union and Russia, its inability to make a significant contribution towards solving the problem of growing GHG emissions—and the unwillingness of major developed countries to meaningfully support its implementation—gave rise to concerns about what would happen to the climate regime post 2012, once its 'first commitment period' ended.

In order to help resolve this issue, COP-11 launched a dual-track process to not only discuss the post-2012 'second commitment period' mitigation targets of the Annex I parties that had ratified the Kyoto Protocol (the KP track), but also a separate 'dialogue' on 'long-term cooperative action' (the LCA track). This dialogue sought to discuss the future commitments of those countries that had either refused to ratify the Kyoto Protocol (such as the USA or Australia), or had no binding emission reduction obligations under it, that is developing nations (UNFCCC 2006).

This was, again, a period when India and other large developing countries came under sustained pressure from the developed world, including via the global media, to do more to demonstrate their commitment towards fighting climate change. A slew of influential global reports released at this time—including the United Kingdom (UK) Government's 2006 Stern Review, the International Energy Agency's (IEA) World Energy Outlook 2007, and the UNDP's Human Development Report 2007/08—also focused increased attention on the rising emissions trajectories of India and China in particular. This was also the time when climate change began to be discussed not only within the UNFCCC, but also in other important political arenas. For example, in June 2007, Germany, as the host of the G8 Summit, invited the leaders of the five largest emerging economies (China, India, Brazil, South Africa, and Mexico) to attend the summit—in an enlarged G8+5 setting—and made climate change a key focus of its agenda.

At this G8+5 Summit held in Heiligendamm, Prime Minister Manmohan Singh, who was representing India, restated and defended the country's core positions on this issue. Singh underscored that India's GHG emissions were 'among the lowest in per-capita terms' and that, even if considered in aggregate terms, it would account for 'only around 4 per cent of the world's emissions'. In response to the growing Western pressure on it to accept greater mitigation obligations, he stressed that the 'process of burden sharing must be fair' and should 'not perpetuate poverty among the developing countries'. He further underlined that the time was 'not ripe for developing countries to take quantitative targets as these would be counter-productive on their development processes'. However, at the same time, he emphasized that India 'recognise[d] wholeheartedly' its 'responsibilities as a developing country' and would 'add [its] weight to global efforts to preserve and protect the environment'. In a significant show of flexibility, Singh also unilaterally pledged that 'India's per-capita GHG emissions are *not going to exceed* those of developed countries even while pursuing policies of development and economic growth' (Singh 2007; emphasis added).

This was for the first time in the entire history of climate talks that India had made such a voluntary offer to accept a curb of any sort on its future potential emissions. However, a careful reading of this pledge also clearly shows that it was as much a challenge to the developed world to reduce its own per capita emissions first, given the vast gap that existed between their emissions and those of India. Moreover, it was also essentially consistent with India's longstanding position on 'per capita convergence', and hence did not reflect a major change in its international stance as such (Sengupta 2012a).

That India was unwilling to brook any dilution in the fundamental architecture of the UNFCCC also became clear during the negotiation of the Bali Action Plan during COP-13 in December 2007. This was a crucial document that aimed to set the terms for an 'agreed outcome' on 'long-term cooperative action' on climate change—including a 'long-term global goal for emission reductions'— which was to be reached by COP-15 in Copenhagen in 2009. Accordingly, India worked closely with other developing countries to ensure that its content remained as consistent as possible with the framework and principles of the UNFCCC and the Kyoto Protocol (UNFCCC 2008). It particularly tried to ensure that a clear 'differentiation', or 'firewall', was maintained between what developed and developing countries would each be required to do on climate mitigation in the future, insisting, especially, that the latter was made contingent on the provision of external support from the former. Likewise, on the issue of international measurement, reporting, and verification of developing country mitigation efforts—a key Western concern—it ensured that such external scrutiny was contemplated only for those actions that were externally supported by the developed world, and not generally. The two years that followed, between COP-13 and COP-15, remained essentially a period of North–South negotiating deadlock. Although the Indian government took a number of significant steps domestically during this time, its international positions remained largely unaltered.

Recent Changes in India's Climate Positions (2007–17)

Regardless of the deadlock at the international level, the two-year period between Bali, Indonesia, and Copenhagen, Denmark, witnessed considerable activity on the issue of climate change within India, as in other countries around the world. Around the time of the Heiligendamm summit, in June 2007, Prime Minister Manmohan Singh constituted the Prime Minister's Council on Climate Change (PMCCC) to evolve a coordinated multistakeholder response to climate change issues at the national level (PMO 2007). In April 2008, he appointed the country's former foreign secretary, Shyam Saran, as his special envoy on climate change to help coordinate the country's international negotiations on this issue. Shortly thereafter, in June 2008, India also published a National Action Plan on Climate Change (NAPCC). The NAPCC outlined a number of measures that the government intended to undertake in key areas—ranging from solar energy expansion, energy efficiency, and sustainable habitats through to agriculture, water management, and afforestation—via 'Eight National Missions' that aimed to promote 'development objectives while also yielding *co-benefits* for addressing climate change effectively' (PMCCC 2008, emphasis added). Cumulatively, these moves signalled the growing importance that India was now according to the issue of climate change at the domestic level as compared to before.

At the international level, the first significant shifts in India's foreign policy on climate were witnessed in July 2009, when Prime Minister Manmohan Singh—following the return to power of the United Progressive Alliance (UPA) in the 2009 general elections—signed the 'Major Economies Forum (MEF) Leaders Declaration on Energy and Climate' at a meeting held alongside the G8 Summit in L'Aquila, Italy. This declaration specifically recognized, for the first time, that the rise in global temperature 'ought not to exceed 2 degrees C', and that MEF countries would work together to identify a 'global goal' to reduce 'global emissions by 2050' (MEF 2009). Although, only a political declaration, and not legally binding, India's signing on to this '2 degree C' temperature rise limit nevertheless signalled its willingness to concede, in theory at least, an implicit cap on its future emissions, even though this was left ambiguous and unstated (Ramachandran 2009).

However, the fact that India's political leadership was now willing to reconsider its international stance on climate change became further clear when Jairam Ramesh, the country's newly appointed minister for environment and forests, actively attempted to reframe India's traditional position on this issue in the six months leading up to the Copenhagen summit. Stressing repeatedly that India was highly vulnerable to climate change—and also that it needed to be seen internationally as 'a leader, as a proactive player, as somebody who is shaping the solution' on this issue— Ramesh argued that it was now in the country's own interest to go beyond its original 'per capita convergence' position, and adopt a more aggressive 'per-capita plus' approach (Ghosh 2009). He asserted that specific 'performance targets' could be assigned through domestic legislation, or executive action, to key sectors of the country's economy (Ghosh 2009). He also suggested taking a more flexible stance on the question of allowing external reviews of India's domestic mitigation actions, including through more frequent and detailed national communications to the UNFCCC and IMF/WTO-style reviews (Sethi 2009).

These new ideas provoked a great deal of domestic debate in the country, including within government, which saw strong concerns about the seemingly unilateral nature of these concessions being expressed by senior members of India's official climate negotiating team itself (TNN 2009). It also led to India's foreign policy on climate change being extensively debated in Parliament on at least three separate occasions (Prabhu 2012; Sengupta 2013). In the final Parliamentary debate held just prior to COP-15, the environment minister declared that India would go to Copenhagen with a 'positive frame of mind', prepared to be 'flexible'. However, he stressed that there were three 'non-negotiables' that it would not compromise on: (*i*) it would not accept any 'legally binding emission reduction cut'; (*ii*) it would not accept any 'peaking year'—a concept that had started emerging at this time; and (*iii*) it would not allow unsupported mitigation actions to be subject to the same type of scrutiny as those that were externally supported. He also announced—in a clear shift of position from India's opposition to 'voluntary commitments' in the pre-Kyoto period, and even from the prime minister's 2007 statement at Heiligendamm—that India would voluntarily reduce the 'emissions intensity' of its GDP by 20–5 per cent by 2020 compared to its 2005 level through domestic mitigation actions, arguing that to do so would be in India's own best interests (Lok Sabha 2009). This was for the first time that India formally put forward a concrete numerical pledge in relation to climate mitigation on the table.

At COP-15 in Copenhagen, India coordinated extremely closely with a core group of similarly placed large developing nations (China, Brazil, and South Africa)—through the newly-formed BASIC alliance—to jointly resist the mounting pressure that they now each came under from a largely unified U.S.-led North. The latter insisted that the BASIC states not only accept stronger mitigation commitments, but also that the Kyoto Protocol, which they considered as fundamentally flawed, be replaced by a new, more 'undifferentiated', international agreement on climate change, where all major GHG emitters, developed and developing alike, would have similar mitigation obligations subject to similar levels of international scrutiny.

This Northern attempt to bypass the Kyoto Protocol, and dilute the foundational norm of 'differentiation' that had been hardwired into the UNFCCC, was strongly opposed by the BASIC group and most other developing nations. It was in this intractable situation that the 'Copenhagen Accord' was uneasily born on the final night of COP-15, as a last-minute compromise between the BASIC countries and the USA at their heads of state and government level. In the accord negotiations, India worked actively to ensure that none of the three 'non-negotiables' that it had promised to its Parliament were fundamentally violated (Sengupta 2012a). India also played a key role in brokering agreement on the sensitive question of international measurement, reporting, and verification by suggesting a less intrusive alternative of 'international consultations and analysis' to review the unsupported mitigation actions of developing countries (Chauhan 2010). The BASIC countries collectively also ensured that some of the fundamental principles and provisions of the UNFCCC (such as 'CBDRRC'; 'equity'; 'new and additional' finance; and recognition for the 'overriding priorities' of poverty eradication and development) were suitably acknowledged and referenced in the accord. A 'differentiated' framework for recording the 'quantified economy-wide emissions targets' of developed countries and the 'nationally appropriate mitigation actions' of developing countries that both agreed to submit under the accord was also ensured (UNFCCC 2010).

These understandings reached under the Copenhagen Accord, which had been 'taken note of' but not officially agreed on at COP-15, were formally anchored in the UNFCCC process only at COP-16 in 2010 as part of the Cancun Agreements. However, the push by the developed countries to substitute the 'top-down', 'strictly differentiated', 'legally binding', 'targets and timetables'-type approach—exemplified by the UNFCCC and its Kyoto Protocol—with a 'less differentiated', 'more voluntary', 'bottom-up', 'pledge and review'-type system that treated developed and developing countries similarly with respect to their mitigation and reporting obligations continued unabated over this period.

A critical milestone in this regard was reached at COP-17 in Durban in 2011 when—through a result of concerted Northern unity and growing

Southern fragmentation, including within BASIC—a decision was taken to terminate the ongoing negotiating process held under the terms of the 2007 Bali Action Plan by the end of 2012. At the same time, this decision launched an entirely new negotiating process that called for the development of a 'protocol, another legal instrument or an agreed outcome with legal force under the Convention' (UNFCC 2012) by COP-21 in 2015, which would be 'applicable to all Parties' and take effect from 2020 onwards. Significantly, unlike the Bali mandate, which had maintained a clear 'firewall' between developed and developing countries, this new 'Durban Platform for Enhanced Action'—despite India's solitary last-minute efforts—made no obvious distinction between developed and developing nations. Indeed, unlike the Copenhagen Accord and the Cancun Agreements, which had explicitly reaffirmed the core UNFCCC norms of 'equity' and 'CBDRRC', the 'Durban Platform' text made no reference whatsoever to either of these foundational regime principles (Sengupta 2012b). Although the Kyoto Protocol continued to survive on paper—with developed countries agreeing at COP-18 in Doha the following year to a 'second commitment period' that would extend from 2012 to 2020—the fact that few industrialized states were willing to make any serious commitments under Kyoto underscored the extent to which it remained marginal.

The period between 2012 and 2015 focused primarily on designing a new global climate agreement based on the new terms defined at Durban, South Africa. COP-19 in Warsaw, Poland, in 2013, all parties to the UNFCCC were invited to voluntarily prepare and communicate their 'bottom up' national-level 'pledges' on climate action—or 'Intended Nationally Determined Contributions (INDCs)'—in support of the 2015 agreement. The COP-20, held in Lima in 2014, continued to develop the contours of this new agreement. At this juncture, a renewed pushback from the developing world —particularly the BASIC group and a newly created Southern alliance called the Like-Minded Developing Countries (LMDCs), of which India was an active member—brought the issue of 'differentiation' back on the table, through their insistence that the 2015 agreement had to remain fully consistent with the agreed provisions and principles of the UNFCCC, which could not undergo 'rewriting, revising or reinterpreting' (Kallbekken, Sælen, and Underdal 2015, 42).

A compromise was ultimately agreed to in Lima, Peru, building on a U.S.–China bilateral understanding, that the 2015 agreement would 'reflect the principle of CBDRRC', albeit 'in light of different national circumstances'. In other words, no longer would the original Rio concept of 'differentiation'—as understood in terms of a strict divide between Annex I and non-Annex I parties' obligations and treatment—apply. Consequently, the Paris Agreement on climate change that was finally adopted at COP-21 in December 2015 incorporated the principle of differentiation within its text in a very different manner than had been originally conceptualized under the UNFCCC and the Kyoto Protocol. Although intense negotiations, including by the BASIC and LMDC groups, ensured that ideas of 'equity' and 'differentiation' remain registered in different operational parts of this new treaty, the Paris Agreement imposed a far more uniform set of obligations for mitigation and reporting on all parties—developed and developing alike—than had previously been the case, which India ultimately had to acquiesce to.

Publicly however, India—represented at COP-21 by a new BJP government led by Prime Minister Narendra Modi—welcomed the adoption of the Paris Agreement. Indeed, just prior to COP-21, in October 2015, India communicated its own updated national pledge, or INDC, to the UNFCCC. In this, India significantly enhanced its earlier pre-Copenhagen pledge of 2009, agreeing to reduce the 'emissions intensity' of its GDP by 33–5 per cent by 2030 from 2005 levels (GOI 2015). Moreover, India's INDC also included other specific time-bound targets to increase both the share of the country's national energy that would be derived from non-fossil fuel sources, and its national tree and forest cover. It, however, took care to note that successful implementation of these measures would remain contingent on the provision of additional means of implementation from developed countries, in accordance with their UNFCCC obligations.

At COP-21 itself, Prime Minister Modi made active efforts to position India as a country that was fully aware of its global responsibilities on this issue, and guided as much by its ancient beliefs on environmental stewardship as by notions of equity and climate justice. Indeed, as a mark of its commitment towards addressing climate change, the Modi government launched a new initiative together with France, called the International Solar Alliance, which aimed to significantly expand the global adoption of solar energy, especially across tropical zone countries. This was in addition to the domestic decision that the Modi government had also taken in June 2015, to increase India's national solar power generation capacity fivefold—from 20 GW to 100 GW by 2022—compared to the original goal that had been set in 2008 under the National Solar Mission of India's NAPCC.

Following COP-21, India has continued to reiterate its support for the Paris Agreement. This was observed, for instance, through the remarkably rapid decision of the Indian government to officially ratify the Paris Agreement in October 2016, which subsequently formally entered into force in November 2016. Likewise, India publicly also voiced its strong support for the agreement in June 2017—after the Trump administration's announcement to withdraw the USA from the treaty—with Prime Minister Modi noting at a joint press conference with President Macron of France that the 'protection of the environment and the mother planet is an article of faith' (De Clercq 2017).

Explaining India's Climate Foreign Policy Behaviour—A Multilayered Analysis

What drives India's global conduct on climate change? The following section attempts to explain the continuities and changes seen in the country's foreign policy on climate over the last two and a half decades by applying the multilayered analytical framework proposed in this book. It thus examines, in turn, the particular role that interests, institutions, and ideas each played across different spatial scales—international, regional, and domestic—in shaping India's external engagement on this issue.

Interests

India's international behaviour on climate change over time has been intimately shaped by how it conceptualized its overall national interest on the topic. At the domestic level, India's primary national purpose, since Independence in 1947, has been to eradicate its deep-rooted poverty and achieve modernization and development through industrialization and economic growth (Gadgil and Guha 1992). With regard to climate change, there was a realization very early on within the government that any international agreement to curb GHG emissions—which were intrinsically correlated to national energy use, economic growth, and development—could impinge upon the country's future development prospects. There was a clear understanding among Indian negotiators participating in the convention negotiations in the early 1990s that the UNFCCC would not just be an environmental treaty but rather a 'major multilateral economic agreement', where '[t]he sharing of costs and benefits implied ... could significantly alter the *economic destinies* of individual countries' (Dasgupta 1994, 131, emphasis added). This particular interest-based understanding of the climate regime—and India's desire to secure enough 'policy space' and 'carbon space' within it to ensure its future development—was a key underlying factor driving its international behaviour.

However, India's understanding of what its domestic interests are in relation to climate change have not remained static over time. This can be seen, for example, on the CDM, where India shifted its position in the late 1990s from opposition to support. This was based, in part, on a revised understanding among key policy makers in government—supported by domestic industry groups and research think tanks—that participating in this mechanism could yield greater material benefits and advantages for India (Jakobsen 1998).

Likewise, some of the more recent changes seen in India's foreign policy on climate—including the submission of unilateral mitigation pledges by it—also reflect how India's understandings of its domestic interests on this topic have broadened over time. There is a far greater appreciation today, for instance, of the risks that climate change—and global inaction on it—poses to the country's future welfare and security. Be it the potential adverse impacts of climate change on India's critically monsoon-dependent agriculture, or the effects of melting Himalayan glaciers on its major river systems in the heavily populated Gangetic plains, or the exposure of its 7,500 km long coastline to rising sea level and extreme-weather events, there is significantly greater awareness among policy makers—enabled, in part, by the growing scientific knowledge encapsulated in successive IPCC reports—of the country's intrinsic vulnerabilities on this issue, and the need, therefore, to support climate action in its own interest.

This impetus for change has, equally, also been facilitated by a growing understanding that taking action on climate change can yield other material co-benefits for the country, whether in terms of improving local health by tackling household, vehicular, and industrial emissions, or enhancing the country's energy security by lowering its dependence on fossil fuel imports and minimizing foreign exchange outflows for the same. Likewise, the fact that alternative climate-friendly technologies, such as solar energy, have become significantly cost-competitive over time compared to traditional energy options such as coal—and offer realistic 'leapfrogging' pathways as well as newer business opportunities for the country to achieve clean development—has also altered India's interest calculus, and fed into the changes seen in its external policies on this issue.

In terms of regional-level factors influencing India's interests on climate change, these have not been particularly salient. Although India has sought the support of its South Asian neighbours for its international negotiating positions—and these have been reflected, in part, in the climate change statements that have emanated periodically from the South Asian Association for Regional Cooperation (SAARC)—its overall success has been limited in this regard. The fact that many SAARC countries are much smaller, have different international power-political positions and ambitions, and face unique vulnerabilities of their own in relation to climate change means that their external preferences on it are not identical to those of India. This is directly reflected in the fact that different SAARC countries belong to different coalitions within the international climate negotiations—with Nepal and Bangladesh part of the Least Developed Countries (LDCs) group and Maldives a member of the Alliance of Small Island States (AOSIS)—even while all being common members of the larger G77 and China bloc.

Global-level considerations, by contrast, have indeed had a discernible impact on India's interests and external positions on climate change. Traditionally, India's foreign policy in the post-colonial period rested fundamentally on a determination to safeguard its sovereignty against external interference, maximize its space for autonomous action, and regain what it considered to be its 'rightful place' in the world (Saran 2006). This it sought to fulfil at the international stage primarily through policies based on 'non-alignment' and Third World solidarity. These precepts informed its external positions and thinking on climate change as well for much of the UNFCCC negotiations.

However, in recent years, there have been notable changes in how India has viewed its global interests and positioning in the world, given its own emergence as a rising power in a more multipolar landscape that has witnessed the even greater rise of China. These changes in its broader foreign policy thinking have, in turn, contributed to the shifts seen in its external positions on climate change. These include, for instance, the enhanced value that India has attached to building a closer bilateral relationship with the USA in particular, and the material and security benefits that it has secured in return—such as the 2005 Indo-US nuclear deal—and India's willingness, in turn, to be more accepting of US framings of the global climate regime (Raghunandan 2012).

Likewise, India has also valued the global power-political status associated with invitations received from traditional Western powers to participate in exclusive global governance clubs such as the G8+5, MEF, or G20. These were recognitions that it had long sought as a marker of its arrival on the global stage. However—in the context of climate—this has often meant that it is less able to defend its traditional positions, or shape the final outcomes, in these more elite minilateral settings. These are some of the global-level interest-based trade-offs that have fed into its recent international climate policy making.

Institutions

India's external positions on climate change have also been directly influenced and shaped by a number of institutional factors. At the domestic level, the central government has been the primary institutional determinant of India's foreign policy on climate over the last quarter century. Until the mid-2000s, the Ministry of Environment and Forests (MoEF)—recently renamed as the Ministry of Environment, Forests and Climate Change—and the Ministry of External Affairs (MEA) were the major government agencies in charge of representing India in the international climate negotiations. Indeed, it can be argued that for much of these negotiations, a core group of serving and retired MoEF and MEA officials held a near-monopoly in terms of determining what India's interests on this issue were, and what its negotiating positions should be. Indeed, a key reason behind the long continuity in India's foreign policy on climate was a strong belief among these officials that their reasoning and positions were right, and required no changing, especially given the unwillingness of the North to abide by their prior promises under the UNFCCC and the Kyoto Protocol. Another reason was the natural tendency of India's climate bureaucracy—given internal capacity constraints—to stick to existing and agreed defendable positions, rather than propose or consider any new concepts or approaches.

However, as climate change became more prominent on the international agenda, and began to feature more frequently in discussions at the heads of state and government levels, it received closer attention within higher levels of government within India too. This was principally through the greater engagement of the PMO, the deputy chairman of the Planning Commission, and newly created institutions and positions such as the PMCCC and the Prime Minister's Special Envoy on Climate Change, set up specifically for this purpose. The emergence of new voices within government—and, particularly, the internal shifting of the balance of power between India's political and bureaucratic leadership on this issue—was exemplified most prominently in the lead up to the 2009 Copenhagen Summit, with the ascendancy of Ramesh, who expressed a significantly differing world view, threat perceptions, and normative commitments on this issue than those traditionally in charge of Indian policy making on climate. This was an instrumental factor in bringing about major changes in India's international climate positions at that time.

Though the traditional voices within government—and their underlying arguments against unilateral concessions and international policy changes—have continued to remain powerful and relevant (Dasgupta 2011), there has nevertheless been a significant institutional broadening on this issue within government in India. This can be seen, for instance, in the greater engagement of other ministries and departments— such the Ministry of New and Renewable Energies (MNRE) or the Bureau of Energy Efficiency (BEE)—within the negotiations. More importantly, it can also be seen in the continued willingness within the country's highest political leadership—beyond just Ramesh—and cutting across party-lines to take political risks and to consider and accept options that extend well beyond India's traditional negotiating positions. This was clear, for instance, in the more direct role that the PMO, led by Prime Minister Modi himself, played in formulating India's foreign policy on climate—and in making and approving the political judgement calls, trade-offs, and compromises that were seen both at and in the immediate lead up to COP-21. Although how much this broadening has better served India's interests on this issue remains debatable (King 2016), what is clear is that, unlike the past, the final shots were now not called by officials at the MoEF or MEA. Furthermore, this institutional broadening can also be seen in the growing engagement, and range of views, seen on this topic within India's Parliament. Likewise, across state governments in India, many of whom have formulated their own State Action Plans on Climate Change in response to this challenge.

More generally, similar changes can be observed within Indian society at large too. In recent years, there has been a far greater proliferation of domestic actors both conscious of and more actively engaged in the climate change debate than previously. Until the mid-2000s, the landscape of research think tanks and non-governmental organizations working on this issue was dominated largely by The Energy Research Institute (TERI) and the Centre for Science and Environment (CSE), which typically endorsed and provided intellectual and normative support for India's traditional positions on this issue. Similarly, domestic business and industry groups such as the Confederation of Indian Industry (CII) and the Federation of Indian Chambers of Commerce and Industry (FICCI) also tended to rally behind the government's positions, albeit only to the limited extent that they were engaged with the issue.

However, domestic consensus within India on this topic is no longer as solid as it used to be (Sengupta 2012a) with the emergence of a range of new think tanks and civil society organizations in recent years. Often with strong transnational connections, these groups—such as Greenpeace India—have expressed strong challenges to some of the core precepts that India has traditionally espoused on climate change (Ananthapadmanabhan, Srinivas, and Gopal 2007). Likewise, new voices have emerged within a more open and globalized Indian industry as well, which have pointed out the business opportunities and advantages that stem from taking greater and early domestic action on climate change (Godrej and Steer 2016; PTI 2018). Cumulatively, these have represented a widening set of domestic interest groups and voices on climate change within the country.

At the regional level, institutional factors and fora, such as the SAARC environment ministers' meetings, have not really played a prominent role in the determination of India's external behaviour on climate change. However, at the global level, institutions have been much more influential. For example, the institutional rules, decisions, and mechanisms formally agreed to under the UNFCCC—such as requirement to submit GHG inventories at regular intervals, develop CDM projects in conformity with internationally agreed upon procedures, and develop and communicate INDCs—have substantively shaped India's behaviour with regard to these. The need to comply with these institutional requirements of the climate regime has moreover also led India to invest in significant domestic-level infrastructure- and capacity-building measures.

Another set of institutional factors that has played an important role in shaping India's foreign policy on climate are the negotiating groups and fora that it has been part of. As we have seen, India's traditional positions on climate change were largely determined and defended in coordination with key Southern partners, working through coalitions such as the G77 and China, and, in more recent times, the BASIC and LMDC groups. However, the fragmentation and weakening of these traditional Southern coalitions in recent years have inevitably led to greater constraints being placed upon India. An associated factor is the 'peer pressure' that India has come under from the actions taken by some of its core traditional partners. A good example of this was in the lead up to the 2009 Copenhagen Summit, where the other members of the BASIC coalition—China, Brazil, and South Africa—announced voluntary mitigation pledges of their own, eventually making it politically impossible for India to not do so too.

The choice of negotiating fora has had an important institutional impact as well. India's traditional institutional preference for conducting the climate negotiations has always been multilateral settings—such as the UNGA or the UNFCCC—where collective Southern bargaining power could be maximized. However, since the mid-2000s, with the developed world increasingly seeking to hold these discussions in smaller minilateral settings—such as G8+5, MEF, G20, and the UNSC—this has had a constraining effect on India as well, in terms of its ability to defend its traditional positions. Even within a multilateral setting such as the UNFCCC, its desire to be viewed as a 'responsible member' of the international community—and avoid being isolated and blamed in the event of any failure in the climate talks—has been an additional element constraining its behaviour.

Ideas

In terms of the ideational factors that have informed India's external policies on climate change, securing equity and justice were core normative concerns for India since the very beginning of the climate talks. Its negotiators sought to operationalize these principally through ideas of 'historical responsibility', 'per capita convergence', and 'equitable access to carbon space' (Dasgupta 2014). Within the climate negotiations, India was a key proponent of the concept that every human being was entitled to an equal share of the Earth's atmosphere, and that industrialized countries not only needed to reduce their GHG emissions to allow developing countries the necessary 'carbon space' to grow—but also that the only acceptable metric of ensuring equity, ultimately, was an equalization of per capita emissions across the globe (Oberthur and Orr 1999, 46; Agarwal, Narain, and Sharma 1999, 45). This directly aligned also with post-colonial India's long-held support for the principle of the 'right to development'.

In terms of its origins, these ideas emanated, in significant part, from Indian NGOs such as CSE, which published a powerful critique in 1991 against an influential report by the U.S.-based World Resources Institute (WRI) that was setting the terms of the debate at that time (WRI 1990). Not only did the CSE report (Agarwal and Narain 1991) question some of the basic scientific assumptions and methodologies that had been used by the WRI, it drew a clear distinction between categories such as historical/current emissions; per capita/aggregate emissions; and luxury/survival emissions, which had been entirely overlooked until then. Given that these were fully in harmony with India's underlying interests—to ensure that the emerging climate regime had minimal obligations for it, and did not encumber its future development prospects or foreign policy ambitions in any significant manner—it was entirely rational for India's negotiators to pick up and use these principled arguments to advance their formal positions.

However, in recent years, these ideas—never popular in the West—have seen some challenges emerge at the domestic level within India too. This is not only within the government—as previously seen with Ramesh advocating for India to consider a 'per capita plus' approach in the lead up to Copenhagen—but also from within civil society itself. This was evident most clearly, for instance, in the influential and provocative report published by Greenpeace India in 2007, which suggested that by using the 'per capita convergence' principle as the bedrock of India's negotiating positions, richer and more environmentally profligate Indians were essentially—by dint of the country's large population—'hiding behind the poor' (Ananthapadmanabhan, Srinivas, and Gopal 2007). Although subsequently challenged by CSE (2009), this nevertheless had the effect of blunting, at least partially, the moral arguments that were being traditionally advanced by Indian negotiators internationally in support of their positions—and revealed the presence of a more diverse ideational landscape on this issue within the country.

More recently, the ideas of equity and justice have been actively supported by the Modi-led BJP government as well in the climate negotiations—although arguably much more as rhetorical devices rather than in any consequential terms. Indeed, both in the lead up to and at COP-21, Prime Minister Modi publicly made 'climate justice' a key plank of what India sought from the Paris Agreement, stressing that 'advanced countries must leave enough room for developing countries to grow'. However, he also noted that developing countries 'must strive for a lighter carbon footprint on our growth path' (Modi 2015a), and that India's development would be guided by its 'ancient belief that people and planet are inseparable; that human well-being and Nature are indivisible' (Modi 2015b).

Furthermore, a proclivity to reference Hindu scriptures and practices as evidence of the intrinsic environmental consciousness that supposedly exists at a cultural and religious level within Indian society is an additional ideational feature that has also been put forward by the current BJP government in support of its external positions at the political level (Chemnick 2016). This is illustrated, for example, both within the Indian INDC, and in the various speeches that Prime Minister Modi himself made on this issue, as also in the book that he previously wrote on climate change as the chief minister of Gujarat (Modi 2011). This has been in addition to citing the more secular Gandhian maxims of sustainable living and environmental stewardship—long a standard motif in India's interventions at international environmental fora—which have also been co-opted and actively used by the Modi government in this regard (Modi 2015c).

However, what became clear in the Paris negotiations is the very limited appeal that these ideational notions—whether based on equity, justice, Gandhianism, or Hinduism—held for India's negotiating counterparts in the North, whose positions were driven by far more hard-headed power/interest calculations that aimed at fundamentally recasting the climate regime than anything else. Although references to 'climate justice' and 'sustainable lifestyles' were indeed included in the preambular section of the Paris Agreement (UNFCCC 2015), the fact that they have very little operational meaning testifies to the extent that these were, essentially, inconsequential throwaway concessions made to India to help it save face and claim victory at home—even while ceding significant ground in the actual negotiations abroad.

From an operational point of view, a more powerful ideational narrative in India that has been influential in driving both its external and internal behaviour on climate change—and also gained global traction—is, however, the 'co-benefits' discourse (Dubash 2013; Thaker and Leiserowitz 2014). This is the growing understanding that taking action to address climate change can simultaneously provide a range of other economic, social, and environmental benefits. And also, importantly, the converse, that is, of promoting those development objectives, measures, and approaches that yield 'co-benefits for addressing climate change effectively'—as framed in India's 2008 NAPCC (PMCCC 2008). In other words, the idea that achieving development and modernization—which have long been non-negotiables for India—did not necessarily have to be compromised in order to take meaningful action on climate change, and that practical 'win-win' pathways and choices were available.

In terms of regional-level ideas informing India's foreign policy making on climate, these have not been particularly prominent as such, beyond shared understandings of vulnerability and North–South justice. In more recent times, however, newer ideas of greater South–South collaboration, with India in the lead, have emerged—such as the creation of a new SAARC climate change fund (PTI 2010) or, most recently, of the India–UN Development Partnership Fund; but these are yet to reach their full maturity.

At the global level, it is clear that India has played a major role in shaping the international norms, rules, and institutions that have governed global action on climate change. This was especially evident in the earlier period, when many of the ideas and approaches that it espoused—in terms of equity, 'common but differentiated responsibilities', developed world leadership, et cetera—were clearly reflected within the UNFCCC. As the world's third largest GHG emitter in aggregate terms—and with growing national emissions—its participation and views will continue to remain critical for the successful implementation of any international climate agreement.

However, in more recent years, India's external policies and thinking on climate change have arguably been shaped more by international/transnational factors rather than the other way around. In a more globalized world, and a more liberal and open Indian economy and society, a large number of external ideas—whether transmitted or supported by international institutions, donors, foreign businesses, global media, international scientific bodies, think tanks, or NGOs— have contributed significantly to the policies and actions that India has undertaken on climate change, both internationally and domestically. Despite increases in India's material wealth and power over the last two and a half decades, these have not necessarily translated—as we have seen—into influence in the recent climate negotiations. On the contrary, the new position that it has occupied as an 'emerging power' has, ironically, imposed additional constraints and responsibilities upon it, and exposed some of the limitations that it has faced in getting its own way (Hurrell and Sengupta 2012).

***

As this chapter has attempted to show, India's foreign policy on climate change is, ultimately, the net result of the balancing out of a number of different factors and considerations. This chapter has attempted to systematically tease these out by not only presenting a detailed overview of how the country's international engagement on this topic has evolved over the last 25 years, but by providing a breakdown and analysis of the specific roles that interests, institutions, and ideas have each played across different levels—domestic, regional, and international—in driving the same. It showed the relative importance that each of these explanatory factors have had at different junctures in time, and how they were interlinked with each other and operated simultaneously across different spatial levels. Overall, the application of this multilayered analytical framework helps to provide a deeper and more comprehensive understanding of India's external behaviour on this key global challenge.

References

Agarwal, Anil and Sunita Narain. 1991. *Global Warming in an Unequal World: A Case of Environmental Colonialism*. New Delhi: Centre for Science and Environment.

Agarwal, Anil, Sunita Narain, and Anju Sharma (eds). 1999. *Green Politics: Global Environmental Negotiations*, vol. 1. New Delhi: Centre for Science and Environment.

Ananthapadmanabhan, G., K. Srinivas, and Vinuta Gopal. 2007. *Hiding behind the Poor: A Report by Greenpeace on Climate Injustice*. Bangalore: Greenpeace India.

Chauhan, Chetan. 2010. 'US, China Close in on Carbon Accord', *Hindustan Times*, 3 December.

Chemnick, Jean. 2016. 'India's Conservative Prime Minister Proves Unlikely Climate Ambassador', *Scientific American*, 10 June. Available at: https://www.scientificamerican.com/article/india-s-conservative-prime-minister-proves-unlikely-climate-ambassador/ (accessed 29 November 2017).

CSE (Centre for Science and Environment). 2009. 'Richest Indians Emit Less than Poorest Americans'. New Delhi: Centre for Science and Environment. Available at: http://www.indiaenvironmentportal.org.in/files/richest_poorest_emissions.pdf (accessed 4 November 2019).

Dasgupta, Chandrashekhar. 1994. 'The Climate Change Negotiations', in Irving M. Mintzer and J. Amber Leonard (eds), *Negotiating Climate Change: The Inside Story of the Rio Convention*, pp. 129–48. Cambridge University Press, Cambridge.

———. 2011. 'Sweet Surrender: Jairam Ramesh has Turned India's Climate Change Policy on its Head', *The Telegraph*, 17 January.

———. 2014. 'Raising the Heat on Climate Change', *Business Standard*, 7 July.

De Clercq, Geert. 2017. 'France, India to Cooperate in Fighting Climate Change', *Reuters UK*, 3 June. Available at: https://uk.reuters.com/article/uk-france-india/france-india-to-cooperate-in-fighting-climate-change-idUKKBN18U051 (accessed 29 November 2017).

Dubash, Navroz K. 2013. 'The Politics of Climate Change in India: Narratives of Equity and Co-Benefits', *WIREs Climate Change*, 4 (3): 191–201.

Gadgil, Madhav and Ramachandra Guha. 1992. *This Fissured Land: An Ecological History of India*. New Delhi: Oxford University Press.

Ghosh, Padmaparna. 2009. 'I Want to Position India as a Proactive Player: Jairam Ramesh', *Mint*, 29 September.

Godrej, Jamshed and Andrew Steer. 2016. 'Obama and Modi Must Work Together to Fight Climate Change', *Time*, 7 June. Available at: http://time.com/4359888/modi-obama-climate-change/ (accessed 29 November 2017).

GOI (Government of India). 2015. *India's Intended Nationally Determined Contribution: Working towards Climate Justice*. Available at: https://www4.unfccc.int/sites/submissions/INDC/Published%20Documents/India/1/INDIA%20INDC%20TO%20UNFCCC.pdf (accessed 4 November 2019).

Hurrell, Andrew and Sandeep Sengupta. 2012. 'Emerging Powers, North–South Relations and Global Climate Politics', *International Affairs*, 88 (3): 467–9.

Jakobsen, Susanne. 1998. 'India's Position on Climate Change from Rio to Kyoto: A Policy Analysis', *CDR Working Paper 98.11*.Copenhagen: Centre for Development Research.

Kallbekken, Steffen, Hakon Sælen, and Arild Underdal. 2014. *Equity and Spectrum of Mitigation Commitments in the 2015 Agreement*. Copenhagen: Nordic Council of Ministers.

King, Ed. 2016.'Why Did Modi Decide to Ratify the Paris Climate Deal?'. *Climate Home News*, 26 September. Available at: http://www.climatechangenews. com/2016/09/26/why-did-modi-decide-to-ratify-the-paris-climate-deal/ (accessed 29 November 2017).

Lok Sabha. 2009. *Transcript of the Minister's Response in the Lok Sabha*, 3 December, pp. 228–247. New Delhi: Parliament of India.

MEF (Major Economies Forum). 2009. *Declaration of the Leaders of the Major Economies Forum on Energy and Climate*, 9 July. L'Aquila, Italy: Major Economies Forum.

Modi, Narendra. 2011. *Convenient Action: Gujarat's Response to Challenges of Climate Change*. Delhi: Macmillan.

———. 2015a. 'PM's Speech at the "Mission Innovation" in COP21', Paris. Available at: http://www.pmindia.gov.in/en/news_updates/speech-by-prime-minister-at-the-innovation-summit-in-cop-21-parisnovember-30-2015/ (accessed 29 November 2017).

———. 2015b. 'Statement by Prime Minister at COP21 Plenary', Paris, 30 November. Available at: http://unfccc.int/files/meetings/paris_nov_2015/ application/pdf/cop21cmp11_leaders_event_india.pdf (accessed 29 November 2017).

———. 2015c. 'The Rich World Must Take Greater Responsibility for Climate Change', *Financial Times*, 29 November. Available at: https://www.ft.com/ content/03a251c6-95f7-11e5-9228-87e603d47bdc?mhq5j=e2 (accessed 29 November 2017).

MoEF (Ministry of Environment and Forests, Government of India). 1990. 'Greenhouse Effect and Climate Change: Issues for the Developing Countries', in *Proceedings of the Conference of Select Developing Countries on Global Environmental Issues*. New Delhi: Government of India.

Newell, Peter and Adam Bumpus. 2012. 'The Global Political Ecology of the Clean Development Mechanism', *Global Environmental Politics*, 12 (4): 49–67.

Oberthur, Sebastian and Hermann E. Ott. 1999. *The Kyoto Protocol: International Climate Policy for the 21st Century*. Berlin: Springer.

PMCCC (Prime Minister's Council on Climate Change). 2008. *National Action Plan on Climate Change*, 30 June. New Delhi: Government of India.

PMO (Prime Minister's Office). 2007. *Prime Minister's Council on Climate Change*, 6 June. New Delhi: Government of India.

Prabhu, Suresh. 2012. 'Climate Change and Parliament', in Navroz K. Dubash (ed.), *Handbook of Climate Change and India: Development, Politics and Governance*, pp. 230–45. New Delhi: Oxford University Press.

PTI (Press Trust of India). 2010. 'India Announces SAARC Climate Change Fund', *The Hindu*, 28 April. Available at: http://www.thehindu. com/news/national/India-announces-SAARC-climate-change-fund/ article16373139.ece (accessed 29 November 2017).

———. 2018. 'Climate Change Next Century's Biggest Biz Opportunity: Anand Mahindra', *The Economic Times*, 25 January. Available at: https:// economictimes.indiatimes.com/news/company/corporate-trends/ climate-change-next-centurys-biggest-biz-opportunity-anand-mahindra/ articleshow/62652949.cms (accessed 18 September 2018).

Raghunandan, D. 2012. 'India's Official Position: A Critical View Based on Science', in Navroz K. Dubash (ed.), *Handbook of Climate Change and India: Development, Politics and Governance*, pp. 170–9. New Delhi: Oxford University Press.

Rajamani, Lavanya. 2012. 'The Reach and Limits of the Principle of Common but Differentiated Responsibilities and Respective Capabilities in the Climate Change Regime', in Navroz K. Dubash (ed.), *Handbook of Climate Change and India: Development, Politics, and Governance*, pp. 118–29. New Delhi: Oxford University Press.

Rajan, Mukund Govind. 1997. *Global Environmental Politics: India and the North–South Politics of Global Environmental Issues*. New Delhi: Oxford University Press.

Ramachandran, R. 2009. 'Climate Change and the Indian Stand', *The Hindu*, 28 July.

Saran, Shyam. 2006. 'Present Dimensions of the Indian Foreign Policy', January 11. Address by Foreign Secretary, Shanghai Institute of International Studies, China.

Sengupta, Sandeep. 2012a. 'International Climate Negotiations and India's Role', in Navroz K. Dubash (ed.), *Handbook of Climate Change and India: Development, Politics and Governance*, pp. 101–17. New Delhi: Oxford University Press.

———. 2012b. 'Lessons from the Durban Conference', *The Hindu*, 14 February. Available at: http://www.thehindu.com/opinion/lead/lessons-from-the-durban-conference/article2890130.ece (accessed 29 November 2017).

———. 2013. 'Defending "Differentiation": India's Foreign Policy on Climate Change from Rio to Copenhagen', in Kanti P. Bajpai and Harsh V. Pant (eds), *India's Foreign Policy: A Reader*, pp. 389–414. New Delhi: Oxford University Press.

Sethi, Nitin. 2009. 'India Ready for Global Scrutiny on Emissions', *The Times of India*, 28 September.

Singh, Manmohan. 2007. 'PM's Intervention on Climate Change at the Heiligendamm Meeting of G8 Plus 5', 8 June. Available at: http://mea.gov.in/in-focus-article.htm?18822/PMs+intervention+on+Climate+Change+at+the+Heiligendamm+meeting (accessed 29 November 2017).

Thaker, Jagadish and Anthony Leiserowitz. 2014. 'Shifting Discourses on Climate Change in India', *Climatic Change*, 123 (2): 107–19.

TNN (Times News Network). 2009. 'Jairam Persuades Negotiators to Join Climate Talks'. *The Times of India*, 7 December.

UNFCCC (United Nations Framework Convention on Climate Change). 1992. *United Nations Framework Convention on Climate Change.*

———. 1995. 'Berlin Mandate', Decision 1/CP.1 in FCCC/1995/7/Add.1, 6 June.

———. 1997. *Kyoto Protocol to the United Nations Framework Convention on Climate Change.*

———. 2006. 'Dialogue on Long-term Cooperative Action', Decision 1/CP.11 in FCCC/CP/2005/5/Add.1, 30 March.

———. 2008. 'Bali Action Plan', Decision 1/CP.13 in FCCC/CP/2007/6/Add.1, 14 March.

———. 2010. 'Copenhagen Accord', Decision 2/CP.15 in FCCC/CP/2009/11/Add.1, 30 March.

———. 2012. 'Establishment of an Ad Hoc Working Group on the Durban Platform for Enhanced Action', Decision 1/CP.17 in FCCC/CP/2011/9/Add.1, March 15.

———. 2015. 'Paris Agreement', United Nations. Available at: http://unfccc.int/files/essential_background/convention/application/pdf/english_paris_agreement.pdf (accessed 29 November 2017).

UNGA (UN General Assembly). 1988. *United Nations General Assembly Resolution 43/53*, 6 December.

———. 1989. *United Nations General Assembly Resolution 44/207*, 22 December.

WRI (World Resources Institute). 1990. *World Resources, 1990–91*. Oxford: Oxford University Press.

7 Democracy Promotion

Christian Wagner[1]

For many decades, the promotion of democracy has been a very important topic in the foreign policy agendas of the United States and European countries. The ideational foundation is the democratic peace debate that dates back to the writings of Immanuel Kant. His analysis of the foreign policies of 'republics' in the eighteenth century has been substantiated by a variety of empirical studies which have highlighted the fact that 'democracies do not go to war with each other' (Sharma 1992). The third and fourth wave of democratization in many parts of the world seemed to indicate a consolidation of democratic governance and the 'end of history' (Fukuyama 1989) after the end of the Cold War.

But the United States and Europe have pursued different strategies for the promotion of democratic governance (Kopstein 2006). The foreign policy of the European Union (EU) and most of its member states have emphasized the need for dialogue and collaboration with authoritarian regimes. The strengthening of civil societies has aimed to initiate reforms and changes from within that should lead to a democratic transition. American administrations, for instance under President George W. Bush, have also advocated military interventions that aimed for regime change, as was the case in Afghanistan and Iraq.

After the end of the Cold War, new regional and global institutions came up in order to promote democratic governance. The Community of Democracies (CoD) was formed in Warsaw, Poland, in 2000, the Bali Forum

[1] The author thanks Claudius Engeling for his inputs in this chapter.

of Democracy was established in 2008. But these intergovernmental institutions have remained weak and have never achieved a vital importance in the context of global governance.

The evaluation of civilian and military interventions for the sake of democracy has shown mixed results. Moreover, the rise of new powers and the debate about a multipolar world order, the renewed emphasis on national interest in many countries, and the growing mistrust against international organizations and regimes have negatively affected the idea of democracy promotion as an instrument of foreign policy in recent years.

India, as the largest democracy, has shown remarkably little interest in promoting its democratic ideals in its foreign policy. The emphasis of common democratic values has helped to strengthen the political relations with the United States, Western Europe, Australia, and Japan. But the promotion of common values has hardly been translated into common interests or a joint foreign policy agenda.

Considerations on democracy have been a factor in India's relations with individual countries, especially in its neighbourhood, but have never been a consistent feature in its foreign policy. Like in most other countries which pursue strategies of democracy promotion, security interests often gain the upper hand vis-à-vis democratic ideals (Muni 2009; Wagner 2009). On the global level, the discourse on democracy promotion became prominent in the context of the rapprochement with the United States in the 2000s. In this period the topic came up for the first time in the academic debate as well (Chellaney 2005; Mohan 2007). But it seems that this debate was only a short episode and has lost much of its importance since then. While the rhetorical emphasis on democracy will continue, it remains a rather weak instrument in New Delhi's foreign policy tool box, both on the bilateral level and with regard to the collaboration with major powers in third countries.

In order to elaborate the argument, this chapter will first look at the ideas, interests, and institutions of democracy promotion on the domestic level. The second part will look at the regional level in South Asia and analyse some of India's interventions in which democratic considerations came into play. Drawing on the insights gained through the analysis of domestic and regional institutions, interests, and ideas related to democracy support, the third part will look at India's interaction in the field of democracy on the global level.

Domestic Level

India is often termed the world's largest democracy. The constitution of 1950 set up a Western style system of democratic institutions that contrasted with India's unique version of Soviet-style socialism and planned economy. The successes and challenges of 'India's unlikely democracy' (Ganguly 2007) have initiated a controversial political and academic debate.

Ideationally, India's foreign policy was shaped by the anti-colonial and anti-imperialist discourse in its early period. The Indian government supported various anti-colonial movements in Africa and Asia in their struggle for Independence. The treaty with China on Tibet in 1954 laid out the five principles of peaceful coexistence (Panchsheel) that became the normative guideline for India's foreign policy: mutual respect for territorial integrity and sovereignty, non-aggression, non-interference in internal affairs, equality and mutual benefit, and peaceful coexistence.

Later foreign policy doctrines that are linked with individual prime ministers, such as the 'Indira' or 'Gujral' doctrines, formulated India's interests vis-à-vis its neighbours in South Asia (Hagerty 1991; Gujral 1998). A common feature was that India's ambitions for regional hegemony were mostly based on concepts of security, stability, or economic cooperation but hardly on the idea of promoting democracy. The support for democratic governance played a role in the relations with individual countries but did not gain a sustained importance in the national debates on foreign policy.

In order to understand India's approach to the topic, it is important to differentiate between 'democracy promotion' and 'democracy support'. The former indicates the Western, pro-active approach which does not necessarily need the consent of the concerned government in a third country. In contrast to this, democracy support indicates the Indian approach which facilitates, if officially requested, the process of democratization in a third country.

A screening of the annual reports of the Ministry of External Affairs (MEA) since 2000 for the context of 'democracy promotion/support' shows 5 hits in the reports of 1999/2000, 23 in 2008/09, and 3 in 2015/16 (Ministry of External Affairs 2000, 2009, 2016). The report of 2008/09 with the highest number of hits shows that the wording 'support' or 'assistance' was mostly being used whereas 'promotion' was only used in two instances. These findings correspond with quotes from politicians such as former External Minister Pranab Mukherjee who, in 2007, pointed out that India was not interested in exporting ideology (Varadarajan 2007). In 2012, the academic document *Non-Alignment 2.0* stated clearly that India was not interested in promoting democracy (Khilnani et al. 2012, 31).

India's foreign policy interests have always centered on development, security, and great power status. Prime Minister Jawaharlal Nehru saw his country as one of the leading powers that would shape the international system after the Second World War along with the United States, the Soviet Union, and China (Nehru 1946, 535). Since the beginning, Nehru pursued an autonomous and independent foreign policy. He wanted to raise India's status internationally in the context of the ideological conflict between the United States and the Soviet Union. Security concerns, especially vis-à-vis China, often superimposed considerations about the support of democratic rule in other countries. Indian foreign policy makers have a conventional understanding of great power status. They see their country as a future centre of gravity in a multipolar world with a focus on hard power capacities such as nuclear weapons, military strength, and economic power.

Institutionally, foreign policy decision-making in India became the realm of the executive. The process was fostered by at least two developments. First, Nehru not only became prime minister, but also took over the office of the foreign minister. Although his idealistic foreign policy and his rapprochement with China was sometimes criticized, the dominance of the Congress Party at the centre and in the states until the 1960s prevented a more controversial debate on foreign policy issues. Second, the Constitution gave hardly any authority to Parliament with regard to international affairs. For instance, international treaties did not require a separate ratification by the Parliament (Jetly 1979). Hence, many foreign policy decisions were made by a small group of people including the prime minister and his advisors. Even the cabinet played a minor role in most foreign policy decisions (Appadorai 1981, 81). This pattern of important foreign policy decisions being taken by the prime minister and a small group of advisors has continued until today. Among prominent examples of this are Nehru's decision to intervene militarily in Goa in December 1961, Indira Gandhi's decision for the Friendship

Treaty with the Soviet Union in August 1971 and Prime Minister Atal Bihari Vajpayee's decision for the nuclear tests in May 1998.

The dominance of coalition governments has changed this pattern partially since 1991. For example, the United Progressive Alliance (UPA) could not get a majority for the Indo-American Nuclear Treaty in 2007/08 because the legislation was opposed by the Communist Party of India (Marxist) [CPI(M)], which supported the government then. Therefore, the Congress Party had to look for new political partners to get the legislation passed through Parliament. The rise of regional parties, for instance in West Bengal and Tamil Nadu, has also affected India's foreign policy vis-à-vis Bangladesh and Sri Lanka (Jacob 2016).

India not only lacked the ideas and institutions, but also the proper instruments for democracy promotion. Since 1964, the Indian Technical and Economic Cooperation (ITEC) became India's main tool for development cooperation with other developing countries. But political considerations such as democracy promotion/support have never played a prominent role in the ITEC programme. India does not officially support societal organizations to work for democracy in a third country. However, in 2011, the Election Commission established the India International Institute of Democracy and Election Management (IIIDEM), which offers various capacity-building programmes for developing countries. The IIIDEM has given 'election management support' to countries such as Bhutan, Nepal, Afghanistan, Cambodia, South Africa, Kenya, and Nigeria (Bhagbanprakash 2011, 75).

The domestic level shows that democracy promotion has entered the foreign policy agenda only for a short period. Today, the ideational discourse on the topic is close to non-existent, and economic and security interests continue to shape foreign policy decisions of the Prime Minister's Office and the MEA. As we will see, all this influences India's approach to the issue of democracy promotion as a field of global governance.

Regional Level

India's relations with its neighbours in South Asia show the limited role of democracy promotion in the context of her foreign policy. The bilateral relationships with Nepal, Bangladesh, Myanmar, and Sri Lanka underline that security concerns have mostly trumped democratic considerations in India's foreign policy.

Nepal

Nepal is probably the best test case for the ups and downs of India's approach towards democracy promotion. No other country has experienced such a long history of Indian interference at various levels in its domestic affairs. Because of Nepal's strategic location vis-à-vis China and Tibet, no Indian government could afford to be indifferent with regard to the internal developments in the Himalayan country. In July 1950, the peace and friendship treaty, a trade agreement and various secret agreements corroborated India's influence on Nepal (Muni 1973, 283–7).

Nepal's internal power struggle between the ruling Rana dynasty, the monarchy, and the political parties triggered India's first intervention. In November 1950, King Tribhuvan requested asylum at the Indian Embassy in Kathmandu, Nepal. India negotiated a compromise (called the Delhi Settlement) between the conflicting parties in February 1952. The absolute monarchy of the Ranas was replaced by a constitutional monarchy under King Tribhuvan. In addition, members of the Nepali Congress (NC), whose leaders had partly operated from India, were given cabinet seats (Kraemer 1996, 78–82). In his address to the Indian Parliament in December 1950 during the negotiation process, however, Nehru declared that India's main interest was peace and security but not necessarily the installation of a democratic government (Nehru 1991, 436). In this first half of the 1950's, the Indian ambassador in Kathmandu and the political advisor at the royal palace executed great influence on Nepalese politics (Upadhyaya 1989, 311).

India's 'special relationship' (Muni 1973, 67) with Nepal ended when King Mahendra succeeded to the throne in March 1955. He normalized relations with Tibet and the People's Republic of China and concluded a trade agreement with China in 1956. After the first democratic elections in February 1959, the Nepali Congress took over the government. But Nepal's first democracy was only short lived. On 16 December 1960, the king dissolved parliament, removed the government of Prime Minister Bishweshwar Prasad Koirala, banned the parties and arrested their political leaders. The new Nepali constitution of 1962 abolished the democratic system, turned Nepal into a Hindu state, and introduced the panchayat system which was devoid of political parties. Although Nehru criticized these political changes, his government was not able to put pressure on the Nepali monarchy to return to the status quo ante. Because of India's deteriorating relations with China and the military defeat in the border war in 1962, security concerns rather than democracy dominated New Delhi's policy vis-à-vis Nepal (Muni 2009, 38–43).

In the second phase of Nepal's transition to democracy in 1989/90, the domestic constellations in India and Nepal were more complex. In Nepal, the opposition against the panchayat system had created widespread discontent among the population. In India, the Congress government of Rajiv Gandhi was replaced by the minority government of the National Front under Prime Minister V.P. Singh in 1989. His coalition included divergent political forces such as the communist parties as well as Hindu nationalist parties such as the Bharatiya Janata Party (BJP).

In the same year, relations with Nepal deteriorated because of disagreements over the renewing of the trade agreement in spring 1989. During the negotiations, the Rajiv Gandhi government ordered the closure of the border posts with Nepal in March 1989. The shortage of supplies fuelled the opposition against the king in Nepal. The new Indian government lifted the blockade against Nepal in November 1989. In January 1990, the Nepali parties formed a joint opposition against the monarchy that started their protests in February 1990 (Sharma 1992; Raeper and Hoftun 1992). In April, after violent demonstrations, the monarchy agreed to hold elections early in 1991.

The joint opposition was also supported by Indian leaders. But the Indian coalition parties had different priorities vis-à-vis Nepal with regard to the democracy movement and the prolongation of the trade agreement. Parts of the BJP supported the king and the concept of a Hindu monarchy, whereas the Janata Dal refused to continue negotiations with the king. In spring 1990, the Indian draft of the new trade agreement underlined that India was more interested in pursuing her security interests vis-à-vis China rather than in the question of a democratic Nepal (Kumar 1992). Because of its own domestic challenges in this period, India was only indirectly involved in Nepal's second transition towards democracy in 1989/90.

The civil war between the Maoists and the Nepali government between 1996 and 2006 marked a third phase in which Indian involvement in Nepal became critical (Destradi 2010). In February 1996, the Maoists who had their support base among the ethnic minorities and lower castes started an armed struggle against the monarchy and the democratic government, which mostly belong to the upper castes. India was also affected because the Maoists in Nepal cooperated with Maoist groups in India (Naxalites). The king utilized the civil war to cut back democratic achievements. In 2002, he dismissed the prime minister and dissolved parliament and in February 2005, he declared a state of emergency. During this period, India tried to pursue a national consensus in Nepal by employing its informal channels to the different actors (Muni 2009, 89–90). After the state of emergency was declared, the Indian government cancelled its military cooperation with Nepal. But the arms embargo included the risk that the king would turn to China again (Varadarajan 2005). The state of emergency in Nepal was also one of the reasons why India demanded a postponement of the SAARC summit in Dhaka. In summer 2005, India changed its strategy and established links with the Maoists, who were regarded as a terrorist group. In November 2005, the Nepalese political parties and the Maoists reached a 12-point agreement. This paved the way for the popular movement in 2006 that forced the monarchy to resign in 2007. The first elected constituent assembly finally abolished the monarchy in 2008.

India's engagement for a peaceful resolution of the civil war in Nepal was not only based on its security interests vis-à-vis China, but also on its interest at that time to see whether it was possible to integrate militant movements such as that of the Maoists' in a democratic framework. Since the 1970s, India had been confronted with various militant Maoist groups (Naxalites). Their activities had also increased since the late 1990s and the Ministry of Home Affairs categorized them among the biggest threats the country was facing. Hence, Nepal also became a test case for the Indian government in how far political solutions can be reached with Maoist groups. This aspect was also confirmed in interviews by Prachandra, the leader of the Nepalese Maoists and later prime minister (*The Hindu* 2006).

Nepal is an interesting case study to show India's capacities and limitations with regard to the promotion of democracy, and it is relevant because India's ambivalent regional experiences have shaped its global approaches towards democracy promotion. First, India's main goals seemed to be to protect its security interests and to maintain political stability in the often turbulent and violent political development in the Himalayan nation. Therefore, India cooperated not only with democratic forces, such as the political parties, but also with authoritarian actors—the monarchy or militant groups—such as the Maoists, in order to achieve these goals. Second, India's domestic constellations also affected its approach towards democracy promotion. India's support for the Nepali Congress came to an end during the Emergency in the mid-1970s because Indira Gandhi feared that her opponents would use Nepal to fight her regime (Muni 2009, 59). During the National Front government after 1989, India's strategy was not consistent because the different coalition parties were pursing divergent strategies vis-à-vis Nepal.

Interestingly, India's various interferences in Nepal—be it in the name of stability, security, or democracy—have not contributed to a positive image in the country vis-à-vis its southern neighbour. In the domestic debates in Nepal, India is always a contentious issue and all important Nepali parties have internal controversies over their relationship with India.

Bangladesh

In 1970, the first democratic election in Pakistan resulted in a massive victory for the Awami League (AL) from East Pakistan which demanded greater autonomy. But the military and political elite in West Pakistan refused the transfer of power. When Mujibur Rahman, the leader of the AL, was imprisoned in March 1971, the unrest in East Pakistan escalated into a civil war between the West Pakistani army and the East Pakistani guerilla groups. In the wake of the war, millions of people fled to India (Sisson and Rose 1990). Because of its rivalry with Pakistan, India supported the East Pakistani opposition. In December 1971, India intervened militarily in the Pakistani civil war, which in turn also led to the third Indo-Pakistan war. After two weeks, the Pakistani army surrendered and the independence of East Pakistan culminated in the formation of the new state of Bangladesh.

The Indian government gave extensive political and economic support for the creation of the new state of Bangladesh. Its constitution was oriented towards the Indian model with its principles of democracy and secularism. In 1972, the two countries signed mutual friendship and trade treaties. These assured India of having a voice in the development of the first democratic system of government in Bangladesh.

In spite of her strong involvement, India was not able to stabilize the internal situation in Bangladesh. Prime Minister Mujibur Rahman developed authoritarian tendencies and his government was not able to improve the economy. Relations with India became strained and the initial gratefulness of Bangladeshis for India's support was replaced by a deep mistrust. The Indian perspective on Bangladesh in the early phase seemed to have been marred because the government in New Delhi 'mistook the Bengali incompatibility with, and hatred for Pakistan to be love for India' (Bajpai 1990, 124). There was also considerable resentment against India among the armed forces of Bangladesh (Pattanaik 2013, 38). It was, therefore, not surprising that the military changed Bangladesh's foreign policy after the coup in 1975. In 1977, the military rulers included Islam in the previously secular constitution in order to promote the concept of Bangladeshi nationalism which was clearly distinct from the common Bengali culture with India. Since then, the bilateral relations are shaped by a variety of conflicts, such as the distribution of the Ganges water, illegal immigration, and militant groups in India's Northeast that operated out of Bangladesh.

The return to democracy in Bangladesh in 1990/91 became possible because the political parties and their respective student organizations were able to overcome their rivalries and form a joint opposition against the military regime. India was supportive of the democratic opposition in Bangladesh and helped to promote unity among the student organizations. But Indian officials conceded the role of their country as having been 'not crucial, but supportive and opportune' (Muni 2009, 76). The bilateral relationship improved after the democratic transition especially under AL governments. But AL governments have also intensified the political, economic, and military cooperation with China much to India's discontent. Like in the case of Nepal, the relationship with India has continued to be a controversial issue in Bangladesh's national debates.

Sri Lanka

The year 1971 saw not only India's military intervention in the civil war in East Pakistan but also its military support for the Sri Lankan government to suppress the rebellion of the then Marxist Janatha Vimukthi Peramuna [JVP (People's Liberation Front)]. In reaction to the abatement of the rebellion, the Sri Lankan government under the leadership of the Sri Lanka Freedom Party (SLFP) passed a new constitution in 1972. Newly introduced constitutional provisions such as the special role of Buddhism and the new quota system for higher education privileged the Singhalese majority and further fuelled the conflict with the Sri Lanka Tamil minority.

After her return to power in 1980, Indira Gandhi became more critical against the pro-Western government of President Jayawardene (DeVotta 2004, 171). Indira Gandhi's ambition was to settle conflicts in India's neighbourhood only with the involvement of India and not by outside powers (called the Indira Doctrine). The conflict in Sri Lanka also had domestic repercussions for India when more than 100,000 Sri Lankan Tamils fled to Tamil Nadu after the riots in Colombo in July 1983. India's foreign intelligence agency, the Research and Analysis Wing (RAW), trained Tamil militant groups such as the Liberation Tigers of Tamil Eelam (LTTE) against the democratically elected government in Colombo, whereas the Indian government tried to reach a solution by negotiations.

In July 1987, India and Sri Lanka signed an agreement which envisaged a political solution to the civil war. Moreover, the deployment of the Indian Peace Keeping Forces (IPKF) was the first military engagement of Indian troops on the basis of a bilateral agreement and not on the basis of a mandate by the United Nations. India had also reached an agreement with the LTTE, which was supposed to be given a special role in implementing the treaty and in the reconstruction of the north and east of Sri Lanka (Muni 1993, 102).

Though, India's most comprehensive attempt to mediate an internal conflict in a neighbouring country so far ended in a military and political fiasco. The LTTE cancelled older cooperation from September 1987 and engaged with the IPKF in a guerilla war. Moreover, elections in India and Sri Lanka in 1989 changed the political constellations that had agreed on the accord in 1987. The new governments in both countries agreed on a withdrawal of the IPKF which then left the country in March 1990. In May 1991, the Indian Prime Minister Rajiv Gandhi, who had been the architect of the treaty, was assassinated by an LTTE suicide attack during an election rally in Tamil Nadu.

Sri Lanka is an interesting test case in the context of India's efforts for the promotion of democracy. First, it is the only case so far in which an Indian government has supported militant groups against another democratically elected government. Second, the treaty of 1987 established the most far reaching constitutional blueprint for a political solution which was incorporated in the 13th amendment in the Sri Lankan Constitution.

But again, as in the cases of Nepal and Bangladesh, India was hardly able to pursue its interests in the long term. India did not have an official role after the ceasefire agreement in 2002 which was mediated by Norway. India was also not one of the so-called co-chairs that consisted of Norway, Japan, the United States, and the European Union, who were named so at the international donor conference held in Tokyo in 2002 for the economic reconstruction of Sri Lanka. However, India supported the Sri Lankan armed forces and their joint intelligence cooperation was important to cut down the maritime supply routes of the LTTE in 2006/07, which ultimately contributed to their military defeat in May 2009.

Burma/Myanmar

India supported the new democratic government in Burma by sending arms, providing financial assistance, and mobilizing international support against rebellions that started after its independence in 1948. India had two security concerns vis-à-vis Burma. First was to suppress the communist rebellion, which was also a challenge in various parts of India in the early 1950s. The second was the fight against militant ethnic groups in India's Northeast, which were operating on both sides of the border. After the military coup in Burma in 1962, the expulsion of many Indians under the policy of Burmanization marred the bilateral relationship. But India did not support the armed struggle of the Burmese opposition against the military regime (Muni 2009, 48–51).

India's efforts for supporting democratic movements in the neighbouring country started again in 1988 when the military regime in Rangoon cracked down on the student rebellion. India welcomed the democratic elections in 1990 which brought a victory of the National League for Democracy (NLD) under the leadership of Aung San Suu Kyi. Suu Kyi had spent a large part of her youth in India and had personal contact with high-level Indian politicians. India also started to criticize the repressions against the democratic movement.

But again, India was not able to sustain a policy of democracy promotion/support vis-à-vis an authoritarian regime. After 1991, India began to accept the military regime in Myanmar and did not join Western efforts for sanctions. Various reasons seemed to have contributed to India's changing policy. First, in order to fight militancy in the Northeast,

India needed good relations with the regime in Rangoon. Second, by accommodating the military regime, India was able to counter the growing Chinese influence in Myanmar. Finally, Myanmar was seen as the land bridge to the Association of South East Asian Nations (ASEAN) in India's new Look East Policy after 1994 (Muni 2009, 83). India's support of the democratic movement at the end of the 1980s thus remained only a short episode. During his visit to Myanmar in March 1993, the Indian Secretary of State J.N. Dixit declared that India is not interested in a 'democratic mission' vis-á-vis any other states (Myint 2003).

The issue of democratization came up in the bilateral relationship only sporadically. In May 1995, the opposition leader, Aung San Suu Kyi, who was under house arrest, received the Nehru prize in India. The military regime reacted angrily to this tribute and broke off joint military activities against rebellious groups that had already started (Egreteau 2008, 941). In March 2006, Indian President Abdul Kalam raised the question of democratization during his visit to Myanmar. Foreign Secretary Shyam Saran emphasized that India wished to help Myanmar to re-establish democracy and the parliamentary process (Press Trust of India 2006). Thereafter, India focused more on internal political reforms rather than on pressure or even sanctions from abroad. With this position, India obviously was trying to justify her policy of cooperation with Myanmar against the severe criticism of the international community.

After the military regime suppressed the demonstrations in 2007 once again, a public debate about supporting the democratic opposition in Myanmar came up in India (Bagchi 2007; Johnson and Kazmin 2007). India asked the military to liberalize the political system, but repudiated sanctions of the international community (Dikshit 2008).

Afghanistan

Traditionally, India and Afghanistan have had good relations resulting from their common rivalry against Pakistan.[2] Afghanistan opposed the

---

[2] Officially India regards Afghanistan as a neighbouring country. The common border of 106 km runs in the northern part of Kashmir, which is seen as an integral part of the Indian Union after its accession in October 1947. Admittedly, this territory has been under the control of Pakistan since the first India–Pakistan War in 1947/48.

creation of Pakistan in 1947, since it claimed the Pashtun territories in the North-West Frontier Province (NFWP). Afghanistan was the only country which opposed the membership of Pakistan in the United Nations. Because of their joint rivalry with Pakistan, the question of democracy never played an important role in the bilateral relationship between India and Afghanistan.

India kept silent after the Soviet occupation of Afghanistan in 1979 because of the close relationship between Moscow and New Delhi. After the withdrawal of the Soviet Union, the Pakistani army leadership strove for control of Afghanistan in order to attain 'strategic depth' for the next conflict with India. Through the support of the Taliban in the Afghan civil war and of Islamist groups in Kashmir, the Pakistani military connected the two trouble spots that had been largely separated until then. After 1992, India worked together with the Rabbani government in Kabul and supported the Northern Alliance against the Taliban that was supported by Pakistan in the Afghan civil war. Since this time, India has established close links with secular groups among the Pashtuns and the minorities in Afghanistan. India has always been an attractive destination for the Afghan elite with regard to education and medical treatment (Abhyankar 2015, 384). Former President Hamid Karzai studied in India and the family of former President Mohammad Najibullah stayed in Delhi after 1992.

After the attacks of 11 September 2001, India did not take part in the international military intervention in Afghanistan that ended the Taliban regime. But India became involved in the civil reconstruction of the country and supplied humanitarian aid, promoted educational programmes, supported infrastructure projects, and trained Afghan diplomats and members of the security forces. Until 2014, India had pledged USD 2.3 billion as bilateral commitments for the rebuilding and reconstruction of Afghanistan (Haidar 2015). In 2013/14, Afghanistan was among the top three countries that received support under India's Technical Cooperation Programme (Ministry of External Affairs 2015, 207). India has always supported stability and democracy in Afghanistan. Some of India's flagship projects, such as the new Parliament building in Kabul, were promoted under the heading of democracy promotion. The IIIDEM has also offered various programmes for the Afghan Election Commission (Election Commission of India 2015). India's economic and political support has therefore contributed to its very positive image in

Afghanistan whereas Pakistan is viewed extremely negatively (Mynott 2010; Moradian 2015, 121).

Like in the case of Nepal, India also pursues its security and geopolitical interests in Afghanistan. First, India supports the Afghan government in its fight against the Taliban, which are seen as allies of Pakistan. In recent years, India has suffered various attacks on its embassy and consulate in Afghanistan conducted by the Taliban or other militant groups that were supported by Pakistan. Hence, India has recently increased its military cooperation with the Afghan security forces. Second, Afghanistan has always been seen as an economic hub to Central Asia. Therefore, India supported Afghanistan's entry into the South Asian Association for Regional Cooperation (SAARC) in 2007.

Bhutan and Maldives

The Friendship Treaty of 1949 gave India a large co-determination in internal and external political developments in Bhutan. Like in the case of Nepal, security considerations vis-à-vis China played an important role for India. Since the 1960s, India supported the Bhutanese security forces. The Himalayan kingdom also became the largest recipient for India's development assistance. The Indian government gave huge loans by which Indian firms developed hydro-power projects in Bhutan. In return, the surplus of power could be easily exported to northern India. The southern parts of Bhutan became a safe haven for militant groups in India's Northeast. In December 2003, the Bhutanese army launched a major offensive against these camps with support of India.

In 2006, King Jigme Singye Wangchuck surprisingly announced that Bhutan would be transformed into a parliamentary democracy under his son Jugme Khesar Namgyal Wangchuck by 2008. It seems that the political developments in Nepal with the civil war and the lingering ethnic tensions in Bhutan between Drupkas and the Nepalis were the main motivations for this move (Greenway 2007). This transition from above was not very popular; so the king had to tour the country in order to convince his people on the necessity of this fundamental change in the country's political system (Muni 2009, 119).

India supported the democratization of Bhutan in various ways. Indian experts helped to draft the new constitution, and Indian election commissioners and election observers supported the first democratic election in Bhutan in 2008 (Cartwright 2009, 412). India's role in Bhutan has sparked some controversies but is seen as less contentious in contrast to Nepal or Bangladesh.

In the Maldives, India had supported the authoritarian government of President Gayoom in suppressing a coup by Tamil mercenaries in 1988. India then observed the democratic opposition movement that started in 2003/04. The Indian government discussed proposals for political reforms, such as the introduction of political parties through diplomatic channels, that were initiated by President Gayoom in 2005 (Muni 2009, 121). It also supported the process of the first elections (Indo-Asian News Service 2006). In 2007/08, India tripled her aid to the Maldives in order to secure their path to democracy (Cartwright 2007, 413). The first democratic election in October 2008 resulted in the victory of opposition leader Mohamed Nasheed over President Gayoom.

Global Level

At the international level, India has been demanding a 'democratization' of multilateral institutions in order to increase its importance since many years. These demands are linked to India's great power ambitions and should not be confused with its position on democracy promotion. But since the end of the 1990s, India has supported various initiatives, both on the global and regional levels, to facilitate democratic governance. Some of these initiatives were closely linked to India's improving relationship with the United States and with Japan.

Multilateral Initiatives: Democracy Promotion in the Context of Indo-US Relations

In 1999, India hosted the inaugural meeting of the World Movement for Democracy (WMD) in New Delhi. The movement brought together organizations, networks, and individuals who work for the proliferation of democratic norms. Within the Commonwealth, India was also active in criticizing military takeovers such as those in Pakistan and Myanmar and in suspending the membership of military regimes (Mazumdar 2014, 15).

Many of India's activities in this period coincided with the improved relations with the United States. In 2000, India supported the founding of the CoD in Warsaw at the urging of the Clinton administration in the United States. The new organization was intended to promote the proliferation of democratic regimes (Raman 2000). The work plan for 2015 included, among other things, issues to 'support and promote regional democracy and human rights instruments; [and] enable old and new democracies to support democracy' (Community of Democracies 2017).

The political, economic, and military collaboration between the 'oldest' and the 'biggest' democracy broadened with the Next Steps in Strategic Partnership (NSSP) initiative in 2004. A new height was reached with the agreement on civil nuclear cooperation in 2005. At the same time, both sides intensified their efforts for democracy promotion in the global arena. In 2004, the states of the CoD founded the Democracy Caucus at the United Nations.

In July 2005, India and the United States proclaimed a common Global Democracy Initiative (GDI) in order to promote democracy and development. In the same year, India was among the founding members of the UN Democracy Fund that aimed at the creation of democratic institutions and the protection of human rights. During the visit in India in March 2006, United States President George W. Bush clearly emphasized his expectations to support the promotion of democracy vis-à-vis India (US Department of State 2009). When president Obama visited India in 2010, both sides signed the Indo-US joint declaration, which mentioned a 'shared international partnership for democracy and development'.

In the beginning, India was among the largest contributors to the UN Democracy Fund. Until 2015, India had spent nearly USD 32 million and is still the second largest contributor after the United States. But since 2013 there is a sharp decline of India's contribution to the fund. India's annual contribution decreased from USD 5,000,000 in 2005 to USD 200,000 in 2014 and 100,000 in 2015 (United Nations Democracy Fund 2017). This seems to correspond with the declining importance that India attaches to the topic.

India's voting behaviour in international institutions depicted its continuing reluctance to support the United States and other Western democracies (Cartwright 2009, 419). India continued its traditional voting behaviour and kept to its principle of non-interference, which is deeply rooted in the afore-mentioned *domestic ideas* about India's foreign policy. India remained critical on Western initiatives, for instance on Responsibility to Protect (R2P), which were not understood as humanitarian instruments for affected populations but rather as instruments for regime change by Western powers. It was only in 2012 that India voted together with Western powers against Sri Lanka in the Human Rights Council of the United Nations for the first time. This change was mainly fostered by the Dravida Munnetra Kazhagam (DMK) from Tamil Nadu, which was then a member of the UPA coalition government.

India pursued various *interests* in its activities for democracy promotion on the international level. First, the context of the United Nations fitted very well into India's strong multilateral traditions. The approach of inter-governmental UN organizations was closer to India's approach to 'support' democracy rather than to 'promote' it. Second, the cooperation with the United States in UN institutions strengthened India's great power ambitions and the bilateral relations between the two democracies. A welcome side effect was probably that India could thereby show its credibility for the support of democracy and counter American requests to actively support regime changes in third countries.

Asian Approaches: The Quad Initiative and the Bali Democracy Forum

Asia saw various initiatives to deepen the cooperation among democratic states in recent years. In 2006/07, Japan's Prime Minister Shinzō Abe propagated a 'values-oriented diplomacy' with the goal of strengthening the cooperation between the democracies in Asia (Aso 2006). One of Abe's main reasons was to counterbalance China with a stronger collaboration of Asian democracies. The Indian government of Prime Minister Manmohan Singh was also sympathizing with this idea as a new pillar in its relationship with Japan (Raman 2006).

On the regional level, the United States intensified the trilateral security dialogue with Japan and Australia during the Bush administration. In 2007, United States Vice President Dick Cheney suggested including India in this dialogue. In May 2007, for the first time the members of this quadrilateral initiative ('Quad') met on the sidelines of the ASEAN Regional Forums (ARF) (Loewen 2008). The four states pursued different interests with the new grouping. Japan and the United States understood the Quad as a counterbalance to China. In contrast, during his visit to India in 2007, the Australian Defense Minister Brendan Nelson emphasized that his country was most interested in expanding cooperation in areas such as trade and culture (Chellaney 2007). The Indian government remained cautious about the Quad initiative in order to avoid any open confrontation with China. The political and economic relations between the two Asian giants had improved since the 1990's despite the unresolved border issue and China's extensive cooperation with Pakistan. Nevertheless, in September 2007 India participated in the first combined fleet manoeuvre of the Quad states in the Gulf of Bengal, which was seen as a signal against China's growing military presence in the Indian Ocean.

India also participated in the Bali Democracy Forum (BDF) that was founded on the initiative of the Indonesian government in 2008. The grouping includes various democracies from Asia such as Indonesia, India, and Japan but also autocracies such as China and Iran. In the context of India's foreign policy, the BDF will probably only play a minor role.

***

India's Democracy Support

It seems that the heyday of democracy promotion in the foreign policies of Western countries has come to an end. Democracy still enjoys the highest normative reputation and is regarded as the most preferred form of governance. But based on past experiences, there is a growing awareness that external interventions for promoting democracy can also lead to unintended consequences.

Indian foreign policy makers will not be disappointed over this turn of events. First, India's own interventions in its neighbourhood brought ambivalent results at best when democratic considerations were involved. The mostly sobering experiences from the *regional* level therefore contributed to shape India's *ideas* and *interests* concerning democracy support. Second, these new developments correspond much more with India's own *domestic ideational* approach, which has focused on the (technical) 'support' rather than on the (political) 'promotion' of democracy. For India, the 'best program for democracy promotion is its own success' (Metha 2011, 111).

In Western debates, it is often overlooked that India's foreign policy discourse across party lines is mostly determined by the notion of sovereignty and the norm of non-interference. In India, the Western understanding of democracy promotion was, therefore, often equated with regime change. Moreover, India simply lacks resources and adequate instruments for such policy initiatives. The support of democracy is not a very important part of India's soft power toolbox. Like in other countries which pursue similar strategic security interests, political concerns and economic considerations will often outweigh the normative aspects of democracy.

India's support for (and not its promotion of) democracy is also a signal to its neighbouring countries that all approaches are in line with her South Asia strategy, which highlights non-reciprocity and economic cooperation since the 1990s. India may, if required, technically support the process of democracy, for instance by capacity-building programmes of the election commission, without necessarily interfering politically in internal affairs. Political interventions may still happen but, as in the past, are then driven by the individual interests of the different players rather than by a consistent foreign policy strategy.

Internationally, India's support for democracy underlined by its engagement in the UN Democracy Fund conforms to its long-standing multilateral traditions. Moreover, the notion of democracy as a common value will continue to be mentioned in the declarations between India and Western democracies (Kugiel 2012). So far, common values have not been translated into common interests or joint foreign policy agendas. But the differences between the Western policy of promotion and India's strategy for support of democracy are not necessarily exclusive. They can also be regarded as complementary approaches which may open new avenues for collaboration.

References

Abhyankar, Rajendra M. 2015. 'Afghanistan after the 2014 U.S. Drawdown. The Transformation of India's Policy', *Asian Survey*, 55 (2): 371–97.

Appadorai, Angadipuram. 1981. *The Domestic Roots of India's Foreign Policy, 1947–1972*. Delhi: Oxford University Press.

Aso, Taro. 2006. 'Minister for Foreign Affairs on the Occasion of the Japan Institute of International Affairs Seminar "Arc of Freedom and Prosperity: Japan's Expanding Diplomatic Horizons"', 30 November. Available at: www.mofa.go.jp/announce/fm/aso/speech0611.html (accessed 11 March 2009).

Bagchi, Indrani. 2007. 'US, EU Want India to Put Pressure on Myanmar', *The Times of India*, 28 September.

Bajpai, U.S. 1990. 'Indira Gandhi and India's Neighbours', in A.K. Damodaran and U.S. Bajpai (eds), *Indian Foreign Policy. The Indira Gandhi Years*, pp. 115–31. New Delhi: Radiant Publishers.

Bhagbanprakash. 2011. *India International Institute of Democracy and Election Management (IIDEM): Towards Professionally Managed Elections, Participatory Democracy and Social Development. Concept Framework cum Project Document.* New Delhi.

Cartwright, Jan. 2009. 'India's Regional and International Support for Democracy. Rhetoric or Reality?', *Asian Survey*, 49 (3): 403–28.

Chellaney, Brahma. 2005. 'India Adopting Double Standard on Democracy in Neighboring States', *South Asia Tribune*, 6 March. Available at: www.satribune.com/archives/200503/P1_bc.htm (accessed 24 March 2005).

———. 2007. '"Quad Initiative": An Inharmonious Concert of Democracies', *The Japan Times*, 19 July. Available at: http://search.japantimes.co.jp/cgi-bin/eo20070719bc.html (accessed 3 September 2007).

Community of Democracies. 2017. 'Work Plan 2015'. Available at: https://www.community-democracies.org/Visioning-Democracy/Work-Plan-2015 (accessed 10 February 2017).

Destradi, Sandra. 2010. 'A Regional Power Promoting Democracy? India's Involvement in Nepal (2005–2008)', *Giga Working Paper No. 138*, June. Hamburg.

DeVotta, Neil. 2004. *Blowback: Linguistic Nationalism, Institutional Decay, and Ethnic Conflict in Sri Lanka*. Stanford: Stanford University Press.

Dikshit, Sandeep. 2008. 'India Asks Myanmar to Expedite Reconciliation', *The Hindu*, 12 February.

Egreteau, Renaud. 2008. 'India's Ambitions in Burma. More Frustration than Success?', *Asian Survey*, 48 (6): 936–57.

Election Commission of India. 2015. *New Initiatives 2015*. New Delhi. Available at: https://eci.nic.in/eci_main1/current/ECI-NewInitiatives2015.pdf (accessed 5 October 2018).

Fukuyama, Francis. 1989. 'The End of History?', *The National Interest*, Summer: 1–18.

Ganguly, Sumit. 2007. 'India's Unlikely Democracy: Six Decades of Independence', *Journal of Democracy*, 18 (2): 30–40.

Greenway, H.D.P. 2007. 'Change Nears for Bhutan', *The Boston Globe*, 14 June.

Gujral, Inder Kumar. 1998. *A Foreign Policy for India*. New Delhi: Ministry of External Affairs, Government of India.

Hagerty, Devin T. 1991. 'India's Regional Security Doctrine', *Asian Survey*, 31 (4): 351–63.

Haidar, Suhasini. 2015. 'India Rebuffs Afghanistan on Strategic Meet', *The Hindu*, 29 August. Available at: http://www.thehindu.com/news/national/india-rebuffs-afghanistan-on-strategic-meet/article7592059.ece (accessed 27 February 2017).

Hindu, The. 2006. 'Multiparty Democracy in Nepal Will Be Message to Indian Naxalites', 10 February. Available at: www. hindu.com/2006/02/10/stories/2006021005161100.htm (accessed 11 February 2006).

Indo-Asian News Service. 2006. 'Maldives Seeks India's Help to Build Democracy', 24 October. Available at: www. siliconindia.com/shownews/Maldives_seeks_Indias_help_to_build_democracy-nid-33643.html/1 (accessed 13 March 2009).

Jacob, Happymon. 2016. *Putting the Periphery at the Center: Indian States' Role in Foreign Policy*. Washington: Carnegie Endowment for International Peace.

Jetly, Nancy. 1979. *India–China Relations, 1947–1977: A Study of Parliament's Role in the Making of Foreign Policy*. Kalkaji: Radiant Publ.

Johnson, Jo and Amy Kazmin. 2007. 'India Pressed to Take Lead on Democracy, *The Financial Times*, 30 September.

Khilnani, Sunil, Rajiv Kumar, Pratap Bhanu Mehta, Prakash Menon, Nandan Nilekani, Srinath Raghavan, Shyam Saran, and Varadarajan Siddharth. 2012. 'Non-Alignment 2.0: A Foreign and Strategic Policy for India in the Twenty First Century'. Available at: http://www.cprindia.org/system/tdf/policy-briefs/NonAlignment%202.pdf?file=1&type=node&id=3572&force=1 (accessed 15 August 2017).

Kopstein, J. 2006. 'The Transatlantic Divide over Democracy Promotion', *The Washington Quarterly*, 29 (2): 85–98.

Kraemer, Karl-Heinz. 1996. *Ethnizität und nationale Integration in Nepal. Eine Untersuchung zur Politisierung der ethnischen Gruppen im modernen Nepal* (Ethnicity and national integration in Nepal: an analysis of the politicization of ethnic groups in modern Nepal). Stuttgart: Franz Steiner Verlag.

Kugiel, Patryk. 2012. 'The European Union and India: Partners in Democracy Promotion?', The Polish Institute of International Affairs, Warsaw, Policy Paper No. 25, February.

Kumar, Dhruba. 1992. 'Asymmetric Neighbours', in Dhruba Kumar (ed.), *Nepal's India Policy*, pp. 5–33. Kathmandu: Tribhuvan University.

Loewen, Howard. 2008. 'The "Quadrilateral Initiative": A New Security Structure in Asia?', *Südostasien aktuell—Journal of Current Southeast Asian Affairs*, 27 (1): 101–10.

Mazumdar, Arijit. 2014. 'Democracy Promotion in India's Foreign Policy: Emerging Trends and Developments', paper presented at the WPSA Annual Meeting, Seattle, Washington, 17–19 April. Available at: https://wpsa. research.pdx.edu/papers/docs/Democracy%20promotion%20and%20 India%20~%20Arijit%20Mazumdar.pdf (accessed 16 February 2017).

Metha, Pratap Bhanu. 2011. 'Reluctant India', *Journal of Democracy*, 22 (4): 101–13.

Ministry of External Affairs. 2000. *Annual Report 1999–2000*. New Delhi.

———. 2009. *Annual Report 2008–2009*. New Delhi.

———. 2015. *Annual Report 2014–2015*. New Delhi.

———. 2016. *Annual Report 2015–2016*. New Delhi.

Mohan, C. Raja. 2007. 'Balancing Interests and Values: India's Struggle with Democracy Promotion', *The Washington Quarterly*, 30 (3): 99–115.

Moradian, Davood. 2015. 'Indo-Afghan Relationship: Afghan Expectations and Indian Reluctance', in Vishal Chandra (ed.), *India and South Asia: Exploring Regional Perceptions*, pp. 119–27. New Delhi: Pentagon Press.

Muni, S.D. 1973. *Foreign Policy of Nepal*. Delhi: Saraswati Printing Press.

———. 1993. *Pangs of Proximity: India and Sri Lanka's Ethnic Crisis*. New Delhi: Sage Publications.

———. 2009. *India's Foreign Policy: The Democracy Dimension (with Special Reference to Neighbours)*. Delhi: Foundation Books.

Myint, Soe. 2003. 'India Must Review Myanmar Policy', *The Hindu*, 13 June. Available at: www.hindu.com/2003/06/13/stories/ 2003061303231200. htm (accessed 14 June 2003).

Mynott, Adam. 2010. 'Afghans More Optimistic for Future, Survey Shows', *BBC News*, 11 January. Available at: http://news.bbc.co.uk/2/share/bsp/hi/ pdfs/11_01_10afghanpoll.pdf (accessed 20 September 2012).

Nehru, Jawaharlal. 1946. *The Discovery of India*. Calcutta: Signet Press.

———. 1991. *India's Foreign Policy. Selected Speeches (September 1946–April 1961)*. New Delhi: Publications Division, Government of India.

Pattanaik, Smruti S. 2013. 'Bangladesh Army: Evolution, Structure, Threat Perception, and its Role', in Vishal Chandra (ed.), *India's Neighbourhood: The Armies of South Asia*, pp. 27–68. New Delhi: Pentagon Press.

Press Trust of India. 2006. 'India Offers Myanmar Help to Set up Democratic Structure', 3 September.

Raeper William and Martin Hoftun. 1992. *Spring Awakening: An Account of the 1990 Revolution in Nepal*. New Delhi: Viking.

Raman, B. 2000. 'Community of Democracies', South Asia Analysis Group, Noida, Paper 119. Available at: www.southasiaanalysis.org/%5Cpapers2%5 Cpaper119.html (accessed 30 February 2008).

———. 2006. 'India and Japan. Democracy as a Strategic Weapon', South Asia Analysis Group, Noida, Paper 2064.

Russett, Bruce. 1993. *Grasping the Democratic Peace: Principles for a Post–Cold War World*. New York: Princeton University Press.

Sharma, Prem. 1992. *50 Days of Pro-Democracy Movement in Nepal—1990*. Kathmandu: Tribhuvan University.

Sisson, Richard and Leo E. Rose. 1990. *War and Secession: Pakistan, India, and the Creation of Bangladesh*. Oxford and New York: Oxford University Press.

United Nations Democracy Fund. 2017. 'Status of Contributions by Cumulative Amount as at 26 January 2017'. Available at: http://www.un.org/democracyfund/sites/www.un.org.democracyfund/files/Contributions-2017.pdf (accessed 21 February 2017).

Upadhyaya, Devendra Raj. 1989. 'The Role of the Monarchy and the Political Institutions in Nepal', in Kamal Prakash Malla (ed.), *Nepal: Perspectives on Continuity and Change*, pp. 309–32. Kirtipur: Malla Press.

US Department of State. 2009. 'President Discusses Strong U.S.–India Partnership in New Delhi', India, 3 March. Available at: https://2001-2009.state.gov/p/sca/rls/rm/2006/62517.htm (accessed 10 February 2017).

Varadarajan, Siddharth. 2005. 'Arms for Nepal Part of Quid Pro Quo', *The Hindu*, 26 April. Available at: www.thehindu.com/2005/04/26/stories/2005042603961200.htm (accessed 27 April 2005).

———. 2007. 'India Not Interested in Exporting Ideology: Pranab', *The Hindu*, 20 January. Available at: http://www.thehindu.com/todays-paper/tp-international/India-not-interested-in-exporting-ideology-Pranab/article14708785.ece (accessed 20 January 2007).

Wagner, Christian.2009. 'Promotion of Democracy and Foreign Policy in India', *SWP Research Paper 13*, October Berlin.

Conclusion

Patterns, Sequences of Change, and Implications

Johannes Plagemann, Sandra Destradi, and
Amrita Narlikar

We began this volume with the observation that India as a rising power has come to play an increasingly important role in a range of fields of global governance, but that its approach displays substantial differences across policy areas. The preceding chapters illustrated the breadth of India's global policies. The purpose of their collection in this volume was threefold. First, we sought to identify similar patterns in order to make a statement about the driving forces of Indian foreign policy on the global level beyond individual policy fields. A second, and equally important, concern was to discern how the interplay of ideas, interests, and institutions affects change in Indian foreign policy. Finally, our aim was to explore some of the possible broader implication of our findings for a better understanding of rising powers' approaches to global governance. This concluding chapter addresses each of these three aims by drawing on the findings of the collected chapters.

The first aim was the *identification of patterns in the driving forces of Indian foreign policy across policy fields*. We believe that a more precise notion of the interplay of ideas, interests, and institutions in Indian foreign policy greatly contributes to our understanding of the latter.

Amongst the most striking features is India's desire for global power status. Of course, status-seeking in the Indian case is anything but a novel phenomenon (Basrur and Sullivan de Estrada 2017); since Independence,

Indian foreign policy has been driven by the conviction that India deserved status as a major power, her 'rightful place in the world', as Nehru put it (Schaffer and Schaffer 2016, 1). Since the advent of multipolarity, this idea has emerged as an ever stronger component of Indian foreign policy, as illustrated by Sullivan de Estrada, Ebert, and Sengupta in this volume (in Chapters 1, 4, and 6 respectively). Interestingly, its implications have varied across issue areas. In the case of nuclear non-proliferation, India managed to stick to its rejection of the Non-Proliferation Treaty (NPT), while at the same time ultimately contributing to the stability of the regime through its desire for the status of a constructive and responsible global player. In climate change negotiations, a similar desire contributed to a shift in New Delhi's approach towards a more amenable negotiating position, which made compromises more likely. And in the cyber domain, status-seeking contributed to India's tendency of calling for a 'third way' or intermediate position, rather than aligning with either the United States (U.S.) or Russia camp—a stance that mirrors the tradition of Indian foreign affairs since Nehru's partaking in the establishment of the Non-Aligned Movement (NAM).

Thus, efforts to achieve a much-desired status as a major power have made India, on the one hand, more responsive towards the demands articulated by external actors, but also more vulnerable to their pressures, and, therefore, more amenable to changes in its previous negotiating positions. As a consequence, India's climate policies have become affected more directly by global institutions, other countries' policies, and global ideas. This also illustrates the difficulty in distinguishing clearly between what we termed interests and ideas. In other words, it may be in the long-term interest across a variety of fields for India to possess the superior status its foreign policy community has been feeling entitled to for decades; yet, the very quest for status may also undermine short-term material interests. On the other hand, the quest for status has led to creative policy solutions in fields such as non-proliferation and cyber governance, which have allowed for a greater global influence of domestic ideas and institutions in these fields.

It may not be surprising that regional institutions across policy fields have played close to no role, according to our contributors, given the numerous tensions and conflicts among South Asian countries. Yet, one of the paradoxes of the region is the unwillingness of a self-proclaimed regional leader such as India in promoting meaningful regional cooperation (Destradi 2012; Michael 2013). Faced with an increasingly expansionary China, the Modi government, with its renewed interest in the Bay of Bengal Initiative for Multi-Sectoral Technical and Economic Cooperation (BIMSTEC) and even the Indian Ocean Rim Association (IORA), apparently seeks to remedy that. Its success will depend not least on the abandonment of some of India's traditional foreign policy ideas—amongst which the preference of bilateralism over multilateralism in regional affairs and a feeling of entitlement to exclusive regional hegemony figure most prominently.

Related to that, another global institution—the NAM—has been notably absent from the policy fields explored in the preceding chapters. In fact, non-alignment has not been mentioned in any of Modi's foreign policy speeches and the prime minister himself did not attend the last summit held in Venezuela in 2016. One may argue that support for the NAM has always been more rhetorical and that this ultra-broad umbrella of 120 mostly developing nations had lost its raison d'être with the end of the Cold War. Yet, this seems to point at another factor also highlighted across the policy fields collected in this volume. Alliance-building in a multipolar world is a messy and often contradictory affair (Narlikar 2012; Narlikar and Narlikar 2014). Arguably, in global politics India is most regularly (and most fundamentally) in disagreement with China. On top of a simmering conflict over land boundaries and trade imbalances, Beijing continues to veto India's accession to the Nuclear Suppliers Group; New Delhi has been unusually outspoken with regard to Beijing's renunciation of the United Nations Convention on the Law of the Sea (UNCLOS) ruling on the South China Sea; and the Belt and Road Initiative with the China–Pakistan Economic Corridor as the single largest project is described as an outright violation of Indian sovereignty by officials from the Indian Ministry of External Affairs (MEA). And yet, New Delhi and Beijing have cooperated closely on climate and trade negotiations; India is the second largest contributor to the Chinese-led Asian Infrastructure Investment Bank; Indian policy makers continue to describe BRICS (Brazil, Russia, India, China, and South Africa) as the international forum that fits Indian aspirations and interests most closely; and the Modi government in 2017—together with Pakistan—accessed the Shanghai Cooperation Organization (dominated by China and Russia). Other great power relations have become more complicated too. Amongst India's strategic community, Russia has long been regarded as India's most reliable partner on the global level. Yet, collaboration with Moscow has not played a significant role in any of the policy fields looked at in this volume. Meanwhile, security cooperation with the USA (and Japan) intensified to a degree difficult to imagine two decades ago and alongside widely diverging interests in climate and trade, among others. In line with geostrategic calculations, alignment with the USA in other fields seems to be less controversial today than it used to be. Hence, compromises in climate negotiations and beyond will not be understood as impinging on national sovereignty and/or bowing down to Western attempts in domination as swiftly as was the case earlier.

In relative terms, which of the three factors considered in this volume matter most? As mentioned, regional institutions have not played an important role in any of the seven policy fields. By contrast, global multilateral organizations and their institutional histories has shaped New Delhi's approach to nuclear proliferation, climate change mitigation, and cyber security. For India, combatting terrorism remains a national affair, despite frequent attempts to put Pakistani support of Islamist terrorists in Jammu and Kashmir on the agenda in the UN and even BRICS. Here, observing how far the accession of India and Pakistan to the Shanghai Cooperation Organization (SCO) in 2017 affects New Delhi's approach to combatting terrorism will be insightful (but was not possible within this volume, given the limited time span). Despite India's growing enmeshment in international institutions, also including IORA and BIMSTEC on the regional level, South Asia remains one of the world's least integrated regions. When compared with European, African, and arguably even Latin American countries, India's involvement in and foreign policy making through international organizations is limited. Correspondingly, they shape Indian foreign policy in isolated cases only. Yet, as demonstrated by Sullivan de Estrada for the nuclear non-proliferation regime, they did so in highly relevant ways. The latter corresponds with existing research on rising and regional powers, which despite or, perhaps, because of their regional predominance have been involved in global institutions more forcefully but have remained less than enthusiastic supporters of effective regional organizations.

How about ideas and interests, factors that are, as mentioned earlier, not always easy to separate clearly? Obviously, material interests—in terms of binding emission targets in climate negotiations or status as a nuclear power—have decisively shaped Indian policies in the fields of climate change and nuclear policy. In maritime security too, India's security interests in the face of fast-growing Chinese naval capacities go a long way in explaining New Delhi's desire for cooperation with other littoral states and external actors, as well as some renewed emphasis on its naval capabilities domestically. And India's increasingly obvious vulnerabilities in the cyber domain induced New Delhi to engage more proactively globally.

More interestingly, however, is the overarching and well-established ideational component of India's desire for global status. As laid out in more detail later, status concerns emerge in all policy areas and they may even lead to a re-interpretation of material interests in cases where a greater international role only comes with accepting additional responsibilities in the provision of public goods. The chapter on democracy promotion (Chapter 7 by Wagner) may be read in the context of it being a field in which ideas dominate interests. In fact, despite the widely held belief amongst India's strategic community that more democratic neighbours ultimately are in India's security interest, the actual promotion of democracy continues to be a matter of low profile engagements combined with outspoken pronouncements about India's adherence to the principle of non-interference. Given the shallow roots of democracy across South Asia, risky investments in democracy promotion may easily backfire. Hence, the very importance of functioning bilateral ties with countries such as Bangladesh, Myanmar, or Sri Lanka may add a strong component of material interest to India's ideational commitment to non-interference.

Rather than being suggestive of a clear hierarchy of factors, analyses presented in the preceding chapters inform us about the sequencing of ideas and interests throughout the process of foreign policy change. Indeed, another commonality across several policy fields concerns the emergence of change. As noted in the Introduction, since the BJP's election victory in 2014, scholars have been debating whether Modi— elected for his promises of domestic reforms—brought about change in India's foreign policy (see, for example, Chatterjee Miller and Sullivan de Estrada 2017; Hall 2015, 2016). Whereas BJP officials point at Modi's foreign policy activism (as he travels frequently), the expansion of foreign policy beyond security and economic matters, or a more eastward-focused perspective (*Swarajya* 2017), most analysts conclude that actual change has been more visible in the foreign policy making process, rather than its content, where changes were mostly incremental in nature (Ganguly 2017; Plagemann and Destradi 2018). That said, wherever actual change occurred—whether in nuclear policy, climate change negotiations, trade, maritime security, or the cyber domain—it originated from the highest political level. It may not come as a surprise to most readers that bureaucrats are unlikely sources of change; our analysis confirms what the study of diplomacy and bureaucratic politics in foreign policy suggests (Cooper, Heine, and Thakur 2013, 18; Greenstock 2013, 114; Neumann 2007, 196): leaving foreign policy matters to—however empowered—bureaucrats is unlikely to generate change. Yet, in the context of Indian foreign policy, this is a non-trivial finding. India for long has been famed for the power its bureaucrats wield. In foreign policy too, diplomats within the notoriously thin-staffed MEA have been described as remarkably independent (Staniland and Narang 2015, 205). Hence, one could have presumed that such power includes the capacity and occasional willingness to change policies. By contrast, contributions to this volume confirm that actual change only happened once the political interest had been aroused—as in the cyber and climate cases—or once the political interest had changed, as in the cases of maritime security, trade, and nuclear non-proliferation. The remarkable continuity in the fundamentals of Indian foreign policy thought, in turn, is not least a result of the limited attention traditionally devoted to foreign policy by India's political leadership.

This leads us to the second concern of this volume: *to discern how the interplay of ideas, interests, and institutions affect change in Indian foreign policy.* Moments of change are particularly revealing when studying the interplay of ideas, interests, and institutions in foreign policy: new ideas unfold, old institutions (formal and informal) crumble, and long-held interests are questioned. With the emergence of new institutions, ideas and interests stand the chance of gaining permanent and structural salience. The chapters in this volume illustrate the frequency of changes—both incremental and somewhat more radical—throughout the past two decades.

Interestingly, the sequence of change in foreign policy—once looked at in the abstract terms of ideas, interests, and institutions—is often similar across issue areas. In climate change, interests (and their perceptions) have changed over the decades preceding the Paris climate agreement. With an ever less-reliable monsoon, air and water pollution reaching worrying heights, and more frequent natural disasters across South Asia, Indians' understanding of their vulnerability to climate change has been transformed profoundly. At the same time, a global discourse around the economic potentials of renewables and other climate friendly technologies—underlined by Chinese industrial success in solar panels, amongst others—became ever more pervasive. Finally, climate change negotiations due to their global visibility emerged as an appropriate venue for the demonstration of India's global leadership. Yet, institutional factors, in this case a relatively exclusive and insulated group of negotiators drawn from India's powerful bureaucracy, rather than politics, inhibited a changing negotiating position, whereby ensuring a remarkable degree of continuity and insistence on the principles defended since the early 1990s. As Sengupta argues in this volume,

> a key reason behind the long continuity in India's foreign policy on climate was a strong belief among these officials that their reasoning and positions were right, and required no changing, especially given the unwillingness of the North to abide by their prior promises under the UNFCCC and the Kyoto Protocol. Another reason was the natural tendency of India's climate bureaucracy—given internal capacity constraints—to stick to existing and agreed defendable positions, rather than propose or consider any new concepts or approaches. (Chapter 6, p. 183)

Enhanced political attention following a changing balance of interest, and combined with a growing influence of global ideas, led to change, most visible in the reframing of India's negotiating position by incoming Minister for Environment and Forests Jairam Ramesh. Only when new ideas such as Modi's rhetorical linkage of climate change mitigation and ancient Hindu tradition, or such policies' untapped economic potential became influential did compromise become possible.

The domain of maritime security is another particularly illustrative case. Ideas around India as an ancient trading and sea-faring nation, a global power necessitating the capacity for maritime power projections in the high seas and, in particular, across the entirety of the Indian Ocean Region ranging from East Africa to South East Asia and the Pacific had been nurtured by Indian naval circles for decades. Since the early 2000s, the Indian Navy has published a series of open access documents, maritime doctrines, and strategies underlining India's strategic need for naval power projection, notably including non-traditional security threats—from piracy, to disaster response—and the navy's value as a diplomatic actor on its own ('naval diplomacy'). Yet, India's most immediate security challenges—Pakistan and disputed borders with China—remained land based with little role for the Indian Navy. As a consequence, naval strategists often referred to India's strategic circle's 'sea blindness'. Maritime security's marginal role has also been reflected in institutional terms, as noted by Roy-Chaudhury (Chapter 3). Within the MEA, for instance, until 2016 Indian Ocean countries were spread across six geographic and at least three thematic divisions, with little coordination and considerable bureaucratic tussles.

The 2004 tsunami has often been described as a moment of change. With Indian naval vessels first to arrive and carrying a significant share of the relief burden to Indonesia, the Maldives, and Sri Lanka, and India invited to partake in the 'Tsunami Core Group', which orchestrated the immediate response to the crisis by Japan, Australia, and the U.S., New Delhi unexpectedly experienced the soft power of international assistance and its potential for global and regional status-making. According to one think tank report, Indian efforts 'catapulted the country to a leading seat in major global disaster relief initiatives' (IDSA 2012). Since then, the Navy participated in several rescue missions in West Asia, all of which were widely publicized within India.[1] Other instances—such as perpetrators of the 2008 terrorist attack in Mumbai entering the city via boat, or the capturing by Somali pirates of the Hong Kong-flagged commercial vessel Stolt Valor, whose crew consisted mainly of Indian nationals—further fuelled the navy's attempts for greater visibility. However, it is the growing fear of Chinese intrusion into South Asia and the Indian Ocean and a concomitant high-level political interest which changed India's strategic debate most profoundly and, among others, boosted India's naval build-up. Again, a changing balance of interests allowed for new or hitherto marginalized ideas to develop salience. Relentless investment in the Chinese navy, Beijing's uncompromising stance regarding the South China Sea, combined with appearances of

[1] Ahead of the 2006 Israel–Hizbollah war, the navy evacuated 2,280 Indians, Sri Lankans, and Nepalese civilians from Lebanon. In 2011, the navy evacuated around 15,000 Indians from war-torn Libya and the navy's Operation Rahat rescued over 4,000 Indians and 900 foreign nationals from Yemen in 2015.

Chinese submarines in Sri Lanka and significant Chinese investments in port facilities across South Asia, contributed to New Delhi assigning a new significance to its navy. Not only does India remain energy-dependent on secure sea lanes from West Asia, but increasingly, China's strategic weakness—its access to world markets via the Malacca Strait and across the Indian Ocean—is being considered more seriously than ever. As a result, core elements of the navy's strategic debate have been popularized and are now resonating strongly within India's political sphere. And despite New Delhi's traditional preference for bilateral over multilateral relations regionally, India has infused new energy into the long dormant IORA and BIMSTEC as well as established new cooperative frameworks, such as the Indian Ocean Naval Symposium or meetings of national security advisors from BIMSTEC member states (in March 2017).

Interestingly, these developments also include elements beyond the immediate confines of maritime security. Officials from the MEA are quick to underline Hindu (and Indian) presence across the Indian Ocean, thereby justifying India's claims to an increased power status in the region. Its maritime capabilities are now regularly mentioned in officials' portraits of India's aspiration to global-power status. Albeit having gained little visibility, 'Project Mausam', initiated in 2014 by India's Ministry of Culture, sought to revive the central position that India enjoyed in ancient times within the Indian Ocean Region in both economic and cultural terms. According to the ministry, the project's aim was to 'reconnect and re-establish communications between countries of the Indian Ocean world' while focusing on 'understanding national cultures in their regional maritime milieu' (IGNCA 2014). Ostensibly, as a complement to India's Act East initiative, the project also contrasts with China's Silk Road initiative. Moreover, the focus on ancient maritime trade routes amplifies India's expanding understanding of its maritime neighbourhood with an emphasis on the Indian Ocean's expanse towards East Africa and South East Asia.

Hannes Ebert's (Chapter 4) contribution on cyber security provides another set of evidence with regard to the sequence of change in foreign policy making. As long as leadership-level interest remained shallow, domestic institutions' diverging perspectives resulted in bureaucratic turf wars and an oscillation between the U.S.-led position ('multistakeholderism') and the more state-centric Russia-led position, both of which reconnect with domestic ideas. Once in power, Prime Minister Modi tilted the balance towards the more tech and business friendly position. Not only was this much in line with Modi's electoral mandate for modernization and his self-representation as a tech-savvy leader, it also addressed an increasing sense of vulnerability to security threats emanating from the cyber domain. Leadership-level attention not only ended the cacophony of domestic voices but also ensured a distinguishable global policy by way of transforming India's role as a 'norm taker' into a 'norm shaper' and promoting a 'middle way' of global internet governance. As we have seen from other cases discussed earlier, the promotion of a middle way conforms to India's tradition of foreign policy thinking from non-alignment to exceptionalism.

Only after high level political attention is secured, alternative ideas may emerge. Political attention, in turn, is most likely if core interests—either domestic electoral interests (as in tariff protection of Indian agriculture) or security-related ones (as in the case of maritime security)—are involved. Do our findings hence state that interests precede ideas? Not necessarily. Sullivan de Estrada (Chapter 1, p. 42) puts the relation between the two succinctly: 'Many within India's foreign policy elite are invested in the key norms of the nuclear non-proliferation regime. This is not to suggest, however, that it would be impossible, or even particularly difficult to overturn, for example, the norm of non-testing if considerations of security or autonomy should so demand.'

However, our findings do not assign an entirely secondary role to ideas either. Consider that political leaders enter the field of global politics with a complete agenda—that is, coherently formulated interests and underlying ideas—only in a few cases. Instead, such moments of political attention and willingness to change allow for alternative ideas that developed across a variety of domestic agents (often including significant external influences) to be selected over other, more established ones.[2] Therefore, the kind of ideas on offer will co-determine the formulation of interests and, thus, India's foreign policies on the global level.

---

[2] The current dynamic in India's foreign policy think tank environment is an interesting confirmation of this. Since 2014, the Vivekananda Foundation, whose former director is the current National Security Advisor Ajit Doval, and the India Foundation run by BJP General Secretary Ram Madhav, have become a lot more visible.

Of course, such alternative new ideas will rarely be adopted fully. Biswajit Dhar (Chapter 5) shows that India went beyond the requirements for lowering tariffs at the regional and global levels—presumably because a new set of ideas had taken hold and one that induced non-reciprocal measures. Yet, the narrative on trade liberalization initiated by the government in 1991 did not conform to the interests of both small farmers and the automobile industry. Here, the political economy of domestic electoral contest overrode the diffusion of alternative ideas. Or consider democracy promotion. The long-held conviction that India was not a democracy promoter has been only very superficially compromised in insular cases, and only when in the interest of other foreign policy objectives (rapprochement to the U.S.). This is not surprising, perhaps, given Indian foreign policy makers' conviction that the norm of non-interference trumps India's abstract interest in democratization and coincides with India's immediate foreign policy interests in a regional environment where democratic governments are the exception, not the norm (the lack of institutional capacities for democracy support follows from the earlier discussion). In their treatment of terrorism in India, Ganguly and Miliate (Chapter 2) expose the limits of global ideas' influence too. By choosing the three most virulent episodes of domestic terrorism (Punjab in the 1980s, Kashmir throughout the 1990s, and the Naxalites in the 2000s), they exhibit the determinants of Indian counterterrorism along the variables established in our framework. The three cases show the limited influence global ideas have had—to be sure, regional factors, the conflict with Pakistan in particular, greatly contributed to the Kashmir conflict and the Naxalites continue to follow an orthodox reading of Marxism–Leninism and Maoism—arguably 'global ideas' par excellence. Yet, in all three conflicts, decidedly local conditions are the conflicts' main causes and the Indian government's responses have hardly been shaped by global factors.

What does the above tell us about the extent to which India's rise has been paralleled by a growing influence of Indian *ideas* in global politics? The analyses in this volume suggest a mixed picture at best. The chapters on trade and terrorism, perhaps for reasons inherent to the issues areas themselves, have not provided evidence for successful Indian entrepreneurship in ideational terms. In nuclear proliferation, India remains an 'exception' not replicated by others so far. Although its status as a nuclear power has been ever more widely recognized,

India is far from being a norm-setter within the global nuclear non-proliferation regime. In climate change, Sengupta concludes that in recent times, global or transnationally communicated ideas have had a stronger impact on India's policy formulation than Indian ideas have had on the global discourse. In maritime security, the Modi government has welcomed the notion of an Indo-Pacific region, put forward by the USA. Whereas this has contributed to New Delhi's growing interest in maritime security affairs, it has hardly changed its preferred modus operandi, including a prioritization of bilateralism over multilateralism in dealing with India's neighbours or its persistent suspicion towards military alliances. Moreover, rather than initiating a new discourse, New Delhi embraced external powers' ideas as an opportunity for its prevailing geopolitical interests.

In trade, global ideas have shaped the very opening of India's economy since the beginning. Since then, however, the narrative on trade liberalization never fully captured India's thinking about its agricultural sector. Here, core domestic interests prevailed, a fact that strengthened India's leadership position amongst developing countries within global trade negotiations. In that sense, Indian arguments (if not ideas) have been taken up by other developing countries, in line with India's traditional role as a self-ascribed leader of the developing world (also see Narlikar 2017). Yet, New Delhi's growing immersion in the global economy and its political investment in the WTO process also put considerable pressure on Indian negotiators to eventually come to an agreement, including at least some compromises of its material interest.

Democracy promotion—or support—is another interesting case in which we see a tacit approval of some elements of global ideas without fully succumbing to them. Rather than explicitly promoting its own model of parliamentary democracy, India carefully describes its support for elections in Afghanistan and elsewhere as primarily administrative and pragmatic. Although met with sympathy in recipient countries, so far there is little to suggest that this peculiar approach has been copied by other donors elsewhere. Given India's strengths in the IT sector, it may be little surprising that it is in the domain of cyber security that of all the contributions in this volume New Delhi was found to be most successful in developing the role of a 'norm-maker', rather than 'norm-taker'. Yet, the promotion of a middle way between the USA and Russia, as laid out by Ebert, may be less than an entirely novel and original contribution. Again, it seems that whereas India's voice has become more prominent on the global level, New Delhi's quest for international recognition combined with growing expectations externally have induced India primarily to engage with transnationally communicated ideas, rather than forcefully projecting its own. Where there is a middle way (as in case of the cyber or, arguably, the case of democracy promotion) between other major powers' positions, India tends to adopt that.

Finally, with this volume we sought to *explore the broader implications of our findings for a better understanding of rising powers' approaches to global governance* and thereby—in turn—evaluate our framework for future comparative analyses beyond the case of India. One of the peculiarities of the Indian case is the extremely difficult and conflictive regional neighbourhood in which India is placed, and which has made the impact of regional-level factors relatively limited in most issue areas (with the obvious exception of regional-related security interests in the fields of terrorism and maritime security). In other, more cooperative regional settings such as Latin America, we can expect shared ideas, for example, on matters of trade liberalization or regional cooperation, to play a greater role. At the same time, there are several aspects that emerged from the analysis of India's global policies that can be expected to matter for comparative analyses of rising powers. Among them are the paradoxical coexistence of conflict and cooperation among rising powers across levels of analysis, and obviously the aspiration for enhanced international status that has been a powerful driver for countries such as China and Russia as well (Larson and Shevchenko 2010). The analytical framework adopted in this volume has helped highlight some of the more complex implications of rising powers' quest for enhanced global status and some of the mechanisms through which status-seeking, interacting with other factors, leads to innovative contributions to global governance.

The inclusion of domestic institutional factors in the analysis has revealed the noticeable impact of bureaucratic politics on India's foreign policy. This focus on the nitty-gritty details of policy making has remained rather underexplored in the literature on rising powers so far. Indeed, much of the literature on foreign policy making processes is focused on the USA and other Western countries, often authored by former foreign policy officials. Among the comparable elements that promise new insights on the policies of emerging powers are issues such as the declining role of foreign ministries and a corresponding increase in the centralization of decision making, which seems to be emerging across regime types. Another line of inquiry might focus on the emergence of middle classes across rising powers, and on the question of whether this leads to the inclusion of new voices in the political process, and also in the field of foreign policy and on issues of global governance that are of immediate relevance to such social groups.

Looking into sequences of change—changing interests and the kind of ideas they bring to the fore—may be the single most fascinating insight from the chapters of this volume. Amongst the alternative ideas gaining in prominence within rising powers (India and China most visibly) are those that relate the country's international posture to ancient and historical roles. Of course, this includes novel interpretations—if not entirely pseudo-historical—of the respective nation's foreign relations in the past, and such interpretations are often used as a device to generate domestic support for otherwise unpopular policy measures, as in the field of climate change mitigation. Among the other potentially comparable ideational elements among today's rising powers are issues like these countries' foreign policy outlook, or what Luttwak (2012, 13–23) has termed 'great state autism' with reference to China; the way (populist) nationalism fuelled by great power status or aspirations to such status has emerged and has been dealt with politically; but also the discrepancy between rising powers' claims to autonomy and independence, and their growing sense of vulnerability (as witnessed for India in the fields of climate change and cyber security).

Finally, the analyses in this volume also yield potentially policy-relevant conclusions for outside powers dealing with rising powers. Status-seeking may, in many cases, contribute to a less hard-line negotiating position on the part of rising powers. The desire to present and promote moderate alternatives with—superficial or not—country-specific characteristics (as illustrated in India's climate, nuclear, and cyber policies) is a potential avenue for finding compromises in areas of entrenched conflicts of interest. Not least, since an ideational commitment to autonomy—a key driver of Indian foreign policy—is also shared across rising powers. For instance, according to Wagner, the Western policy of democracy promotion and India's strategy for support of democracy are not necessarily mutually exclusive. Similar potential complementarities in other fields and with different countries might open up new avenues for collaboration.

References

Basrur, Rajesh and Kate Sullivan de Estrada. 2017. *Rising India: Status and Power*. London and New York: Routledge.

Chatterjee Miller, Manjari and Kate Sullivan de Estrada (eds). 2017. 'India's Rise at 70', *International Affairs* (Special Issue), 93 (1): 1–198.

Cooper, Andrew F., Jorge Heine, and Ramesh Thakur (eds). 2013. *The Oxford Handbook of Modern Diplomacy*. Oxford: Oxford University Press.

Destradi, Sandra. 2012. *Indian Foreign and Security Policy in South Asia: Regional Power Strategies*. Abingdon and New York: Routledge.

Ganguly, Sumit. 2017. 'Has Modi Truly Changed India's Foreign Policy?', *The Washington Quarterly*, 40 (2): 131–43.

Greenstock, Jeremy. 2013. 'The Bureaucracy: Ministry of Foreign Affairs, Foreign Service, and Other Government Departments', in Andrew Fenton Cooper, Jorge Heine, and Ramesh Chandra Thakur (eds), *The Oxford Handbook of Modern Diplomacy*, pp. 106–21.

Hall, Ian. 2015. 'Is a "Modi Doctrine" Emerging in Indian Foreign Policy?', *Australian Journal of International Affairs*, 69 (3): 247–52.

———. 2016. 'Multialignment and Indian Foreign Policy under Narendra Modi', *The Round Table*, 105 (3): 271–86.

IDSA (Institute of Defence Studies and Analyses). 2012. *Net Security Provider: India's Out-of-Area Contingency Operations*. Delhi: Military Affairs Centre.

Larson, Deborah Welch and Alexei Shevchenko. 2010. 'Status Seekers: Chinese and Russian Responses to US Primacy', *International Security*, 34 (4): 63–95.

IGNCA (Indira Gandhi National Centre for the Arts). 2014. 'Project "Mausam"—Mausam/Mawsim: Maritime Routes and Cultural Landscapes'. Available at: http://ignca.gov.in/project-mausam-3/about-the-project/ (accessed 21 October 2019).

Luttwak, Edward N. 2012. *The Rise of China vs. the Logic of Strategy*. Cambridge, Massachusetts: Harvard University Press.

Michael, Arndt. 2013. 'Sovereignty vs. Security: SAARC and Its Role in the Regional Security Architecture in South Asia', *Harvard Asia Quarterly*, 15 (2): 41.

Narlikar, Amrita. 2012. 'Collective Agency, Systemic Consequences: Bargaining Coalitions in the WTO', in Amrita Narlikar, Martin Daunton, and Robert Stern (eds), *The Oxford Handbook on the WTO*. Oxford: Oxford University Press, pp. 184–212.

———. 2017. 'India's Role in Global Governance: A Modi-fication?' *International Affairs*, 93 (1): 93–111.

Narlikar, Amrita and Aruna Narlikar. 2014. *Bargaining with a Rising India: Lessons from the Mahabharata*. Oxford: Oxford University Press.

Neumann, Iver. 2007. '"A Speech That the Entire Ministry May Stand for", or: Why Diplomats Never Produce Anything New', *International Political Sociology* 1 (2): 183–200.

Plagemann, Johannes and Sandra Destradi. 2018. 'Populism and Foreign Policy: The Case of India', *Foreign Policy Analysis*, 15 (2): 283–301.

Schaffer, Teresita C. and Howard B. Schaffer. 2016. *India at the Global High Table: The Quest for Regional Primacy and Strategic Autonomy*. Washington, DC: Brookings Institution Press.

Staniland, Paul and Vipin Narang. 2015. 'State and Politics', in David Malone, Raja Mohan, and Srinath Raghavan (eds.), *The Oxford Handbook of Indian Foreign Policy*, pp. 205–18. Oxford: Oxford University Press.

Swarajya. 2017. 'Swarajya Exclusive: Ram Madhav on Kashmir, North East, Foreign Policy and Going Back to the Roots', 2 September. Available at: https://swarajyamag.com/politics/swarajya-exclusive-ram-madhav-on-kashmir-north-east-foreign-policy-and-going-back-to-the-roots (accessed 11 October 2017).

Editors and Contributors

Editors

Sandra Destradi is Professor of International Relations and Regional Governance at the Helmut Schmidt University, Hamburg, Germany. She also heads the research programme 'Power and Ideas' at GIGA German Institute of Global and Area Studies in Hamburg. Before joining Helmut Schmidt University, she was a research fellow at GIGA and a Jean Monnet Fellow at the European University Institute in Florence, Italy. Among her research interests are rising powers and their role in global governance and regional crisis management. Her current research focuses on the international implications of the global rise of populism, and, more specifically, on the impact of populist government formation on foreign policy. Her research has been published in journals such as the *European Journal of International Relations, Review of International Studies, Democratization,* and *Asian Survey*.

Amrita Narlikar is the President of GIGA and Professor of International Relations at University of Hamburg. She has earlier been a reader for international political economy at the University of Cambridge and has taught and studied at the University of Oxford, UK. Her research expertise lies in the areas of international trade, rising powers, and multilateral negotiations. She has authored/edited nine books, including *Bargaining with a Rising India: Lessons from the Mahabharata* (co-authored with Aruna Narlikar, 2014). She has also had numerous articles published in leading scholarly journals. She regularly provides her expertise to diverse media outlets such as *FAZ, Welt, Süddeutsche,* and *BBC*. She also writes a monthly column in *Der Tagesspiegel*.

Johannes Plagemann is a political scientist and research fellow at GIGA. He is the spokesperson of the research team 'Ideas and Agency' and coordinator of the research project 'Legitimate Multipolarity' (2018–21). His work focuses on rising powers in international politics and Indian foreign policy in particular. In his latest research he discusses on how populism affects foreign policy and the legitimacy of international organizations in a multipolar world. He is the author of *Cosmopolitanism in a Multipolar World* (2015). His work has been published in journals such as *Review of International Studies, Foreign Policy Analysis, International Studies Review*, and *International Relations of the Asia Pacific*, among others.

Contributors

Biswajit Dhar is Professor, Centre for Economic Studies and Planning, Jawaharlal Nehru University, New Delhi, India. Before that, he was director general of Research and Information System for Developing Countries, a think tank of India's foreign ministry specializing in international economic issues. He also helped in establishing the Centre for WTO (World Trade Organization) Studies of the Government of India and was the head of the centre for several years. He has served as a member of the Indian delegation in several multilateral treaty negotiations, including the WTO, the UN Framework Convention on Climate Change, the World Intellectual Property Organization, and the Convention on Biological Diversity. He was on the board of directors of the Export–Import Bank of India and is currently a member of the Board of Trade, Government of India. Dhar is an advisor to the Asia-Pacific Research and Training Network on Trade of the UN Economic and Social Commission for Asia and the Pacific.

Hannes Ebert is Senior Advisor at the German Marshall Fund (GMF) in Washington DC, USA, and an associate at GIGA. His research focuses on international and cyber security in South Asia and has been published in *International Politics, Third World Quarterly*, and *Rising Powers Quarterly*. As a member of GMF's European Union Cyber Direct Project, he is currently helping to broaden the European Union's cyber dialogues with strategic partners such as Brazil, India, and South Korea. He completed his studies of international politics and law with a master's at the

London School of Economics and Political Science, UK. He acquired his PhD at the University of Hamburg, and worked at the German Federal Foreign Office's Policy Planning Staff and Political Directorate in Berlin, Germany.

Sumit Ganguly is a Distinguished Professor of Political Science and holds the Rabindranath Tagore Chair in Indian Cultures and Civilizations at Indiana University, Bloomington, USA. During 2018–19 he was the Alexander von Humboldt Fellow at Heidelberg University, Germany. He is a member of the Council on Foreign Relations, USA, and a fellow of the American Academy of Arts and Sciences. He has authored/edited twenty books on contemporary South Asian politics. He is currently working on a book that examines the origins and evolution of India's defence policies.

Brandon J. Miliate received his PhD in political science from Indiana University in 2019. He currently works as the South and Southeast Asian Studies Librarian at Yale University, USA. His doctoral dissertation, 'Uncertain Self (Determination): National Movements at the Intersection of India, Myanmar, and Bangladesh', explored the construction of ethnonational identities and movements for self-determination in Mizoram, Manipur, and Chin State (Myanmar). His fieldwork was funded by a Fulbright-Hays Doctoral Dissertation Research Abroad Fellowship.

Rahul Roy-Chaudhury is a Senior Fellow and the Head of the South Asia programme at the International Institute for Strategic Studies (IISS) in London, UK. He has earlier served in the National Security Council Secretariat in the Prime Minister's Office in India and the Institute for Defence Studies and Analyses in New Delhi, India. His research and publications focus on India's foreign and security policies; the Indian Navy and the Indian Ocean; and Pakistan, Afghanistan, India, and regional security. He organizes high-level annual 'Track 1.5' meetings on these issues in Muscat (Oman), Bahrain, Islamabad (Pakistan), New Delhi, and London. He is currently finishing his third book, titled *India's New Maritime Security Strategy*.

Sandeep Sengupta is the Global Coordinator for Climate Change at the International Union for Conservation of Nature (IUCN) in Switzerland, where he leads the organization's engagement on the topic. He has previously worked on a wide range of environment and development issues, both within and outside the government in India, and in international organizations abroad. He is also a visiting lecturer at the Graduate Institute of International and Development Studies (IHEID) in Geneva, Switzerland, where he teaches climate change politics and governance. He holds a doctorate in international relations from the University of Oxford, where his research focused on India's international and domestic engagement on climate change.

Kate Sullivan de Estrada is Associate Professor, International Relations of South Asia, at the Oxford School of Global and Area Studies and the Department of Politics and International Relations, University of Oxford. Her research focuses on India's identity and trajectory as a rising power. Recent publications include her 2017 book with Rajesh Basrur, *Rising India: Status and Power*.

Christian Wagner is Senior Fellow at the German Institute for International and Security Affairs (SWP) in Berlin, Germany. He obtained his MA and PhD degrees from Albert Ludwig University of Freiburg, Germany. From 2007 to 2013, he was a member of the board of directors of the German Association for Asian Studies (DGA) and is a member of the European Association for South Asian Studies (EASAS). He was a visiting fellow at the Observer Research Foundation (ORF), the Jawaharlal Nehru Institute for Advanced Studies (JNIAS), and at the Institute for Defence Studies and Analyses (IDSA) in New Delhi in 2015–16. At present he is a member of the International Research Committee (IRC) of the Regional Centre for Strategic Studies (RCSS) in Colombo, Sri Lanka. His main areas of interest are India and South Asia, with a special focus on foreign policy and security issues.

Index